PRENTICE HALL
LITERATURE

PENGUIN EDITION

English Learner's
Notebook

Grade Twelve

PEARSON
Prentice
Hall

Upper Saddle River, New Jersey
Boston, Massachusetts

ISBN 0-13-165298-2

1 2 3 4 5 6 7 8 9 10   09 08 07 06 05

ACKNOWLEDGMENTS

Grateful acknowledgment is made to the following for copyrighted material:

Jonathan Clowes Ltd.
"No Witchcraft for Sale," from *African Short Stories* by Doris Lessing. Copyright © 1951 by Doris Lessing.

Dutton Signet, a division of Penguin Group (USA) Inc.
From *Beowulf* by Burton Raffel, translator. Translation copyright (C) 1963, renewed (C) 1991 by Burton Raffel.

Encyclopaedia Britannica, Inc.
"Encyclopedia Britannica Online: Cavalier Poets." from Britannica Student Encyclopedia, © 2004 by Encyclopaedia Britannica, Inc.

Faber and Faber Limited
"Journey of the Magi" from *Collected Poems 1909-1962* by T. S. Eliot, copyright 1936 by Harcourt Brace & Company, copyright © 1964, 1963 by T. S. Eliot.

Harlan Davidson/Forum Press, Inc.
Excerpt from "Book I" of *Utopia* by Thomas More, edited and translated by H.V.S. Ogden, pp. 21, 22 (Crofts Classics Series). Copyright © 1949 by Harlan Davidson, Inc. Reprinted by permission.

HarperCollins Publishers, Inc.
"A Devoted Son" from *Games At Twilight And Other Stories* by Anita Desai. Copyright © 1978 by Anita Desai.

A M Heath & Company Limited, Authors' Agents
"Shooting an Elephant" from *Shooting An Elephant And Other Essays* by George Orwell (copyright © George Orwell, 1936).

Michelin Travel Publications
"Tintern Abbey" from *The Green Guide.* Copyright © Michelin et Cie, proprietaires-editeurs, 2001.

The National Gallery
"The Gallery's Role and Objectives" by *The National Gallery, London.* Used with permission.

Penguin Books Ltd. (London)
"The Prologue" to *The Canterbury Tales* by Geoffrey Chaucer, translated by Nevill Coghill (Penguin Classics 1951, fourth revised edition 1977), copyright © 1951 by Nevill Coghill. Copyright, © Nevill Coghill 1958, 1960, 1975, 1977.

Salisbury Post
"Shakespearean expert brings skills to Rowan County" by Cortney L. Hill from *www.salisburypost.com.* Copyright © 2000, 2001 Post Publishing Company, Inc.

Stanley Weintraub
"Queen Victoria's Empire" by Stanley Weintraub from *www.pbs.org/empires/victoria/history/index.html.*

Note: Every effort has been made to locate the copyright owner of material reproduced on this component. Omissions brought to our attention will be corrected in subsequent editions.

Contents

Unit 2 Celebrating Humanity: The English Renaissance Period (1485–1625)

Unit 3 A Turbulent Time: The Seventeenth and Eighteenth Centuries (1625–1798)

Unit 4 Rebels and Dreamers: The Romantic Period (1798–1832)

Unit 5 Progress and Decline: The Victorian Period (1833–1901)

Part 2 Turbo Vocabulary

INTERACTING WITH THE TEXT

As you read your hardcover student edition of *Prentice Hall Literature* use the **Reader's Notebook,** English Learner's Version, to guide you in learning and practicing the skills presented. In addition, many selections in your student edition are presented here in an interactive format. The notes and instruction will guide you in applying reading and literary skills and in thinking about the selection. The examples on these pages show you how to use the notes as a companion when you read.

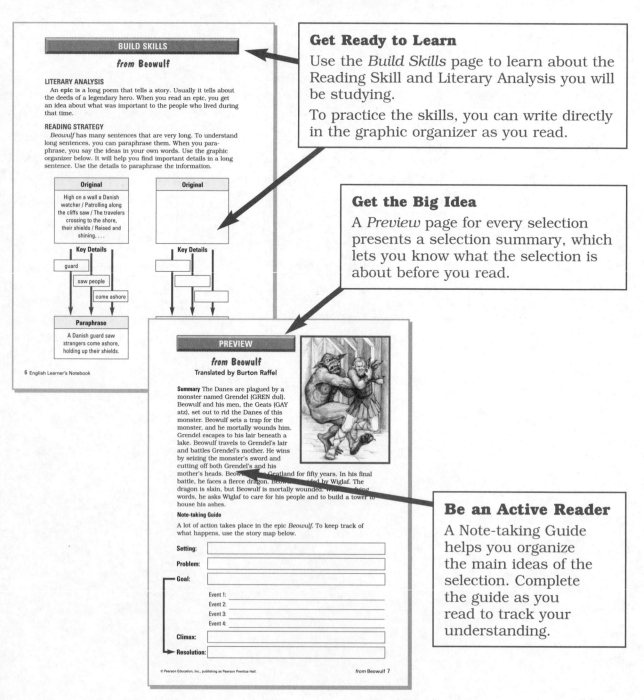

Get Ready to Learn

Use the *Build Skills* page to learn about the Reading Skill and Literary Analysis you will be studying.

To practice the skills, you can write directly in the graphic organizer as you read.

Get the Big Idea

A *Preview* page for every selection presents a selection summary, which lets you know what the selection is about before you read.

Be an Active Reader

A Note-taking Guide helps you organize the main ideas of the selection. Complete the guide as you read to track your understanding.

TAKE NOTES

At the banquet at Herot, the Danes are probably listening to poems like *Beowulf*—epics about heroes and their deeds. What are some poems or songs that celebrate heroes in your native land? Write the name of one on these lines. Be prepared to tell classmates about it.

_____

_____

Vocabulary and Pronunciation

Homophones are words with the same sound but different meanings and spellings. Circle the homophone for *there* that appears a few lines down. Then, write the meaning of each word.

there: _____

homophone: _____

meaning: _____

from Beowulf
Translated by Burton Raffel

Beowulf is a legend that comes out of the early Anglo-Saxon tradition. The story takes place in what today are the nations of Denmark and Sweden. As the selection opens, the Danes are celebrating at Herot, the banquet hall of Danish king Hrothgar.[1] They eat, drink, and listen to poets singing of great heroes. Little do they know that outside in the dark is an evil monster named Grendel. Disturbed by the Danes' singing and jealous of their joy, he wishes to put an end to them.

♦ ♦ ♦

Then, when darkness had dropped, Grendel
Went up to Herot, wondering what the warriors
  Would do in that hall when their drinking was done.
He found them sprawled in sleep, suspecting
Nothing, their dreams undisturbed. The monster's
Thoughts were as quick as his greed or his claws:
He slipped through the door and there in the rush
Snatched up thirty men, smashed them
Unknowing in their beds and ran out with their bodies,
The blood dripping behind him, back
To his <u>lair</u>, delighted with his night's slaughter.
  At daybreak, with the sun's first light, they saw
How well he had worked, and in that gray morning

Vocabulary Development
lair (LAYR) *n.* den; hangout

1. **Hrothgar** (RUHTH guhr).

Take Notes

Side-column questions accompany the selections that appear in the Reader's Notebooks. These questions are a built-in tutor to help you practice the skills and understand what you read.

Mark the Text

Use write-on lines to answer questions in the side column. You may also want to use the lines for your own notes.

When you see a pencil, you should underline, circle, or mark the text as indicated.

APPLY THE SKILLS
from Beowulf

1. **Analyze:** Epics usually tell about a battle between good and evil. Who is the "good" in this epic? Who is the "evil"? Explain how you know.

_____

_____

2. **Literary Analysis:** An epic shows us what people long ago thought was important. The chart below lists a feature in *Beowulf* that people valued and tells why it pleased them. Complete the row to explain what this tells us about the Anglo-Saxons. Then add another feature and complete the chart.

Feature	Why It Is Pleasing	What It Tells About the Anglo-Saxons
boastful speeches	makes hero seem superhuman	

3. **Reading Strategy:** Read the last section of *Beowulf*, starting with the line "Wiglaf, lead my people" (p. 14). **Paraphrase** the lines. In your own words, tell what the lines mean.

_____

_____

4. **Cultural Connection:** The story of *Beowulf* shows how people honored their heroes, long ago. How do we honor heroes today? Write a few sentences that compare honoring heroes in an epic and honoring heroes in today's world.

_____

_____

_____

Check Your Understanding

Questions after every selection help you think about the selection. You can use the write-on lines and charts to answer the questions. Then, share your ideas in class discussions.

PART 1

The Seafarer • The Wanderer • The Wife's Lament

LITERARY ANALYSIS

A lyric poem tells the thoughts and feelings of one person. **Anglo-Saxon lyrics** were written so they could be easily memorized and recited. They have these elements:

- Lines with regular rhythms, usually four strong beats.
- Caesura: rhythmic breaks in the middle of the lines. These breaks let the person saying the poem pause to take a breath.
- Kennings: two-word poetic renamings of people, places, and things. For example, whale's home means the sea.
- Assonance: repeated vowel sounds in unrhymed, stressed syllables (for example, "batter these ramparts")
- Alliteration: the repetition of beginning consonant sounds in words (for example, "smashing surf")

See how the elements add a unique flavor to Anglo-Saxon lyrics.

READING STRATEGY

Learn about the period in which a poem was written. This knowledge will help you understand the poems better. Think about historical background information as you read the poems in this grouping. Use this diagram for "The Wanderer."

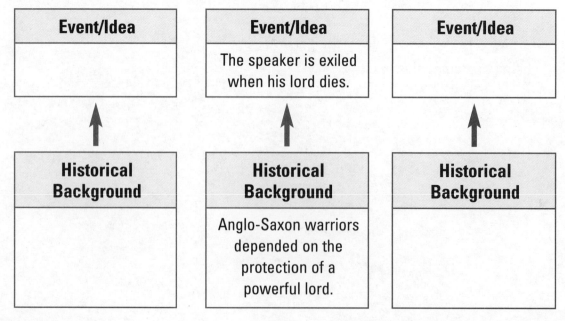

Event/Idea	Event/Idea	Event/Idea
	The speaker is exiled when his lord dies.	

Historical Background	Historical Background	Historical Background
	Anglo-Saxon warriors depended on the protection of a powerful lord.	

The Seafarer
• The Wanderer

Translated by Burton Raffel
• Charles W. Kennedy

Summaries In "The Seafarer," a sailor returns again and again to the sea. He describes the fear and loneliness of such a life. He concludes that the only home he has is the "heavenly home." "The Wanderer" tells of the sad journeying of a man who no longer has a lord. He wants the comforts and companionship of the mead-hall, the place where the men feast and talk. He concludes that the earth is a horrible place.

Note-taking Guide

Use this chart to recall things lost or missed by the persons in these two poems. Record examples of people, things, or experiences lost in each poem. Write the line number in parentheses after each example you find.

The Seafarer	The Wanderer
shelter and quiet of land (line 13)	his lord (line 12)

The Wife's Lament

Translated by Ann Stanford

Summary In "The Wife's Lament," a woman talks about her life in the dark, overgrown place where her husband has sent her to live. She is all alone and friendless. She wishes he would experience the same grief.

Note-taking Guide

Use this chart to recall things lost or missed by the speaker of the poem. Record examples of people, things, or experiences lost. Write the line number in parentheses after each example you find.

The Wife's Lament
her husband's love and frriendship (lines 21-25)

The Seafarer • The Wanderer • The Wife's Lament

1. **Analyze:** Choose one of the poems. Identify two images or details the poet uses to show his or her sadness or isolation.

   _____

   _____

2. **Literary Analysis:** A **kenning** is two-word poetic renaming of a person, place, or thing. Find two kennings in the poems. Explain what each kenning means.

   _____

   _____

3. **Literary Analysis:** What suffering is described in each poem, and what causes it? Use the graphic organizer below to record examples of suffering. Write the lesson or insight you learn about suffering from each example. Follow the example given for "The Seafarer.

Poem	Cause of Suffering	Insight Gained
"The Seafarer"	He feels like an outcast at home and at sea.	We are exiles on earth. Heaven is home.

4. **Reading Strategy:** Anglo-Saxon women did not have many rights. How does understanding the position of Anglo-Saxon women help you understand "A Wife's Lament"?

   _____

   _____

   _____

from Beowulf

LITERARY ANALYSIS

An **epic** is a long poem that tells a story. Usually it tells about the deeds of a legendary hero. When you read an epic, you get an idea about what was important to the people who lived during that time.

READING STRATEGY

Beowulf has many sentences that are very long. To understand long sentences, you can paraphrase them. When you paraphrase, you say the ideas in your own words. Use the graphic organizer below. It will help you find important details in a long sentence. Use the details to paraphrase the information.

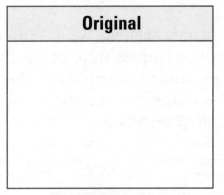

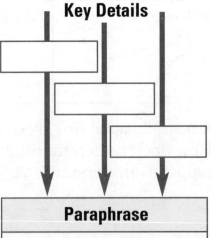

from Beowulf
Translated by Burton Raffel

Summary The Danes are plagued by a monster named Grendel (GREN dul). Beowulf and his men, the Geats (GAY atz), set out to rid the Danes of this monster. Beowulf sets a trap for the monster, and he mortally wounds him. Grendel escapes to his lair beneath a lake. Beowulf travels to Grendel's lair and battles Grendel's mother. He wins by seizing the monster's sword and cutting off both Grendel's and his mother's heads. Beowulf rules Geatland for fifty years. In his final battle, he faces a fierce dragon. Beowulf is aided by Wiglaf. The dragon is slain, but Beowulf is mortally wounded. With his dying words, he asks Wiglaf to care for his people and to build a tower to house his ashes.

Note-taking Guide

A lot of action takes place in the epic *Beowulf*. To keep track of what happens, use the story map below.

Setting:

Problem:

Goal:

Event 1: _____

Event 2: _____

Event 3: _____

Event 4: _____

Climax:

Resolution:

TAKE NOTES

Culture Note

At the banquet at Herot, the Danes are probably listening to poems like *Beowulf*—epics about heroes and their deeds. What are some poems or songs that celebrate heroes in your native land? Write the name of one on these lines. Be prepared to tell classmates about it.

_____

_____

Vocabulary and Pronunciation

Homophones are words with the same sound but different meanings and spellings. Circle the homophone for *there* that appears a few lines down. Then, write the meaning of each word.

there: _____

homophone: _____

meaning: _____

from Beowulf

Translated by Burton Raffel

Beowulf is a legend that comes out of the early Anglo-Saxon tradition. The story takes place in what today are the nations of Denmark and Sweden. As the selection opens, the Danes are celebrating at Herot, the banquet hall of Danish king Hrothgar.[1] They eat, drink, and listen to poets singing of great heroes. Little do they know that outside in the dark is an evil monster named Grendel. Disturbed by the Danes' singing and jealous of their joy, he wishes to put an end to them.

◆　◆　◆

Then, when darkness had dropped, Grendel
Went up to Herot, wondering what the
　　warriors
　Would do in that hall when their drinking was
　　done.
He found them sprawled in sleep, suspecting
Nothing, their dreams undisturbed. The
　　monster's
Thoughts were as quick as his greed or his
　　claws:
He slipped through the door and <u>there</u> in the
　　silence
Snatched up thirty men, smashed them
Unknowing in their beds and ran out with
　　their bodies,
The blood dripping behind him, back
To his <u>lair</u>, delighted with his night's slaughter.
　At daybreak, with the sun's first light, they saw
How well he had worked, and in that gray
　　morning

Vocabulary Development

lair (LAYR) *n.*　den; hangout

---

1. **Hrothgar** (RUHTH guhr).

Broke their long feast with tears and laments
For the dead. Hrothgar, their lord, sat joyless
In Herot, a mighty prince mourning
The fate of his lost friends and companions,
Knowing by its tracks that some demon had torn
His followers apart. He wept, fearing
The beginning might not be the end. And that night
Grendel came again. . . .

♦ ♦ ♦

For twelve long years, Grendel continues to attack the Danes. Stories of their sorrow reach across the sea to the land of the Geats,[2] where Beowulf, nephew of the Geat king, hears of the horror. Beowulf has already won fame and glory for his powerful fighting skills. Hoping to win more, he sails to the land of the Danes to help Hrothgar and his people. That night, Grendel attacks Herot again.

♦ ♦ ♦

Grendel snatched at the first Geat
He came to, ripped him apart, cut
His body to bits with powerful jaws,
Drank the blood from his veins and bolted
Him down, hands and feet; death
And Grendel's great teeth came together,
Snapping life shut. Then he stepped to another
Still body, clutched at Beowulf with his claws,
Grasped at a strong-hearted wakeful sleeper
—And was instantly seized himself, claws
Bent back as Beowulf leaned up on one arm.

Vocabulary Development

bolted (BOHL ted) *v.* swallowed

---

2. **Geats** (GAY atz) a people living in what today is the northern European nation of Sweden.

Reading Strategy

Circle the letter of the choice below that best **paraphrases** the underlined lines.

(a) He cried because he has missed the start of the attack and could do little at the end.

(b) He cried because he was afraid there might be more attacks.

(c) He cried because he feared a different monster would come.

(d) He cried because his rule of Denmark was beginning to end.

English Language Development

From earliest times, English speakers liked to take several descriptive words and shorten them into a **compound adjective**. Here, for example, "sleeper *with a strong heart*" has become "*strong-hearted* sleeper." On the lines below, turn each wordy phrase into a compound adjective before a noun.

blade with a steel edge:

_____

dragon who breathes fire:

_____

Who is the "shepherd of evil" and "guardian of crime"? Write this character's name:

_____

The words *evil* and *crime* stress that he does bad things. What do *shepherd* and *guardian* stress? Circle the letter of your answer.

(a) He does not mean to do bad.

(b) He protects others when he can.

(c) He is in charge of doing bad things.

(d) He does bad things in both the country and the city.

What has happened here? Circle the letter of the best answer below.

(a) Beowulf failed to kill Grendel, who crawls off to fight another day.

(b) Having received a fatal wound, Grendel crawls off to die.

(c) Beowulf killed Grendel on the spot and now goes to Grendel's den.

(d) Beowulf and Grendel fought to a draw and will now make peace.

The word *sword* rhymes with *poured*. Say the word aloud, and circle the silent letter.

That shepherd of evil, guardian of crime,
Knew at once that nowhere on earth
Had he met a man whose hands were harder;
His mind was flooded with fear—but nothing
Could take his talons and himself from that
       tight
Hard grip. . . .
The monster's hatred rose higher,
But his power had gone. He twisted in pain,
And the bleeding sinews deep in his shoulder
Snapped, muscle and bone split
And broke. The battle was over. Beowulf
Had been granted new glory: Grendel
       escaped,
   But wounded as he was could flee to his den,
His miserable hole at the bottom of the
       marsh
Only to die. . . .

♦ ♦ ♦

The Danes are delighted by Grendel's death and honor Beowulf that night in celebrations. But another monster still threatens them—Grendel's mother. Outraged by her son's death, she attacks Herot that very night. She kills Hrothgar's friend and then returns to her lair at the bottom of the lake. Beowulf bravely follows.

♦ ♦ ♦

Then he saw
The mighty water witch and swung his sword,
His ring-marked blade, straight at her
       head; . . .
But her guest

Vocabulary Development

talons (TA luhnz) *n.*   claws
sinews (SIN yooz) *n.*   tendons; cords that connect muscles to bones and other body parts

---

Discovered that no sword could slice her evil
Skin, that Hrunting³ could not hurt her, was useless
    useless
Now when he needed it. They wrestled, she ripped
    ripped
And tore and clawed at him, bit holes in his
    helmet,
And that too failed him; for the first time in
    years
Of being worn to war it would earn no glory;
It was the last time anyone would wear it.
        But Beowulf
Longed only for fame, leaped back
Into battle. He tossed his sword aside,
Angry; the steel-edged blade lay where
He'd dropped it. If weapons were useless he'd
    use
His hands, the strength in his fingers. So fame
Comes to men who mean to win it
And care about nothing else! . . .
Then he saw, hanging on the wall, a heavy
Sword, hammered by giants, strong
And blessed with their magic, the best of all
    weapons
But so <u>massive</u> that no ordinary man could lift
Its carved and decorated length. He drew it
From its scabbard, broke the chain on its <u>hilt</u>,
And then, savage, now, angry
And desperate, lifted it high over his head
And struck with all the strength he had left,

3. **Hrunting** (RUHNT ing) the name of Beowulf's sword. Valuable
swords were often given names.

TAKE NOTES

Reading Check

What two things fail Beowulf in
his battle with Grendel's
mother?

(1)

_____

_____

(2)

_____

_____

Reading Strategy

Circle three or four key details
that you would use in
paraphrasing the
second bracketed
passage. Then, put the
passage into your own
words on the lines below.

_____

_____

_____

_____

_____

English Language Development

The regular past tense of
verbs ends in -*ed*,
but many common
verbs are irregular, or spelled in
different ways. For example, the
past tense of *have* is *had*. Circle
the irregular past tense of *draw*
and *break*.

Literary Analysis

List two ways in which Beowulf's behavior here displays qualities of an **epic hero**.

1. _____

_____

2. _____

_____

Vocabulary and Pronunciation

A long *e* is the sound of /*e*/ as in *be*. The letter combination *ea* sometimes has the sound of long *e*, as it does in *beast*. Circle the next word after *beast* where *ea* again has the long *e* sound.

And struck with all the strength he had left,
Caught her in the neck and cut it through,
Broke bones and all. Her body fell
To the floor, lifeless, the sword was wet
With her blood, and Beowulf <u>rejoiced</u> at the
     sight.

◆   ◆   ◆

     After being honored by Hrothgar, Beowulf and the other Geats return home. There Beowulf eventually becomes king. He rules with success for fifty years. Then a Geat man steals a drinking cup from a treasure in a tower guarded by a fire-breathing dragon. When the angry dragon attacks his kingdom, Beowulf, despite old age, goes to battle the creature.

◆   ◆   ◆

Then Beowulf rose, still brave, still strong,
And with his shield at his side, and a mail
     shirt[4] on his breast,
<u>Strode</u> calmly, confidently, toward the tower,
     under
The rocky cliffs; no coward could have walked
there! . . .
The <u>beast</u> rose, angry,
Knowing a man had come—and then nothing
But war could have followed. Its breath came
     first,
A steaming cloud pouring from the stone,
Then the earth itself shook. Beowulf
Swung his shield into place. . . .

Vocabulary Development

rejoiced (re JOYST) *v.* took joy in; was happy
strode (STROHD) *v.* walked

---

4. **mail shirt** a shirt made out of metal links that give protection in battle.

The Geats'
Great prince stood firm, unmoving, prepared
Behind his high shield, waiting in his
        shining
Armor. The monster came quickly toward
        him,
Pouring out fire and smoke, hurrying
To its fate. Flames beat at the iron
Shield, and for a time it held, protected
Beowulf as he'd planned; then it began to melt,
And for the first time in his life that famous
        prince
Fought with fate against him, with glory
Denied him. He knew it, but he raised his
        sword
And struck at the dragon's scaly hide.
The ancient blade broke, bit into
The monster's skin, drew blood, but
        cracked
And failed him before it went deep enough,
        helped him
Less than he needed. The dragon leaped
With pain, thrashed and beat at him,
        spouting
Murderous flames,spreading them
        everywhere.

◆   ◆   ◆

    All of Beowulf's subjects have fled in
terror except Wiglaf, who fights at Beowulf's
side. But though Beowulf manages to kill the
dragon, he receives a fatal wound himself.
Gasping, he reminds Wiglaf to claim the
dragon's treasure for the Geats. He then
gives his final instructions.

◆   ◆   ◆

Literary Analysis

Circle the detail that shows the early Anglo-Saxon belief in fate guiding human affairs. Based on this passage, what other values does this **epic** reflect?

_____

_____

_____

Reading Strategy

Paraphrase the underlined sentence. Write it on these lines in your own words.

_____

_____

_____

_____

Vocabulary Development

thrashed (THRASHT) *v.* moved wildly

Vocabulary and Pronunciation

The word *tomb,* which refers to a burial place, rhymes with *room.* The *b* is silent. A *b* is almost always silent when it comes after *m* at the end of a word. If the *mb* comes earlier in a word, the *b* is sometimes pronounced. Say these words aloud.

bomb	combine	dumb
bomber	crumb	numb
comb	crumble	tombstone

Culture Note

Like the epic itself, the tower named for Beowulf is a form of lasting fame to honor him after he dies. What are some things today that we often name in honor of people who have died?

_____

_____

_____

Literary Analysis

Based on this closing portion of the **epic,** what do the early Anglo-Saxons seem to admire in their leaders?

_____

_____

_____

"Wiglaf, lead my people,
Help them; my time is gone. Have
The brave Geats build me a <u>tomb</u>,
When the funeral flames have burned me, and build it
Here, at the water's edge, high
On this <u>spit</u> of land, so sailors can see
This tower, and remember my name, and call it
Beowulf's tower. . . ."
Then the Geats built the tower, as Beowulf
Had asked, strong and tall, so sailors
Could find it from far and wide; working
For ten long days they made his monument,
Sealed his ashes in walls as straight
And high as wise and willing hands
Could raise them. And the riches he and Wiglaf
  Had won from the dragon, rings, necklaces,
Ancient, hammered armor—all
The treasures they'd taken were left there, too,
Silver and jewels buried in the sandy
Ground, back in the earth, again
And forever hidden and useless to men.
And then twelve of the bravest Geats
Rode their horses around the tower,
Telling their sorrow, telling stories
Of their dead king and his greatness, his glory,
Praising him for heroic deeds, for a life
As noble as his name, . . .
Crying that no better king had ever
Lived, no prince so mild, no man
So open to his people, so deserving of praise.

Vocabulary Development

spit (SPIT) *n.* a narrow point of land

from Beowulf

1. **Analyze:** Epics usually tell about a battle between good and evil. Who is the "good" in this epic? Who is the "evil"? Explain how you know.

_____

_____

2. **Literary Analysis:** An **epic** shows us what people long ago thought was important. The chart below lists a feature in *Beowulf* that people valued and tells why it pleased them. Complete the row to explain what this tells us about the Anglo-Saxons. Then add another feature and complete the chart.

Feature	Why It Is Pleasing	What It Tells About the Anglo-Saxons
boastful speeches	makes hero seem superhuman	

3. **Reading Strategy:** Read the last section of *Beowulf,* starting with the line "Wiglaf, lead my people" (p. 14). **Paraphrase** the lines. In your own words, tell what the lines mean.

_____

_____

4. **Cultural Connection:** The story of *Beowulf* shows how people honored their heroes, long ago. How do we honor heroes today? Write a few sentences that compare honoring heroes in an epic and honoring heroes in today's world.

_____

_____

from A History of the English Church and People
• from The Anglo-Saxon Chronicle

LITERARY ANALYSIS

Historical writing tells the story of past events using research evidence. A historical writer checks the research to make sure it is accurate. Checking research helps a writer take a step back in time from the beliefs of people around them. You can see this historical "step back" in a sentence from Bede's *History:* "Britain, formerly known as Albion, is an island in the ocean...." Bede left behind his tiny corner of England when he wrote this sentence. He wrote for a wider world that did not know much about Britain.

READING STRATEGY

Bede sometimes writes in very long sentences. **Break down long sentences** into main and related parts. This will help you understand them.

Step 1: Figure out the main action or actions.

Step 2: Find details that answer *who, what, when, where,* or *why.*

Use the chart below to break down long sentences you find. Follow the example given.

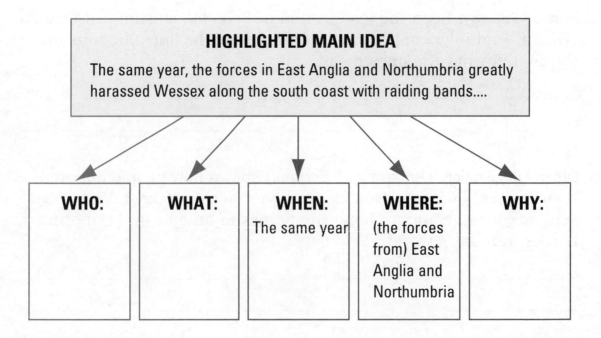

HIGHLIGHTED MAIN IDEA

The same year, the forces in East Anglia and Northumbria greatly harassed Wessex along the south coast with raiding bands....

WHO:	WHAT:	WHEN:	WHERE:	WHY:
		The same year	(the forces from) East Anglia and Northumbria	

from A History of the English Church and People

Bede
Translated by
Leo Sherley-Price

Summary Bede describes Britain's geography and natural resources. He then focuses on its four different nations. Each nation speaks its own language. He tells why each group settled in the area it did. Bede also describes Ireland.

Note-taking Guide

Use the chart below to compare and contrast England and Ireland. In the outer circles, record how England and Ireland are different. In the center, where the circles overlap, note how they are the same.

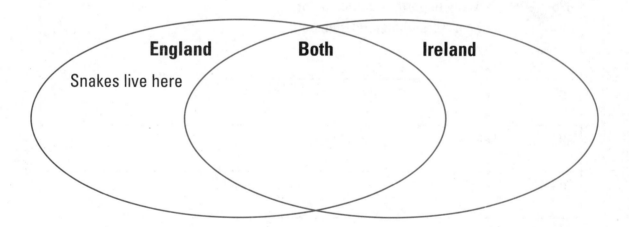

England   Both   Ireland

Snakes live here

from The Anglo-Saxon Chronicle

translated by Anne Savage

Summary In the years between 896 and 906, the Vikings are fighting the English. King Alfred invents long-ships. After Alfred dies, his son Edward takes over. He and his cousin Aethelwald [ATH el WALD] fight for years. Aethelwald dies during this fight. There is an eclipse, a comet, and finally peace.

Note-taking Guide

Use this chart to list the most important event or events of the years provided.

Year	Major Event(s)
896	• Many important thanes died. • King Alfred had long ships built. • •
900	• •
902	• •
903	• •
904	•
905	•
906	•

from History of the English Church and People
• from The Anglo-Saxon Chronicle

1. **Interpret:** What factors are important in uniting a people and giving them a common identity?

_____

_____

2. **Literary Analysis:** Evaluate *The Chronicle* as **historical writing**. Use the chart below. Give examples of where you thought the author provided too little information or evidence. List examples of where the organization helped or did not help understanding. Follow the example given for Bede's *History*.

Necessary Background	Evidence	Clear Organization
"Five languages and four nations"	"English, British, Scots, Picts, & Latin"	The organization makes it easier to understand.

3. **Reading Strategy:** Read this sentence: "As time went on, Britain received a third nation, that of the Scots, who migrated from Ireland under their chieftain Reuda, and by a combination of force and treaty, obtained from the Picts the settlements that they still hold." Which words in this sentence describe the main action?

_____

_____

4. **Reading Strategy:** Reread the sentence in question 4. Answer the questions *who, what,* and *where* about the main action.

_____

_____

ABOUT MAPS

The purpose of a **map** is to present geographical information in a convenient graphic form. To use a map effectively, you should be familiar with the following basic map elements:

- A legend or key defines the symbols on the map.
- A compass rose shows cardinal directions—north, south, east, west.
- A scale shows the ratio between distances on the map and actual distances on Earth.

READING STRATEGY

Using Maps for Verification and Interpretation

To **verify and interpret** information is to check whether it is true and to explore what it means. To verify and interpret information from text using a map, follow the steps below:

1. Identify claims in the text for which geographical information is relevant.
2. Formulate geographical questions based on the text.
3. Obtain a map of the region referenced in the text. Consider whether you need a map that focuses on a specific kind of information.
4. Use the map to answer your questions. Note any additional questions, and consult other sources for answers.

BUILD UNDERSTANDING

Knowing this term will help you read this map.

literary map *n.* map that focuses on the significance of geographical locations as they relate to literary works and authors. These maps often show where important authors were born, lived, and/or wrote.

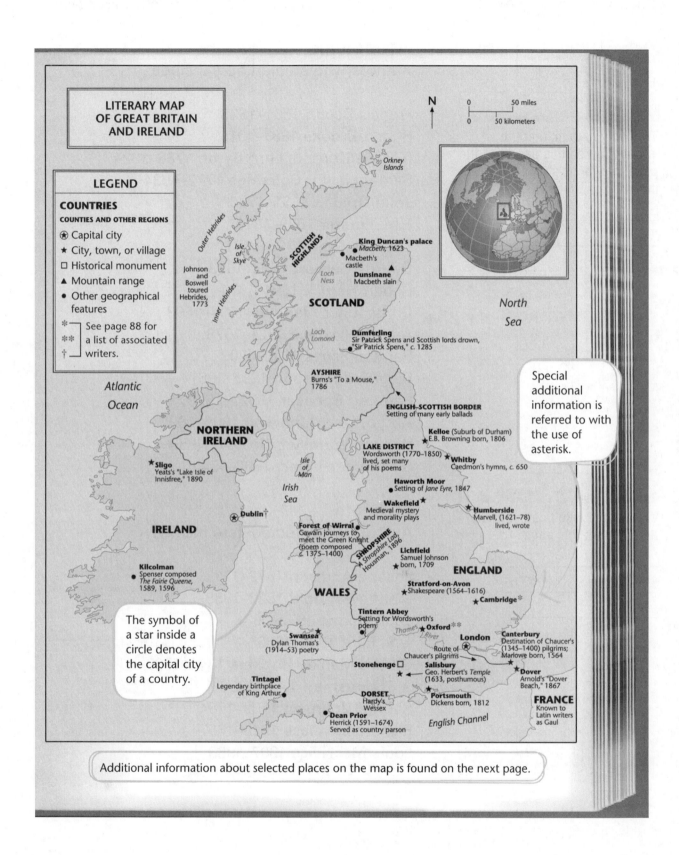

LITERARY MAP OF GREAT BRITAIN AND IRELAND

N

0 ____ 50 miles
0 ____ 50 kilometers

LEGEND

COUNTRIES
COUNTIES AND OTHER REGIONS
⊛ Capital city
★ City, town, or village
□ Historical monument
▲ Mountain range
● Other geographical features
*
** ⎤ See page 88 for
† ⎦ a list of associated writers.

Orkney Islands

Outer Hebrides

Isle of Skye

Inner Hebrides

Johnson and Boswell toured Hebrides, 1773

SCOTTISH HIGHLANDS

King Duncan's palace
Macbeth, 1623

● Macbeth's castle

Loch Ness

Dunsinane
Macbeth slain

SCOTLAND

Loch Lomond

Dumferling
Sir Patrick Spens and Scottish lords drown, "Sir Patrick Spens," c. 1285

AYRSHIRE
Burns's "To a Mouse," 1786

ENGLISH-SCOTTISH BORDER
Setting of many early ballads

North Sea

Kelloe (Suburb of Durham)
E.B. Browning born, 1806

LAKE DISTRICT
Wordsworth (1770–1850) lived, set many of his poems

★ **Whitby**
Caedmon's hymns, c. 650

Haworth Moor
Setting of *Jane Eyre*, 1847

Wakefield ★
Medieval mystery and morality plays

★ **Humberside**
Marvell, (1621–78) lived, wrote

Atlantic Ocean

NORTHERN IRELAND

★ **Sligo**
Yeats's "Lake Isle of Innisfree," 1890

Isle of Man

Irish Sea

⊛ **Dublin** †

IRELAND

Forest of Wirral
Gawain journeys to meet the Green Knight (poem composed c. 1375–1400)

SHROPSHIRE
▲*Shropshire Lad,* Housman, 1896

Lichfield
Samuel Johnson ★ born, 1709

ENGLAND

Kilcolman
Spenser composed *The Fairie Queene*, 1589, 1596

WALES

Stratford-on-Avon
★Shakespeare (1564–1616)

★ **Cambridge** *

Tintern Abbey
Setting for Wordsworth's poem

★ **Oxford** **

Thames River

London
Route of ⊛ Chaucer's pilgrims

Canterbury
Destination of Chaucer's (1345–1400) pilgrims; Marlowe born, 1564

Swansea ★
Dylan Thomas's (1914–53) poetry

Stonehenge □

Salisbury
Geo. Herbert's *Temple* (1633, posthumous)
★

★ **Dover**
Arnold's "Dover Beach," 1867

Tintagel
Legendary birthplace of King Arthur ●

Dean Prior
Herrick (1591–1674) Served as country parson ●

DORSET
Hardy's Wessex

Portsmouth
Dickens born, 1812

English Channel

FRANCE
Known to Latin writers as Gaul

> Special additional information is referred to with the use of asterisk.

> The symbol of a star inside a circle denotes the capital city of a country.

> Additional information about selected places on the map is found on the next page.

Stop to Reflect

Why do you think that the information on this page and the page that follows was not included on the map?

_____

_____

_____

Reading Strategy

What is the significance of the asterisks on this page?

_____

_____

_____

_____

*Cambridge

Authors who studied here include

Francis **Bacon** 1561–1626
Rupert **Brooke** 1887–1915
George Gordon, Lord **Byron** 1788–1824
Samuel Taylor **Coleridge** 1772–1834
John **Dryden** 1631–1700
E.M. **Forster** 1879–1970
Thomas **Gray** 1716–1771
George **Herbert** 1593–1633
Robert **Herrick** 1591–1674
Christopher **Marlowe** 1564–1593
Andrew **Marvell** 1621–1678
Samuel **Pepys** 1633–1703
Siegfried **Sassoon** 1886–1967
Edmund **Spenser** 1552?–1599
Alfred, Lord **Tennyson** 1809–1892
William **Wordsworth** 1770–1850
Sir Thomas **Wyatt** 1503–1542

**Oxford

Authors who studied here include

Joseph **Addison** 1672–1719
Matthew **Arnold** 1822–1888
John **Donne** 1572–1631
T. S. **Eliot** 1888–1965
Gerard Manley **Hopkins** 1844–1889
A.E. **Housman** 1859–1936
Samuel **Johnson** 1709–1784
Richard **Lovelace** 1618–1657
Louis **MacNeice** 1907–1963

Sir Walter **Raleigh** 1552–1618
Percy Bysshe **Shelley** 1792–1822
Sir Philip **Sidney** 1554–1586
Richard **Steele** 1672–1729

†Dublin

Authors associated with the city include

James **Joyce** 1882–1941
George Bernard **Shaw** 1856–1950
Sir Richard **Steele** 1672–1729
Jonathan **Swift** 1667–1745
Oscar **Wilde** 1854–1900
William Butler **Yeats** 1865–1939

TAKE NOTES

Read Fluently

Read aloud the list of authors associated with the city of Dublin. If any of these authors are familiar to you, circle their names.

Reading Informational Materials

In what ways would a tourist **map** of Great Britain and Ireland be similar to and different from this literary map? Write two similarities and two differences.

Similarities:

1. _____

_____

2. _____

_____

Differences:

1. _____

_____

2. _____

_____

THINKING ABOUT MAPS

1. What can you learn from the literary map?

   _____

2. Would people probably travel between Stratford-on-Avon and Northern Scotland on horseback for enjoyment? Why or why not?

   _____

READING STRATEGY

3. Bede guessed the distance from the south to the tip of northern England. What is the difference between his guess and the real distance? _____

4. According to the map and the list of authors, does Great Britain or Ireland have more writers in its past?

   _____

TIMED WRITING: PERSUASIVE ESSAY (20 MINUTES)

Write a **persuasive essay** to convince a literary historian to visit a city. Choose one of the cities on the map. Then, explain why someone might want to visit that city. Follow these steps:

- Look at the map and write down a city and an author.

  _____

- Write down what the map tells you about the author.

  _____

- Go to the library, the Internet, or your textbook and research the author. Find out where in the city the author spent time and why those places were important to the author.

- Then choose the strongest reason and write a topic sentence for your persuasive essay.

from The Canterbury Tales: The Prologue

LITERARY ANALYSIS

As you read the Prologue, look for two kinds of **characterization** — ways of describing character:

- **Direct characterization** uses direct statements are made about character.
- **Indirect characterization** uses actions, thoughts, and speech to show a character's personality.

Each character in *The Canterbury Tales* is from a different part of society in Chaucer's time. By showing the strengths and weaknesses of each, Chaucer gives **social commentary,** writing that makes a point about society, its values, and its customs.

READING STRATEGY

Chaucer's Prologue begins with an eighteen-line sentence. To **analyze difficult sentences** like this one, ask the questions *when, who, where, what,* and *how* to figure out the main information in the sentence. Complete the chart below to finish analyzing Chaucer's first sentence.

When?	in April
Who?	people; palmers
Where?	
What?	
Why?	
How?	

from The Canterbury Tales: The Prologue

Geoffrey Chaucer
Translated by Nevill Coghill

Summary The author joins a group of pilgrims traveling toward the shrine at Canterbury. He describes in detail the people making the trip with him. The characters represent a cross-section of society. Among them are a knight and his son, who is a squire or knight's helper; a yeoman, who is a servant to the squire; a nun, accompanied by another nun and three priests; a well-dressed monk; a jolly friar, a member of a religious order; a merchant; a clergyman who is an impoverished student; and a number of others. They all agree to tell stories on the trip.

Note-taking Guide

Use this chart to list details about the characters.

Characters	Traits and Appearance
1. Knight	
2. Squire	
3. Yeoman	
4. Nun	
5. Monk	
6. Friar	
7. Merchant	
8. Oxford Cleric	

from The Canterbury Tales: The Prologue

Geoffrey Chaucer

People in the Middle Ages often made holy journeys, or pilgrimages, to the city of Canterbury to honor Archbishop Thomas á Becket, killed in 1170. One April in the 1300s, a group of pilgrims, or travelers making this pilgrimage, met at the Tabard Inn just outside London. Chaucer describes each pilgrim, starting with a Knight.

◆ ◆ ◆

There was a Knight, a most distinguished man,
Who from the day on which he first began
To ride abroad had followed chivalry,[1]
Truth, honor, generousness and courtesy.
He had done nobly in his sovereign's[2] war
And ridden into battle, no man more . . .

◆ ◆ ◆

The Knight has fought in the Crusades, the Christian holy wars to gain control of Jerusalem. He makes his pilgrimage to give thanks for surviving. With him is his son, a knight-in-training, or Squire, of about twenty. The Squire likes to joust, or fight in tournaments, but he also likes music, poetry, and showy clothes.

◆ ◆ ◆

He was embroidered like a meadow bright
And full of freshest flowers, red and white.
Singing he was, or fluting all the day;
He was as fresh as is the month of May.
Short was his gown, the sleeves were long and
    wide;
He knew the way to sit a horse and ride.

---

1. **chivalry** (SHIV uhl ree) *n.* the code of behavior for knights, which stressed truth, honor, generosity, and courtesy.
2. **sovereign's** (SOV ruhnz) ruler's; king's.

TAKE NOTES

English Language Development

Remember that in English, the twelve months of the year each begin with a capital letter. Write them in order on the lines below.

_____ _____

_____ _____

_____ _____

April_____ _____

_____ _____

_____ _____

Vocabulary and Pronunciation

In the Middle English spoken in Chaucer's day, the *k* before the *n* in *knight* was pronounced. Today, it is silent. Circle the other letters that are silent in the word *knight*. What other word sounds the same as *knight* but is spelled differently and has a different meaning?

_____

Culture Note

After the Normans conquered England in 1066, many French words were introduced into English. Many of these words have to do with the king's court, the law, and upper-class life. *Chivalry,* the knights' code of honor, comes from French, as does *courtesy,* which originally meant "polite behavior expected in a royal or noble court." In the bracketed passage, circle the part of *courtesy* that shows this original meaning.

He could make songs and poems and recite,
Knew how to joust and dance, to draw and write.

♦   ♦   ♦

The Knight also travels with a Yeoman (YOH man) dressed like a forest hunter. The Yeoman serves as the Knight's attendant. Next Chaucer describes a Nun who is Prioress (PRY uhr uhs), or assistant head, of the nunnery where she lives.

♦   ♦   ♦

And she was known as Madam Eglantyne.
And well she sang a service,[3] with a fine
<u>Intoning</u> through her nose, as was most <u>seemly</u>,
And she spoke daintily in French, extremely,
After the school of Stratford-atte-Bowe;[4]
French in the Paris style she did not know.
At meat[5] her manners were well taught withal;[6]
No <u>morsel</u> from her lips did she let fall,
Nor dipped her fingers in the sauce too deep;
But she could carry a morsel up and keep
The smallest drop from falling on her breast.
For <u>courtliness</u> she had a special zest,
And she would wipe her upper lip so clean
That not a trace of grease was to be seen.

♦   ♦   ♦

The Nun's group includes another Nun and several Priests. There are also other members of the clergy going to Canterbury.

Reading Check

List three of the Squire's talents.

(1) _____

(2) _____

(3) _____

Stop to Reflect

The French spoken in Paris was considered the most proper.

(1) What can you assume about the French that the Nun speaks?

_____

_____

_____

(2) Why do you think the Nun tries to speak French at all?

_____

_____

_____

Vocabulary Development

intoning (in TOHN ing) *n.* chanting; humming
seemly (SEEM lee) *adv.* proper; fitting
morsel (MOHR suhl) *n.* small bite or piece
courtliness (KORT lee nuhs) *n.* elegant manners

---

3. **service** daily prayer.
4. **Stratford-atte-Bowe** a nunnery near London.
5. **At meat** at meals.
6. **withal** (with AWL) *adv.* in addition; nevertheless; besides.

A Monk there was, one of the finest sort
Who rode the country; hunting was his sport.
A manly man, to be an Abbot[7] able;
Many a dainty horse he had in stable.
His bridle, when he rode, a man might hear
Jingling in a whistling wind as clear,
Aye, and as loud as does the chapel bell
Where my lord Monk was Prior of the cell.[8]
The Rule of good St. Benet or St. Maur[9]
As old and strict he tended to ignore;
He let go by the things of yesterday
And took the modern world's more spacious way.

♦ ♦ ♦

Next there is a Friar, or begging Monk,
who likes the company of innkeepers and
barmaids far more than that of the poor. And
there is a Merchant who seems so successful
that no one knows he is in debt. In contrast is
the Oxford Cleric, a student of religion at
Oxford University. He cares only about his
study and his faith.

♦ ♦ ♦

Whatever money from his friends he took
He spent on learning or another book
And prayed for them most <u>earnestly</u>, returning
Thanks to them thus for paying for his learning.
His only care was study, and indeed
He never spoke a word more than was need,
Formal at that, respectful in the extreme,
Short to the point, and <u>lofty</u> in his theme.

Vocabulary Development

earnestly (ER nuhst lee) *adv.* in a sincere way
lofty (LAHF tee) *adj.* elevated; high minded; idealistic

---

7. **Abbot** (AB uht) *n.* a monk in charge of a monastery, or community of monks.
8. **Prior** (PRY uhr) **of the cell** head of a smaller monastery that is part of a larger one.
9. **St. Benet** (buh NAY) **and St. Maur** (MAWR) the French names for St. Benedict, who established the rules for monks, and St. Maurice, one of his followers.

TAKE NOTES

English Language Development

Poetry sometimes uses unusual word order. For example:

Chaucer's order: A Monk there was.

Usual order: There was a Monk.

Rewrite the following sentences using more usual word order.

Chaucer's order: Many a dainty horse he had in stable.

Usual order:

_____

_____

_____

Chaucer's order: His bridle, when he rode, a man might hear jingling in a whistling wind.

Usual order:

_____

_____

_____

Chaucer's order: The Rule of good St. Benet or St. Maur as old and strict he tended to ignore.

Usual order:

_____

_____

_____

English Language Development

Learn and *teach* are sometimes confused. To *teach* is to provide information; to *learn* is to find it out. Complete each sentence below by circling the correct verb in parentheses. Notice that the past tense of *teach* is *taught.*

(1) I (learned, taught) to read some Middle English, the language in which Chaucer wrote.

(2) A professor (learned, taught) me several Middle English words.

(3) The professor will (learn, teach) me more words tomorrow.

Vocabulary and Pronunciation

In English, two vowels often combine to form a single sound. For example, in the word *measure,* the *ea* sounds like the short /e/ in *bed.* Sometimes, however, two vowels in a row do not combine; instead, they each have a separate sound. In *diet,* the *i* has a long /i/ sound, like the *i* in *ride.* But the *e* has its own separate sound, the unstressed vowel sound of the *e* in *taken.* Circle two more words in the bracketed passage in which two vowels in a row have their own separate sounds. Also say the words aloud.

The thought of moral virtue filled his speech
And he would gladly <u>learn</u>, and gladly <u>teach</u>.

♦ ♦ ♦

There is also a Sergeant at the Law, a lawyer for the king's courts; a Franklin, or wealthy landowner; a Skipper, or ship's captain; a Cook; and several tradesmen—a Weaver, a Carpenter, a Carpet Maker, and others. Then there is a Doctor skilled in the medical practices of the day.

♦ ♦ ♦

In his own <u>diet</u> he observed some <u>measure</u>;
There were no superfluities[10] for pleasure,
Only digestives, nutritives[11] and such.
He did not read the Bible very much.
In blood-red garments, slashed with
   bluish-gray
And lined with taffeta,[12] he rode his way;
Yet he was rather <u>close</u> as to expenses
And kept the gold he won in <u>pestilences</u>.
Gold stimulates the heart, or so we're told.
He therefore had a special love of gold.

♦ ♦ ♦

Also traveling to Canterbury is a woman from the English city of Bath, and a Parson, or village priest. The woman, known as the Wife of Bath, has been married and widowed five times. She now spends her days making pilgrimages all over Europe and the Middle East.

♦ ♦ ♦

Vocabulary Development

close (KLOHS) *adj.* stingy
pestilences (PES tuh luhn siz) *n.* contagious diseases; plagues

---

10. **superfluities** (soo puhr FLOO uh teez) *n.* things that are not necessities.
11. **digestives** (duh JES tivs), **nutritives** (NOO truh tivs) foods eaten because they are healthy.
12. **taffeta** (TAF uh tuh) *n.* a fine silk fabric.

Easily on an <u>ambling</u> horse she sat
Well wimpled up,[13] and on her head a hat
As broad as is a buckler[14] or a shield;
She had a flowing mantle[15] that concealed
Large hips, her heels spurred sharply under that.
In company she liked to laugh and chat
And knew the remedies for love's <u>mischances</u>,
An art in which she knew the oldest dances.
A holy-minded man of good <u>renown</u>
There was, and poor, the Parson to a town,
Yet he was rich in holy thought and work.
He also was a learned man, a clerk,
Who truly knew Christ's gospel[16] and would
   preach it
<u>Devoutly</u> to <u>parishioners</u>, and teach it.

♦   ♦   ♦

    Traveling with the Parson is his honest,
hard-working brother, a farmer or Plowman. A
bit less honest is the Miller, a jolly fellow with
a red beard and a wart at the end of his nose.

♦   ♦   ♦

His nostrils were as black as they were wide.
He had a sword and buckler at his side,
His mighty mouth was like a furnace door.

Vocabulary Development

ambling (AM bling) *adj.* moving at a slow, easy speed
mischances (mis CHAN siz) *n.* unlucky accidents;
   misfortunes
renown (ree NOWN) *n.* fame
devoutly (duh VOWT lee) *adv.* in a religious way
parishioners (puh RISH uhn uhrz) *n.* churchgoers in the
   priest's district

Literary Analysis

Circle one example each of **direct** and **indirect characterization** in these bracketed lines. Label them *direct* or *indirect.* What do they reveal about the personality or attitudes of the Wife of Bath or the Parson?

(1) The Wife of Bath is

_____

_____

(2) The Parson is

_____

_____

_____

Reading Check

Because of her great experience with love, what does the Wife of Bath know?

_____

_____

_____

---

13. **wimpled** (WIM puhld) **up** wearing a scarf covering the head, neck, and chin, as was customary for married women.
14. **buckler** (BUCK luhr) *n.* small round shield.
15. **mantle** (MAN tuhl) *n.* cloak.
16. **gospel** (GAHS puhl) a part of the Bible that tells of Christ's life and teachings.

from The Canterbury Tales: The Prologue **31**

Thumb, the word for the thickest, shortest finger, rhymes with *gum;* the *b* is silent. A *b* is often silent after an *m,* but not if it starts a new syllable. In *combine,* for example, the *b* starts a new syllable and is pronounced. Say *thumb* and *combine* aloud. Then practice saying all the words below. Circle any silent *b.*

bomb	dumb	limber
bumble	lamb	tomb
climber	limb	tombstone

Reading Check

What musical instrument does the Miller play as the pilgrims leave the town?

_____

_____

A wrangler and buffoon,[17] he had a store
Of tavern stories, filthy in the main.[18]
His was a master-hand at stealing grain.
He felt it with his <u>thumb</u> and thus he knew
Its quality and took three times his due—
A thumb of gold, by God, to <u>gauge</u> an oat!
He wore a hood of blue and a white coat.
He liked to play his bagpipes up and down
And that was how he brought us out of town.

◆　◆　◆

    The Manciple, or caterer, works at one of the London law schools. Though not a learned man, he manages to cheat all the clever law students. The Reeve, or estate manager, is skilled at managing his master's wealth. He has also managed to stash away quite a bit for himself. The Summoner, who summons people to appear in Church court, is a heavy drinker with a bad complexion. His companion is a Pardoner, an official who sells papal pardons to those summoned to the court. The Pardoner also claims to own several holy relics, or items associated with Jesus, Mary, and the saints.

◆　◆　◆

For in his trunk he had a pillowcase
Which he asserted was Our Lady's veil.[19]
He said he had a gobbet[20] of the sail
Saint Peter had the time when he made bold
To walk the waves, till Jesu Christ took hold.
He had a cross of metal set with stones
And, in a glass, a rubble of pigs' bones.

Vocabulary Development

gauge (GAYJ) *v.* measure; weigh

---

17. **wrangler** (RANG luhr) **and buffoon** (buh FOON) someone who often argues or clowns around.
18. **in the main** mainly; for the most part.
19. **Our Lady's veil** (VAYL) a veil worn by Mary, mother of Jesus.
20. **gobbet** (GAHB it) *n.* piece.

And with these relics, any time he found
Some poor up-country parson to astound,
On one short day, in money down, he drew
More than the parson in a month or two,
And by his flatteries and <u>prevarication</u>
Made <u>monkeys</u> of the priest and congregation.

◆　◆　◆

Having now described everyone,
Chaucer tells of the merry meal at the Tabard
Inn before the group leaves for Canterbury.
The Innkeeper joins the fun and makes an
interesting offer.

◆　◆　◆

"My lords," he said, "now listen for your good,
And please don't treat my notion with <u>disdain</u>.
This is the point. I'll make it short and plain.
Each one of you shall help to make things slip[21]
By telling two stories on the outward trip
To Canterbury, that's what I intend,
And, on the homeward way to journey's end
Another two, tales from the days of old;
And then the man whose story is best told,
That is to say who gives the fullest measure
Of good morality and general pleasure,
He shall be given a supper, paid by all,
Here in this tavern, in this very hall,
When we come back again from Canterbury.
And in the hope to keep you bright and merry
I'll go along with you myself and ride
All at my own expense and serve as guide.
I'll be the judge, and those who won't obey
Shall pay for what we spend upon the way."

◆　◆　◆

Everyone is happy to agree to the
Innkeeper's offer. The stories the pilgrims tell
become the individual stories of the rest of
The Canterbury Tales.

Vocabulary Development

prevarication (pree var uh KAY shuhn) *n.* avoiding the truth
disdain (dis DAYN) *n.* scorn; contempt

---

21. **make things slip** make the time go faster.

TAKE NOTES

English Language Development

"Made monkeys of" means "made fools of." Words ending in a vowel + y, like *monkey*, usually add just *s* to form their plural:

monkey + s = monkeys

Words ending in a consonant + *y* usually change the *y* to *i* and add *es*:

reply + s = replies

On the lines, write the plural form of each listed word.

baby _____

journey _____

cry _____

party _____

donkey _____

toy _____

Reading Strategy

Analyze the long bracketed **sentence** by answering the questions below.

(1) *What* does the Innkeeper propose the pilgrims do in a contest?

_____

_____

(2) *When* will the pilgrims do it?

_____

(3) *Why* should the pilgrims do it?

_____

_____

(4) *Who* will be the judge?

_____

_____

from The Canterbury Tales: The Prologue

1. **Apply:** What modern character types match the characters in the Prologue?

   _____

   _____

   _____

2. **Literary Analysis:** Choose one **character.** Explain what the appearance or actions of the character tell the reader.

   _____

   _____

   _____

3. **Literary Analysis:** Use the chart to reflect on the **social commentary** in the Prologue. What social comment does Chaucer make in his sketch of the Pardoner? What does the sketch of the Knight suggest were some of the excellences promoted by medieval society? Include the details that support the social comment.

Character	Detail	Comment About Society
Pardoner		
Knight		

4. **Reading Strategy:** Analyze the **sentence** in lines 47–50 answering the questions *who, what, how much,* and *how well.*

   _____

   _____

   _____

from The Canterbury Tales: The Pardoner's Tale

LITERARY ANALYSIS

An **allegory** is a type of story. An allegory has both a literal meaning and a deeper, more symbolic meaning. "The Pardoner's Tale" is a type of allegory called an **exemplum**. That is Latin for *example*. This tale is an exemplum about greed. As you read "The Pardoner's Tale," think about how it shows this point.

READING STRATEGY

Rereading passages can help you understand the story. It can help you:

- understand the characters.
- understand the events in the plot.
- figure out the meaning of unfamiliar words.

As you read "The Pardoner's Tale," you might come to a line that you do not understand. Reread the lines that come before. They may have information to help you. The diagram on the left shows an example Use the diagram on the right to clarify a difficult passage.

Passage	Passage
"He gathered lots and hid them in his hand. . . ."	

Reread Earlier Passage	Reread Earlier Passage
"'We draw for lots and see the way it goes; / The one who draws the longest, lucky man, . . .'"	

Clarification	Clarification
"Drawing lots" must be like drawing straws: The one who draws the longest is "it."	

from The Canterbury Tales: The Pardoner's Tale

Geoffrey Chaucer
Translated by Nevill Coghill

Summary The Pardoner tells a tale about "Greed is the root of all evil." Three young people search for Death. An old man directs them to look under a tree. They find a lot of money. The three men try to cheat each other to get more money. Their greed brings a bad result for all of them.

Note-taking Guide

Use this diagram to recall the events of the tale.

Beginning Event

Three men are looking for Death.

↓

↓

↓

↓

Final Event

from The Canterbury Tales: The Pardoner's Tale

1. **Interpret:** The old man said that Death is under the tree. Explain how his words are accurate.

   _____

   _____

2. **Literary Analysis:** Explain how the **allegory** proves that greed is the root of all evil.

   _____

   _____

3. **Reading Strategy:** In line 112, the publican tells the rioters, "He might do you dishonor." **Reread** the previous lines to explain his meaning.

   _____

   _____

4. **Reading Strategy:** In line 319, the Pardoner speaks of "blackguardly excess" as well as people killing each other. Use the following chart to help you clarify the meaning of this passage.

Passage	Reread Earlier Passage	Meaning
"Blackguardly excess"		

The Wife of Bath's Tale

LITERARY ANALYSIS

Sometimes you might read a story *within* a story. The main story serves as a **frame** around the "inner" story. For example:

- In *The Canterbury Tales*, the frame (or main story) is the characters' journey to Canterbury Cathedral. This main story is told in the General Prologue.

- Within the frame, lie the "inner" tales. These tales are told by the characters on their way to the cathedral.

Watch for a tale-within-a-tale as you read. "The Wife of Bath's Tale" is an inner story of *The Canterbury Tales*, but it also serves as a frame for another story.

READING STRATEGY

Context clues are words and phrases in a text that help show what an unfamiliar word means. Common context clues are synonyms and antonyms. The chart below shows an example.

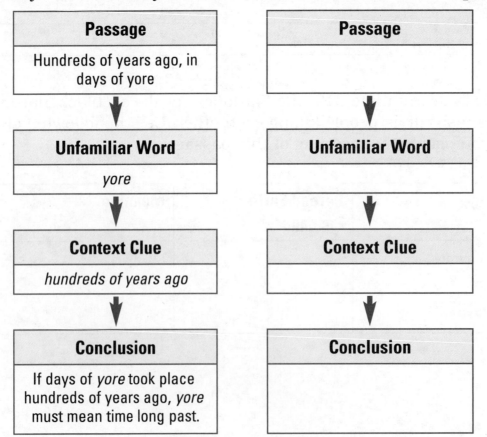

Passage	Passage
Hundreds of years ago, in days of yore	

Unfamiliar Word	Unfamiliar Word
yore	

Context Clue	Context Clue
hundreds of years ago	

Conclusion	Conclusion
If days of *yore* took place hundreds of years ago, *yore* must mean time long past.	

The Wife of Bath's Tale

Geoffrey Chaucer
Translated by Nevill Coghill

Summary A knight goes on a quest to find an answer to the question of what women most want. He meets an old woman. She will give him the answer if the knight promises to marry her. The old woman lectures the knight about all his objections to her as a wife. A surprise ending happens after the knight agrees to do what his wife says.

Note-taking Guide

In this tale, men sometimes dominate women, and the women react. What happens? Explain in the first diagram. Also, in this tale, women sometimes dominate, and the men react. What happens then? Explain in the second diagram.

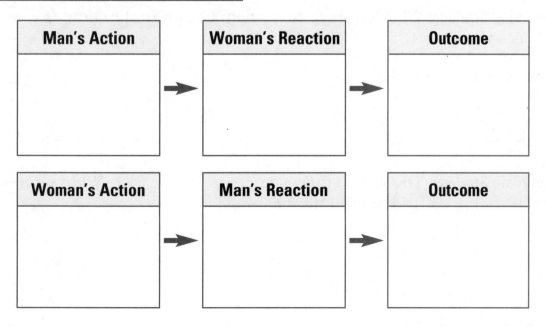

Man's Action	Woman's Reaction	Outcome

Woman's Action	Man's Reaction	Outcome

The Wife of Bath's Tale

1. **Compare and Contrast:** Compare the Wife of Bath described in the Prologue to the old woman in the tale. How are they the same? How are they different?

_____

_____

_____

2. **Literary Analysis:** In the **frame**, the Host says he will judge the pilgrims' tales on their ability to teach a moral lesson and their entertainment value. If you were the Host, how would you respond to the Wife's tale? Use the chart to note details from the tale. Use the details to make a final judgment. One detail is given to you.

Good Morality/ Lesson	General Pleasure/ Entertainment Value	Final Judgment
The knight is forced to marry the old woman.		

3. **Reading Strategy:** What **context clues** help you to understand the word *dejected* in line 135?

_____

_____

_____

4. **Reading Strategy:** The word *suffices* appears in line 381. What context clues help you understand its meaning?

_____

_____

_____

from Sir Gawain and the Green Knight
• from Morte d'Arthur

LITERARY ANALYSIS

Medieval romances are adventure stories. The characters are kings, knights, and damsels in distress. They tell of quests, battles, and love. The stories of King Arthur and his Knights are examples of medieval romances. As you read these stories, look for ideas of love and honor in a mix of realism and fantasy.

READING STRATEGY

When you **summarize** a story, you:

• retell the main parts of a story.

• explain the main ideas.

• do not include all the details.

The chart on the left shows an example. Use the chart on the right to summarize the key ideas and details in a passage.

Passage	Passage
"Ah, traitor unto me and untrue," said King Arthur, "now hast thou betrayed me twice. Who would have weened that thou that has been to me so loved and dear . . . , and would betray me for the riches of this sword."	
Summary	**Summary**
King Arthur charges his knight with betraying him twice out of greed.	

from Sir Gawain and the Green Knight

Translated by Marie Borroff

Summary A huge green knight dares Arthur's knights to cut off his head. The knight who beheads him must have his own head cut off in a year. Sir Gawain accepts the Green Knight's challenge. He cuts off the Green Knight's head. The headless knight survives. A year later, Gawain sets off to find the knight and fulfill his promise. His loyalty and honesty undergo different tests.

Note-taking Guide

Use this diagram to summarize the key events in the story of *Sir Gawain and the Green Knight.*

Passage	Passage
"Ah, traitor unto me and untrue," said King Arthur, "now hast thou betrayed me twice. Who would have weened that thou that has been to me so loved and dear . . . , and would betray me for the riches of this sword."	
Summary	**Summary**
King Arthur charges his knight with betraying him twice out of greed.	

from Morte d'Arthur

Sir Thomas Malory

Summary King Arthur has a dream. In his dream, Gawain warns him not to fight Mordred. Arthur does fight Mordred, and he receives a mortal wound. He knows he is going to die. He asks his knight Bedivere to throw his magic sword into a lake. Bedivere places Arthur on a mysterious barge. The barge sails away. The next day Bedivere finds a new grave. No one knows if Arthur will return to be king.

Note-taking Guide

Use this diagram to summarize the key events in the story of King Arthur's death.

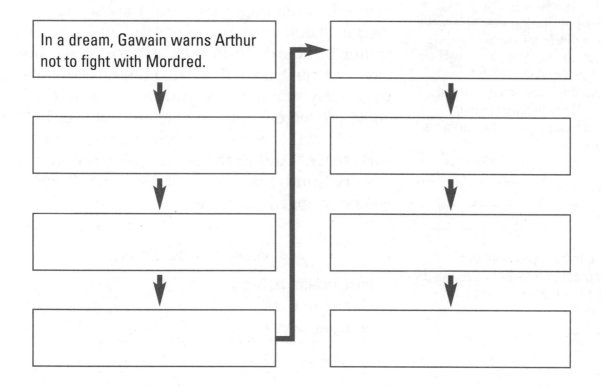

In a dream, Gawain warns Arthur not to fight with Mordred.

from Morte d' Arthur

Sir Thomas Malory

During the Middle Ages, knights swore loyalty to their lord or king. Breaking that oath of loyalty was a great sin. Mordred's close family relationship to Arthur make his sin even worse. What is his relationship to Gawain, who dies because of his actions?

_____

_____

_____

English Language Development

Morte d'Arthur uses many old words not usually used today. What pronoun is used today instead of ye? Use the surrounding words to figure out the meaning of *ye*.

_____

_____

_____

Then, to help you read this paragraph, cross out all the *ye's* and write the modern pronoun instead.

King Arthur creates an ideal kingdom called Camelot where talented knights sit at a Round Table and all feel equal. But jealousy and other human weakness eventually destroy Camelot. Arthur is forced to fight his friend Sir Lancelot in France. While he is away, his illegitimate son Mordred tries to steal the English throne. When Arthur races home to fight Mordred, Arthur's nephew Sir Gawain is killed almost immediately. Gawain returns to Arthur in a dream, surrounded by lovely ladies Gawain has helped in life. He warns Arthur not to fight Mordred the next day. If he does, both sides will take huge losses, and Arthur will die. So Arthur arranges a one-month treaty. The two sides each bring fourteen men to the place where the treaty will be signed.

◆ ◆ ◆

And when King Arthur should depart, he warned all his <u>host</u> that, and[1] they see any sword drawn, "Look ye come on fiercely and <u>slay</u> that traitor Sir Mordred, for I in no wise[2] trust him." In like wise Sir Mordred warned his host that "And ye see any manner of sword drawn, look that ye come on fiercely, and so slay all that ever before you standeth, for in no wise I will not trust for this treaty." And in the same wise said Sir Mordred unto his host, "For I know well my father will be <u>avenged</u> upon me."

Vocabulary Development

host (HOHST) *n.* army; troops
slay (SLAY) *v.* kill
avenged (uh VENJD) *v.* gotten revenge

---

1. **and** if.
2. **wis:** way.

And so they met as their pointment[3] was and were agreed and <u>accorded</u> thoroughly. And wine was fetched and they drank together. Right so came an <u>adder</u> out of a little heathbush, and it stung a knight in the foot. And so when the knight felt him so stung, he looked down and saw the adder. And anon[4] he drew his sword to slay the adder, and thought none other harm. And when the host on both parties saw that sword drawn, then they blew beams,[5] trumpets, horns, and shouted grimly. And so both hosts dressed them[6] together. And King Arthur took his horse and said, "Alas, this unhappy day!" and so rode to his party, and Sir Mordred in like wise.

◆   ◆   ◆

The battle that breaks out is a horrible one. A hundred thousand soldiers are killed. Arthur is horrified to see so many of his noble knights fall.

◆   ◆   ◆

Then King Arthur looked about and was ware[7] where stood Sir Mordred leaning upon his sword among a great heap of dead men.

"Now give me my spear," said King Arthur unto Sir Lucan, "for yonder I have <u>espied</u> the traitor that all this woe hath wrought."[8]

◆   ◆   ◆

Vocabulary Development

accorded (uh KAWR did) *v.* brought into harmony or agreement

adder (AD uhr) *n.* poisonous snake

espied (es PĪD) *v.* spotted; seen

---

3. **pointment** arrangement.
4. **anon** soon after; immediately.
5. **beams** a type of trumpet.
6. **dressed them** prepared to come.
7. **ware** aware.
8. **hath wrought** (RAWT): has made.

TAKE NOTES

Reading Strategy

Circle key ideas and details in the bracketed passage. Then, **summarize** how the fighting begins.

_____

_____

_____

Vocabulary and Pronunciation

The letter combination *ea* has three main sounds, shown on this chart. Say the three examples aloud.

Sound	Example	Rhymes with
1. long /*a*/	great	ate
2. long /*e*/	heap	peep
3. short /*e*/	dead	bed

Say each word below. Then, on the line, write whether it uses long /*a*/, long /*e*/, or short /*e*/.

- already _____
- jealous _____
- break _____
- spear _____
- death _____
- steak _____
- dream _____
- treaty _____

Read the underlined sentence aloud. How do you think Arthur said it? Circle the letter of the best choice below. Then circle the punctuation in the underlined sentence that points to the answer.

(a) in a loud, angry voice

(b) in a tired, weary voice

(c) in a frightened, trembling voice

(d) in a dangerously quiet voice

English Language Development

A famous English spelling rule says:

Use i before e except after c

Or when sounded like A *as in* neighbor and weigh.

Of course, there are exceptions, but *shield* follows the rule. So do all the incomplete words below. Complete each by adding ie or *ei* on the line. Also say the words aloud.

bel___ve   f___rce   rec___ve

c___ling   gr___ve   shr___k

dec___ve   p___rced   v___l

Stop to Reflect

The word *wound* has two different pronunciations. Rhymed with *ground,* it means "twisted or turned." Rhymed with tuned, it means "an injury" or "to injure."

(1) What is the word's meaning here?

_____

(2) How should the word be pronounced here?

_____

Sir Lucan, one of Arthur's knights, advises him not to fight. He points out that Arthur has already won the day and reminds the king of his dream. But Arthur insists on fighting Mordred.

◆   ◆   ◆

Then the King got his spear in both his hands and ran toward Sir Mordred, crying and saying, "Traitor, now is thy deathday come!"

And when Sir Mordred saw King Arthur he ran until him with his sword drawn in his hand, and there King Arthur <u>smote</u> Sir Mordred under the shield, with a thrust of his spear, throughout the body more than a fathom.[9] And when Sir Mordred felt that he had his death's wound, he thrust himself with the might that he had up to the burr[10] of King Arthur's spear, and right so he smote his father King Arthur with his sword holden in both his hands, upon the side of the head, that the sword pierced the helmet and the casing of the brain. And therewith Sir Mordred dashed down stark dead to the earth.

And noble King Arthur fell in a swough[11] to the earth, and there he <u>swooned</u> oftentimes, and Sir Lucan and Sir Bedivere ofttimes heaved him up. And so, weakly betwixt[12] them, they led him to a little chapel not far from the seaside.

◆   ◆   ◆

Vocabulary Development

smote (SMOHT) *v.* struck down or killed; past tense of *smite*

swooned (SWOOND) *v.* fainted

---

9. **fathom** (FATH uhm) *n.* six feet.
10. **burr** hand guard.
11. **swough** (SWŌ) *n.* faint or swoon.
12. **betwixt** (buh TWIXT) *prep.* between.

Sir Lucan and his brother Sir Bedivere decide to bring the wounded Arthur to the safety of a town. They try to lift him up again. But Lucan, who was wounded in battle, collapses and dies. Bedivere weeps at the death of his brother and the likely death of his king.

◆　◆　◆

"Now leave this mourning and weeping gentle knight," said the King, "for all this will not avail me.[13] For wit thou[14] well, and might I live myself, the death of Sir Lucan would grieve me evermore. But my time passeth on fast," said the King. "Therefore," said King Arthur unto Sir Bedivere, "take thou here Excalibur my good sword and go with it to yonder water's side; and when thou comest there I charge thee throw my sword in that water and come again and tell me what thou sawest there."

"My lord," said Sir Bedivere, "your <u>commandment</u> shall be done, and I shall lightly[15] bring you word again."

◆　◆　◆

Sir Bedivere takes the sword to the lake. But he cannot bring himself to throw it in. It simply seems too valuable. There are even jewels in the hilt, or handle. So Bedivere hides the sword under a tree and returns to Arthur.

◆　◆　◆

"What saw thou there?" said the King.

"Sir," he said, "I saw nothing but waves and winds."

"That is untruly said of thee," said the King. "And therefore go thou lightly again and do my commandment; as thou art to me loved and dear, spare not, but throw it in."

◆　◆　◆

Vocabulary Development

commandment (kuh MAND muhnt) *n.*   order; command

---

13. **avail** (uh VAYL) **me** help me; do me any good.
14. **wit thou** know you.
15. **lightly** quickly.

TAKE NOTES

Culture Note

In the early Middle Ages, it was the custom of warriors to give a name to their sword. Why do you think they did this?

_____

_____

_____

English Language Development

Thou and thee are two more old forms of *you*, and *passeth* is an old verb form that would be *passes* today. The selection uses several old verb forms ending in *eth* or *est*. Circle two more in this paragraph. Near each, write the verb form that would be used today.

Literary Analysis

Which element of **medieval romances** does the underlined passage illustrate? Circle the letter of the best answer below.

(a) unusual settings

(b) supernatural events

(c) beautiful ladies in need of help

(d) battles or contests

Reading Strategy

Summarize, or retell briefly in your own words, what happens in the bracketed passage.

_____

_____

_____

Sir Bedivere goes again to the lake. He still cannot throw the sword in. Again he returns to Arthur and pretends he has thrown it in. Again Arthur knows he is lying. Arthur begs Bedivere to obey him.

◆   ◆   ◆

Then Sir Bedivere departed and went to the sword and lightly took it up, and so he went to the water's side; and there he bound the girdle[16] about the hilts, and threw the sword as far into the water as he might. And there came an arm and an hand above the water and took it and clutched it, and shook it thrice[17] and brandished; and then vanished away the hand with the sword into the water. So Sir Bedivere came again to the King and told him what he saw.

"Alas," said the King, "help me hence,[18] for I dread me[19] I have tarried overlong."

Then Sir Bedivere took the King upon his back and so went with him to that water's side. And when they were at the water's side, even fast[20] by the bank floated a little barge with many fair ladies in it; and among them all was a queen; and all they had black hoods, and all they wept and shrieked when they saw King Arthur.

Vocabulary Development

brandished (BRAN disht) *v.* waved in a threatening way
tarried (TAR eed) *v.* waited; lingered
bank (BANK) *n.* the land alongside a lake or river
barge (BAHRJ) *n.* a flat-bottomed boat
fair (FAYR) *adj.* pretty; nice looking

---

16. **girdle** (GER duhl) *n.* the sash or belt used to strap the sword around the hips of the person wearing it.
17. **thrice** (THRĪS) *adv.* three times.
18. **hence** from here.
19. **dread** (DRED) **me** fear.
20. **fast** close.

"Now put me into that barge," said the King; and so he did softly. And there received him three ladies with great mourning, and so they set them down. And in one of their laps King Arthur laid his head.

◆ ◆ ◆

Sir Bedivere weeps as Arthur explains that he must leave him and go to the legendary island of Avilion. He asks Bedivere to pray for him. The next morning, Bedivere meets a hermit who was once the Archbishop of Canterbury. The hermit explains that some women brought him a dead body. They asked him to bury it. So the hermit buried it in the little chapel.

◆ ◆ ◆

Now more of the death of King Arthur could I never find, but that these ladies brought him to his grave, and such one was <u>interred</u> there which the hermit bare witness that was once Bishop of Canterbury. But yet the hermit knew not in certain that he was verily[21] the body of King Arthur; for this tale Sir Bedivere, a knight of the Table Round, made it to be written.

Yet some men say in many parts of England that King Arthur is not dead, but carried by the will of our Lord Jesu into another place; and men say that he shall come again, and he shall win the Holy Cross. Yet I will not say that it shall be so, but rather I would say: here in this world he changed his life. And many men say that there is written upon the tomb this:

HIC IACET ARTHURUS, REX QUONDAM, REXQUE FUTURUS[22]

Vocabulary Development

interred (in TURD) *n.* buried

---

21. **verily** (VER uh lee) *adv.* truly.
22. **HIC . . . FUTURS** Here lies Arthur, who was once king and will be king again.

TAKE NOTES

Reading Check

According to the ending, what has happened or will happen to Arthur? Answer by completing the sentence below.

Either he

_____

_____

_____

or he

_____

_____

_____

from Sir Gawain and the Green Knight
• from Morte d'Arthur

1. **Make a Judgment:** In your opinion, has Sir Gawain failed to live up to his knightly ideals? Explain. Think about his actions throughout the story.

_____

_____

2. **Interpret:** Mordred is Arthur's illegitimate son. How does the conflict between Mordred and Arthur emphasize the theme of betrayal in *Morte d'Arthur*?

_____

_____

3. **Literary Analysis:** Both Sir Gawain and Sir Bedivere face challenges as knights. Compare Sir Gawain and Sir Bedivere. Read the way Sir Gawain reacts to the Green Knight's questioning of his honor in lines 459–477. Then, read about how Bedivere reacts to King Arthur's request to throw the sword in the water. Write your ideas in the chart below.

	Gawain's Reactions	Bedivere's Reactions
What He Says	He confesses to having lied.	
What He Does		
What He Feels		

4. **Reading Strategy:** Pretend you are Sir Bedivere and a curious traveler comes to visit you. **Summarize** the main events leading up to King Arthur's death.

_____

_____

Letters of Margaret Paston • Four Ballads

LITERARY ANALYSIS

A **letter** is written to a specific person or group to be read at a specific time. That is why letters are a great "window" into the past. They save or *preserve* a moment in history.

A **folk ballad** is a story. It is told as a poem and is meant to be sung. Some ballads are funny, while others are more serious. Most ballads have these features:

- Verses (or stanzas) with four lines; the second and fourth lines usually rhyme
- Repeated phrases, or a repeated verse; this is the refrain
- Dialogue.

Letters and ballads can serve as **primary sources.** These are documents from the past that report events or values of the time. Primary sources include letters, legal documents, and songs. Compare the information these selections offer about medieval life.

READING STRATEGY

A **dialect** is a form of language. It is spoken by people in a certain area or group. In these ballads, you will read words in the Scottish-English dialect. To understand them, you can:

- read the words out loud. Listen to how they sound. Do they sound like words you know?

- read the footnotes. Footnotes provide extra help.

Use the chart to help you figure out dialect.

Phrase in Dialect	They made a paction tween them twa.		
Meaning Suggested	**Sound:** twa = two tween = between		
Meaning Given in Footnote	paction = agreement		

Letters of Margaret Paston

Summary These letters provide insights into life in the Middle Ages. Paston describes attacks and impending attacks on the Paston lands.

Note-taking Guide

Use the chart to record the main ideas of each of Paston's letters.

Main Ideas		
Letter Dated 17 October 1465	Letter Dated 27 October 1465	Letter Dated 11 July 1467

Twa Corbies • Lord Randall • Get Up and Bar the Door • Barbara Allan

Summaries In "Twa Corbies," a speaker hears two ravens discussing their next meal. It is a dead knight's corpse. "Lord Randall" presents the last moments in Lord Randall's life. His mother finds out he has been poisoned. "Get Up and Bar the Door" recounts fighting between a man and wife over who will lock the door to their home. "Barbara Allan" tells the story of a woman who visits her love on his deathbed. She shows him no sympathy.

Note-taking Guide

Fill in the chart with details about the main characters in each of the ballads.

Ballad	Main Characters	What the Characters Do
Twa Corbies		
Lord Randall		
Get Up and Bar the Door		
Barbara Allan		

Letters of Margaret Paston • Four Ballads

1. **Generalize:** What do these letters and ballads suggests about life in medieval England? Support your answer with details.

_____

_____

_____

2. **Literary Analysis:** Use the Venn diagram to compare the kinds of historical information you can find in Paston's letters and the ballads. The chart has been started for you.

The Paston Letters | specific details about the raids on the manor. | **Ballads**

3. **Reading Strategy:** Read these words from "Twa Corbies": "And *naebody kens* that he lies there..." The words *naebody kens* are in a **dialect.** What do they mean?

_____

_____

_____

4. **Reading Strategy:** Find two other dialect words in the ballads. Explain their meanings and the strategy you used to figure them out.

_____

_____

_____

Sonnet 1 • Sonnet 35 • Sonnet 75 • Sonnet 31 • Sonnet 39

LITERARY ANALYSIS

These are the elements of the literary form known as a **sonnet:**

- lyric poem, • fourteen lines • single theme
- each line written in iambic pentameter, which means there are five groups of two syllables, with the stress falling on the second syllable

Two types of sonnets are as follows:

Petrarchan (pi TRAHR kuhn)

- First eight lines ("octave")
- rhyme *abba abba*
- often present a problem
- Last six lines ("sestet")
- rhyme *cdecde*
- often give solution

Spenserian (spen SIR ee uhn)

- First 12 lines are three groups of four lines each
- rhyme *abab bcbc cdcd*
- Last two lines ("couplet")
- rhyme *ee*

A **sonnet sequence** is a group of sonnets. They are linked by theme or addressed to the same person. As you read these sonnets, notice their form and how they are linked.

READING STRATEGY

To **paraphrase** a poem, read until you find a complete thought. Then, decide which information is important. Restate important thoughts in your own words. Use this chart to help.

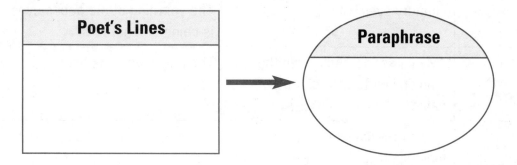

Sonnets 1, 35, 75
Sonnets 31, 39

Edmund Spenser
Sir Philip Sidney

Summary In Sonnet 1, Spenser asks his pages, lines, and rhymes to please his beloved. In Sonnet 35, he says that he cannot gaze upon his beloved without feeling the pain of hopeless desire. In Sonnet 75, he writes his beloved's name in the sand. However, the waves wash it away.

In Sonnet 31, Sidney sees the pale. He asks if the moon is pale because, like him, it is unhappy in love. Sidney asks for the peace and healing of sleep in Sonnet 39. Asleep, he may dream of Stella, his beloved.

Note-taking Guide

One way an author tries to describe something for a reader is to compare it to something else. As you read these sonnets, explain the comparison that the poet is making in each of the listed phrases.

Sonnet	The Comparison, in the Poet's Words	What Two Items Are Being Compared?
1	"lily hands"	The beloved's hands are being compared to
35	"hungry eyes"	The yearning of the poet's eyes is being compared to
1	"My verse . . . shall . . . in the heavens write your glorious name."	The poet's verse is being compared to
1	"With how sad steps, O Moon, thou climb'st . . ."	The moon is being compared to
1	"sleep, the certain knot of peace"	Sleep is being compared to

Sonnet 1 • Sonnet 35 • Sonnet 75 • Sonnet 31 • Sonnet 39

1. **Literary Analysis:** Use this chart to compare and contrast one of Sidney's **sonnets** with one of Spenser's. Some information has been filled in.

Petrarchan/ Spenserian?	Speaker's Situation	Addressed to ...	Types of Images	Speaker's Conclusion
Spenser, Sonnet 1		Leaves, lines and rhymes		
Sidney, Sonnet 31		the moon		

2. **Literary Analysis:** Do Sidney's Sonnets 31 and 39 more closely follow the **Spenserian** or the **Petrarchan** form? Explain

_____

_____

3. **Reading Strategy:** Write a **paraphrase** of lines 1-8 of Sidney's Sonnet 39.

_____

_____

_____

4. **Reading Strategy:** Write a paraphrase of lines 9-14 of Sidney's Sonnet 39.

_____

_____

The Passionate Shepherd to His Love
• The Nymph's Reply to the Shepherd

LITERARY ANALYSIS

A **pastoral** poem celebrates life in the country. It celebrates nature. Many pastoral poems have a shepherd. A shepherd is someone who watches over a flock of sheep. In a pastoral poem, the shepherd usually:

• writes to someone he loves;

• writes about how beautiful nature is.

Pastoral poems were usually written by skilled poets, not by shepherds. The poems were written for people who lived in the city. The poems let city people experience what a simple country life was like. When you read these pastoral poems, look for:

• details in "The Passionate Shepherd to His Love" that describe how beautiful nature in the country is;

• details in "The Nymph's Reply to the Shepherd" that point out what is wrong with the shepherd's ideas about nature.

READING STRATEGY

When you **identify with the speaker of a poem,** you put yourself in the speaker's place. You try to understand the speaker's feelings and goals. Recognizing these feelings and goals can help you figure out a poem's theme. Fill in this chart. It will help you identify with each speaker.

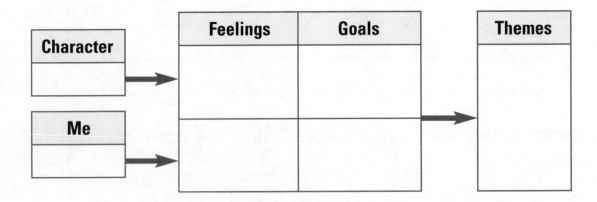

The Passionate Shepherd to His Love

Christopher Marlowe

The Nymph's Reply to the Shepherd

Sir Walter Raleigh

Summary In "The Passionate Shepherd to His Love," a shepherd invites his love to live with him. They will live in nature, surrounded by valleys and hills. The shepherd describes all the beauties they will see and enjoy.

In "The Nymph's Reply to the Shepherd," the shepherd's love answers his passionate request. She turns him down because everything changes and ages. All the beauties he describes will fade. Neither youth nor love will last.

Note-taking Guide

As you read these two poems, record the shepherd's promises and the nymph's replies on this chart. Also, explain who you think is more convincing.

Why Does the Shepherd Promise?	What Does the Nymph Respond?	Who Is More Convincing? Why?

The Passionate Shepherd to His Love
• The Nymph's Reply to the Shepherd

1. **Literary Analysis:** Both poems are examples of **pastoral** poetry. Each poem expresses a different idea. Use the chart to record details that express the shepherd's perfect, idealistic version of nature and the nymph's more realistic view. One item has been filled in for you.

Shepherd's Idealism	Nymph's Realism
We will enjoy the beauty of valley's groves, hills, and fields.	

2. **Reading Strategy:** Do you **sympathize** with the speaker in "The Passionate Shepherd to His Love"? Why or why not?

_____

_____

3. **Reading Strategy:** In "The Nymph's Reply to the Shepherd," how does the speaker reveal a distrustful side to her nature?

_____

_____

_____

4. **Reading Strategy:** What experiences might have shaped the speaker's attitudes in "The Nymph's Reply"?

_____

_____

Sonnet 29 • Sonnet 106 • Sonnet 116 • Sonnet 130

LITERARY ANALYSIS

Shakespeare used a variation of the sonnet form when he composed his poems. A **Shakespearean** (shayk SPIR ee uhn) **sonnet** has fourteen lines, as do all sonnets. However, unlike Petrarchan (pi TRAHR kuhn) and Spenserian (spen SIR ee uhn) sonnets, a Shakespearean sonnet follows this rhyme scheme: *abab cdcd efef gg.* Shakespearean sonnets.

- three **quatrains** (KWAH trayns), or four-line stanzas
- a rhyming **couplet** (KUHP let), which often resolves the central problem of the sonnet

Notice how Shakespeare uses the first twelve lines of each sonnet to present a problem. Then, he resolves or restates the problem in the couplet.

READING STRATEGY

As you read, **relate structure to theme.** In each sonnet, Shakespeare builds on his meaning from quatrain to quatrain. Notice how he uses the couplet to deliver a dramatic final statement. As you read, fill in this chart. Record the main idea in the second quatrain of Sonnet 29. Then, in the third box, show how the ideas in the first two quatrains are related.

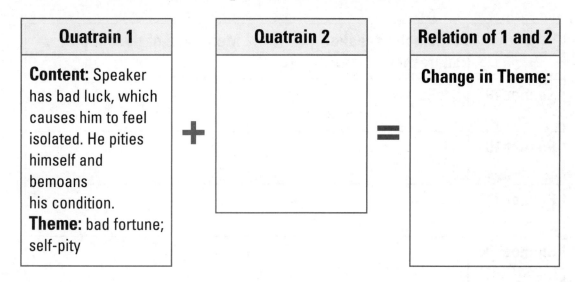

Quatrain 1		Quatrain 2		Relation of 1 and 2
Content: Speaker has bad luck, which causes him to feel isolated. He pities himself and bemoans his condition. **Theme:** bad fortune; self-pity	**+**		**=**	**Change in Theme:**

Sonnet 29 • Sonnet 106 • Sonnet 116 • Sonnet 130

William Shakespeare

Summary The speaker in Sonnet 29 wallows in his own misfortune and wishes he were someone else. However, thinking about his loved one brings him such joy that he is happy to be himself. In Sonnet 106, the speaker says that even the best writers of the past lacked the words and skill to praise his love. Sonnet 116 is about true love and how it never changes. In Sonnet 130, the speaker says that his beloved is not the typical beauty described in many poems.

Note-taking Guide

In some of the sonnets, the speaker seems to be addressing a specific person. In others, the speaker appears to address the general public. For each sonnet, use the chart to record whom the speaker addresses and the main idea of the couplet at the end of the poem.

	Whom the speaker addresses	Main idea of the couplet
Sonnet 29		
Sonnet 106		
Sonnet 116		
Sonnet 130		

Sonnet 29 • Sonnet 106 • Sonnet 116 • Sonnet 130

1. **Literary Analysis:** Identify the three quatrains and the couplet of one of these **Shakespearean sonnets.**

   _____

   _____

2. **Literary Analysis:** Use the chart below to show how Shakespeare conveys his message in the sonnet form in Sonnet 106. One box is filled in for you.

Theme:		
Message of Quatrain 1: When in historical records and old poems I see descriptions of lovely women and handsome knights	**Message of Quatrain 2:**	**Message of Quatrain 3:**
Connection to Theme:	**Connection to Theme:**	**Connection to Theme:**
Message of Couplet:		

3. **Reading Strategy: Relate structure to theme** by listing the main idea of each section of Sonnet 116.

   _____

   _____

   _____

4. **Reading Strategy:** Does each idea in Sonnet 116 correspond to a quatrain or couplet? Explain.

   _____

   _____

from Utopia • Speech Before Her Troops

LITERARY ANALYSIS

The English Renaissance (REN uh SAHNS) took place from 1485-1625. Writers imitated Greek and Roman literature. The literature of the English Renaissance often shows the **monarch as hero.** Writers created heroic portraits of the monarch to make citizens feel loyal. Praising rulers could also help writers make connections with the royal court. Look for this **theme** as you read.

In *Utopia*, Sir Thomas More uses logic to paint a picture of the heroic monarch. He connects the qualities of a monarch with the effects of his or her actions. By contrast, Queen Elizabeth I acts out the part of the heroic monarch as she gives her speech. She wears armor, and she offers to join her troops in battle. Both writers use **persuasive devices,** or methods, to convince their audiences to accept their arguments. The devices include:

- **Reasoned argument**—the use of one idea to logically support another.
- **Charged language**—strong words that convey emotion about an issue.

READING STRATEGY

To **summarize** means to restate the main ideas of a work. Use these charts to note the main ideas of these selections. In your own words, state the main idea from the statement provided.

More's Statement
And that therefore a prince ought to take more care of his people's happiness than his own, . . .

↓

Main Idea

Elizabeth's Statement
I myself will take up arms; I myself will be your general, judge, and rewarder of every one of your virtues in the field.

↓

Main Idea

from Utopia

Sir Thomas More

Summary Subjects choose a king for their own sake, not for the king's. A king should therefore take better care of his subjects than he does of himself. By keeping his subjects poor, a king will only make them more discontented. He should live on the income that he naturally receives and not seize property from his subjects in an unjust manner. Also, he should deal with crime by preventing it, rather than by punishing criminals after they have violated the law.

Note-taking Guide

This chart shows the main idea of the selection. Below the main idea, list the details that the author uses.

Main Idea

Because people choose a king, for their own sake, a king should take better care of his subjects than of himself.

Supporting Details

In a **summary,** you state the main idea of a passage in your own words. Summarize More's main idea in the bracketed passage.

_____

_____

_____

More believes that the answers to the questions in the bracketed passage are obvious. He uses the questions for persuasive effect. Rewrite one of the three questions so that it is in the form of a statement, rather than a question.

_____

_____

_____

Underline two words or phrases that More uses to describe people who are the *opposite* of a **monarch as hero.**

Circle two words identifying vices or defects that cause the people to hate or scorn a ruler.

from Utopia
Sir Thomas More

A good king should be like a shepherd. He should care for his people's happiness more than for his own.

♦   ♦   ♦

Certainly it is wrong to think that the poverty of the people is a safeguard of public peace. Who quarrel more than beggars do? Who long for a change more earnestly than the dissatisfied? Or who rushes in to create disorders [with] such desperate boldness as the man who has nothing to lose and everything to gain?

♦   ♦   ♦

If a king is hated by his subjects, it is better for him to resign. Dignified kings rule over prosperous people, not over beggars.

♦   ♦   ♦

When a ruler enjoys wealth and pleasure while all about him are grieving and groaning, he acts as a jailor rather than as a king. He is a poor physician who cannot cure a disease except by throwing his patient into another. A king who can only rule his people by taking from them the pleasures of life shows that he does not know how to govern free men. He ought to shake off either his <u>sloth</u> or his pride, for the people's hatred and scorn arise from these faults in him. Let him live on his own income without wronging others, and limit his expenses to his <u>revenue.</u>

♦   ♦   ♦

A good king should try to prevent crime. He should not try foolishly to revive outdated laws. He should never take other people's property in cases where a judge would decide that such a seizure was evil.

Vocabulary Development

sloth (SLAWTH) *n.* laziness
revenue (REV uh NYOO) *n.* income

Speech Before Her Troops

Queen Elizabeth I

Summary Queen Elizabeth is speaking to her armed forces, who have assembled to do battle with the Spanish naval fleet. She tells her audience that she has been advised not to appear before them, for fear that she might be attacked. However, she trusts her loyal subjects. She wants to be among them at this critical moment and, if necessary, to give up her life. She may "have . . . the body of a weak . . . woman," but she has the brave "heart of a . . . king of England, . . ." Also, she will reward those who fight well. She tells her listeners to obey her lieutenant general, who will lead the English forces. Then, she predicts that they will soon win a great victory over the Spanish.

Note-taking Guide

Elizabeth's speech has both dramatic arguments and practical messages. In the chart below, list the details that are dramatic arguments and those that are practical messages.

Two Strands of Queen Elizabeth's Argument

Arguments for Dramatic Effect	Practical Message

Elizabeth I uses the pronoun *we* rather than *I* to refer to herself. This usage is sometimes called the "royal *we*." You will also find it used by courtroom judges and newspaper editors. What effect does this choice of words have?

_____

_____

Reading Strategy

Summarize, or restate briefly in your own words, the first paragraph of Elizabeth's speech.

_____

_____

_____

_____

Literary Analysis

How does the comparison in the bracketed paragraph show Elizabeth as a **heroic monarch?**

_____

_____

_____

_____

Stop to Reflect

What effect do you think this speech had on Queen Elizabeth's audience?

_____

_____

_____

Speech Before Her Troops

Elizabeth I

My loving people, we have been persuaded by some, that are careful of our safety, to take heed how we commit ourselves to armed multitudes, for fear of treachery; but I assure you, I do not desire to live to distrust my faithful and loving people. Let tyrants fear; I have always so behaved myself that, under God, I have placed my chiefest strength and safeguard in the loyal hearts and good will of my subjects.

♦ ♦ ♦

Therefore, says Elizabeth, she has come before the troops. She has made a firm decision to live or die with them. She will lay down her honor and her life for God and for the kingdom.

♦ ♦ ♦

I know I have but the body of a weak and feeble woman; but I have the heart of a king, and of a king of England, too.

♦ ♦ ♦

It is disgraceful that any foreign ruler should dare to invade England. Elizabeth says she will fight rather than suffer dishonor. She herself will lead her troops in battle, and she will reward her soldiers for bravery.

♦ ♦ ♦

I know already, by your forwardness, that you have deserved rewards and crowns; and we do assure you, on the word of a prince, that they shall be duly paid you.

♦ ♦ ♦

The lieutenant who represents Elizabeth is noble and worthy. She tells the troops she is sure that their obedience, teamwork, and courage will help them defeat the enemy. They will win a famous victory.

from Utopia • *Speech Before Her Troops*

1. **Apply:** Does the physical presence of leaders count as much today as it did in the time of Queen Elizabeth I?

_____

_____

2. **Literary Analysis:** How realistic is More's presentation of the **theme** of the **monarch as hero**?

_____

_____

3. **Literary Analysis:** Analyze how Elizabeth's appearance in front of her troops is a persuasive device. In the chart below, list the reasons that Elizabeth gives for appearing before her troops.

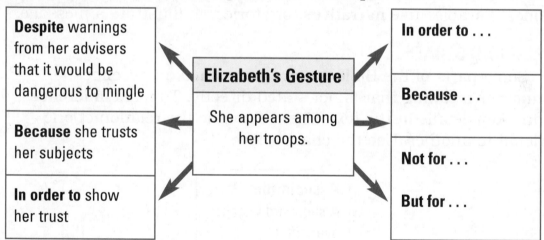

Despite warnings from her advisers that it would be dangerous to mingle

Because she trusts her subjects

In order to show her trust

Elizabeth's Gesture

She appears among her troops.

In order to . . .

Because . . .

Not for . . .

But for . . .

4. **Reading Strategy: Summarize** More's Utopia, listing each main idea.

_____

_____

5. **Reading Strategy:** Summarize Elizabeth's speech.

_____

_____

from The King James Bible

LITERARY ANALYSIS

Faith is a theme that appears in the Bible. It appears in literary forms such as these:

- **Psalms**—sacred songs or lyric poems that praise God. The Old Testament's Book of Psalms contains 150 such pieces.
- **Sermons**—speeches that give religious or instruction. The Sermon on the Mount contains the basic teachings of Christianity.
- **Parables**—simple stories from which a moral or religious lesson can be drawn. The most famous are in the New Testament.

Notice that each type of writing communicates in its own way. As songs, psalms use vivid **metaphors,** comparisons in which one thing is spoken of as if it were another. Sermons may use **analogies,** explanations that compare abstract things to familiar ones. Parables use **narratives,** or stories, to illustrate a message.

READING STRATEGY

Some parts of the Bible require you to **make inferences,** or uncover meaning that is not stated directly. To make inferences, find key details in the text. Then, examine the relation of one detail to another. Use the chart below.

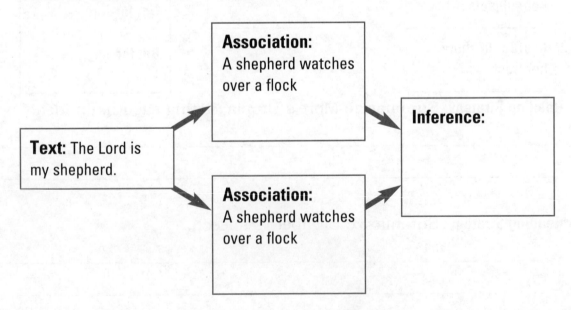

Psalm 23

Summary Psalm 23 is a sacred song or lyric poem that praises God. The speaker compares God to a shepherd who cares for his flock both during and after life. Some of the words do not address God directly. However, this psalm is often used as a prayer requesting God to continue providing loving care for the person praying.

Note-taking Guide

This psalm praises God for acting as a shepherd to his people. As you read, use this chart to record what God does in the left column. Then, in the right column, restate these actions in our own words. One item is already filled in.

Deeds listed in text	How God is Comforting and Protecting
He maketh me lie down in green pastures; he leadeth me beside the still waters.	He provides a place to rest, food, and drink.

from The Sermon on the Mount

Summary The Sermon on the Mount is a speech thought to have been made by Jesus. The sermon includes many basic principles of the Christian religion. This section of the longer speech teaches that people cannot serve both God and money. Also, no one should worry about physical needs because God will provide everything, just as He does for birds and plants.

Note-taking Guide

Use the chart below to record important details from The Sermon on the Mount.

Title: The Sermon on the Mount
Audience:
Purpose:
Advice Given:

from The Parable of the Prodigal Son

Summary The Parable of the Prodigal Son is the story of a man with two sons. One son stays home and works. The other son leaves home, lives wildly, and spends everything. He is the prodigal (PRAH di GUHL), a person who is recklessly wasteful. When that son becomes hungry, he returns home and apologizes. His father is delighted and holds a feast. This angers the brother who stayed home and worked. The father explains that it is worth celebrating when someone who goes astray is found again.

Note-taking Guide

As you read, fill in the chart below with information about the two sons in the story. Then write the overall message in the box at the bottom.

Young Son	Older Son
How he lives his life:	How he lives his life:
What he does at the end:	How he feels at the end:
Message of the story:	

from The King James Bible

1. **Literary Analysis:** Why is the form of a **sermon** suited to the message taught by the Sermon on the Mount?

   _____

   _____

2. **Literary Analysis:** Explain how the **metaphor** of the shepherd in Psalm 23, the **analogy** of the birds in the Sermon on the Mount, and the **narrative** in the Parable of the Prodigal Son are all suited to an audience of simple, rural folk. Enter your reasons in the following chart. Some entries have been filled in for you.

Images: Familiar/Unfamiliar	Simple/Difficult?	Memorable? Why?
Psalm 23: shepherd metaphor	Simple image, familiar to rural folk	Memorable because it expresses God's care in a vivid way

3. **Reading Strategy: Make inferences** about the meaning of this quotation from Psalm 23: "I will dwell in the house of the Lord forever."

   _____

   _____

4. **Reading Strategy:** What inference about Jesus' listeners can you make from the closing of this excerpt from the Sermon on the Mount: "O ye of little faith?"

   _____

The Tragedy of Macbeth, Act I

LITERARY ANALYSIS

Elizabethan drama came into full bloom during the late 1500s. Playwrights stopped writing about religion. They began writing more complicated plays about human nature. Playwrights reintroduced plays called **tragedies** (TRAJ uh DEEZ). These plays tell about a hero or heroine to whom something terrible happens. Playwrights also began writing in carefully structured lines of unrhymed verse. They used rich language and colorful imagery.

A **soliloquy** (suh LIL uh KWEE) is a long speech. It is usually made by a character alone on stage. A soliloquy reveals a character's private thoughts and feelings to the audience. However, other characters do not hear. In Shakespeare's tragedies, characters reveal secret desires or fears though their soliloquies. As you read Lady Macbeth's soliloquy in Act I, use the chart below to note the inner struggles she reveals.

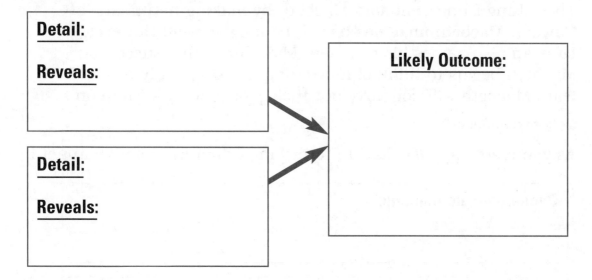

READING STRATEGY

Shakepeare's plays were meant to be performed, not read. Playwrights and editors often add **text aids** to printed versions of the plays. These aids explain how to interpret the play. They include stage directions in brackets and notes on the side of the text. Use these aids when you read.

The Tragedy of Macbeth, Act I

William Shakespeare

Summary Macbeth and Banquo (BANK wo), a fellow noble, have helped win an important battle for King Duncan of Scotland. Returning from the battle, they encounter three witches. The witches hail Macbeth as the Thane of Glamis, the Thane of Cawdor, and King. At the time, however, Macbeth is only Thane of Glamis. The witches also say that Banquo shall father a long line of kings.

Then, King Duncan honors Macbeth by making him Thane of Cawdor. Macbeth imagines he will be king as well. However, Duncan also names his own son, Malcolm, as his successor. Macbeth begins to think of murdering the king. Lady Macbeth fears Macbeth will not carry out their plot. She urges him on.

Note-taking Guide

As you read, use this chart to record important information in Act I.

Background Information:

Witches' Prediction:

Macbeth's Plan:

The Tragedy of Macbeth, Act I

1. **Literary Analysis:** How does Macbeth's meeting with the witches show that this **Elizabethan drama** will probably be a **tragedy?**

   _____

   _____

2. **Literary Analysis:** What does Lady Macbeth's **soliloquy** in Act I, Scene v, lines 1-30 reveal about her thoughts and plans?

   _____

   _____

3. **Reading Strategy:** Use text aids like stage directions and side notes to describe the action in Act I, scene i.

   _____

   _____

4. **Reading Strategy:** Using **text aids**, analyze the details of setting in the lines shown on the chart. Then, in the boxes on the right, indicate how modern sets and lighting could produce such a setting. One box is filled in for you.

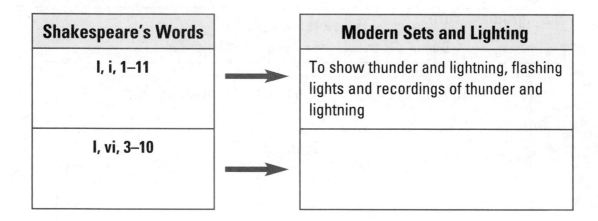

Shakespeare's Words	Modern Sets and Lighting
I, i, 1–11	To show thunder and lightning, flashing lights and recordings of thunder and lightning
I, vi, 3–10	

The Tragedy of Macbeth, Act II

LITERARY ANALYSIS

Lines written in **blank verse** are lines that have a strict meter but do not rhyme. This meter is called iambic (i AM bik) pentameter. Each line is made up of pairs of syllables called iambs. An **iamb** (I am) consists of an unstressed syllable followed by a stressed syllable (indicated by the accent marks ˘ ´). In iambic pentameter, there are five iambs in each line. *Macbeth* is written mainly in blank verse:

Me thought I heard a voice cry, "Sleep no more!" (II, ii, 34)

Shakespeare often changes his meter to make his verse more interesting. Sometimes, he begins lines with a stressed syllable followed by an unstressed syllable. This pair of syllables is called a **trochaic** (troh KAY ik) **foot.** He also sometimes uses an **anapestic** (an uh PES tik) **foot.** This foot has two unstressed syllables followed by a stressed syllable.

Sometimes Shakespeare uses prose. **Prose** is writing that is not divided into poetic lines. Also, prose lacks a regular rhythm. Characters such as servants often speak in prose.

READING STRATEGY

To **read blank verse for meaning,** follow sentences past line endings. Use the chart to distinguish between lines and sentences. Count the sentences and lines. Then, write the meaning.

Passage: II, i, 33-39	
Begins: "Is this dagger which I see before me..."	
Number of Lines	**Number of Lines**
Meaning	

The Tragedy of Macbeth, Act II

William Shakespeare

Summary Macbeth wants to murder King Duncan. He imagines that he sees a dagger before him, yet he cannot seize it. Then, Macbeth kills Duncan while the king sleeps. Lady Macbeth has helped by drugging Duncan's servants so Macbeth will not wake them. Then, she covers the servants with Duncan's blood to make it seem as if they have killed him. Macduff, a nobleman, discovers the king's body. Afraid that they will be murdered next, Duncan's sons flee Scotland. With the king dead and his sons gone, Macbeth is free to seize the throne.

Note-taking Guide

Use the chart below to record important information in Act II.

Macbeth's vision:

Who is murdered:

How Malcolm and Donalbain react:

The Tragedy of Macbeth, Act II

1. **Literary Analysis:** Analyze Shakespeare's use of **blank verse**. Complete this chart by identifying the rhythm of each of the lines indicated. The first row is filled in for you

Line	Iambic Feet	Trochaic or Anapestic Feet
"It is the bloody business which informs. . ."	the BLOO dy BUS / iness WHICH / in FORMS	IT is (trochaic)
"Macbeth does murder sleep'—the innocent sleep, . . ."		

2. **Literary Analysis:** How does the Porter's speech in **prose**, Act II, Scene iii, lines 1-21, offer **comic relief?**

_____

_____

3. **Reading Strategy:** In **reading lines for meaning,** would you pause at any of the line ends in Act II, Scene 1, lines 62-64? Explain.

_____

_____

4. **Reading Strategy:** In your own words, express the meaning of the sentences in Act II, Scene i, lines 62-64.

_____

_____

The Tragedy of Macbeth, Act III

LITERARY ANALYSIS

Conflict

Conflict is a struggle between two people or forces. Conflict creates drama.

- An **external conflict** is a struggle between two characters.
- An **internal conflict** is a struggle within a character.

The **climax** of a play is the moment when the internal and external conflicts are greatest. The action rises to the climax. This is the moment of highest tension. After the climax, the action falls as the conflicts are resolved.

In Act III of *Macbeth*, pay attention to the rising action. Notice how it leads the new king to a state dinner. An unexpected guest is waiting for him there.

READING STRATEGY

Reading between the lines means reading for deeper meanings. You can find such meanings by connecting different parts of the play. Reading *line by line* tells you *what* happens. Reading *between the lines* tells you *why*.

Use this chart to help you read between the lines of Act III. Enter details from the play in the first two boxes. Then, in the third box, show how the link between them suggests future action.

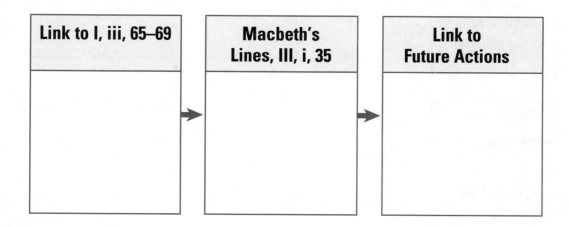

Link to I, iii, 65–69	Macbeth's Lines, III, i, 35	Link to Future Actions

The Tragedy of Macbeth, Act III

William Shakespeare

Summary Fearing the witches' prediction that Banquo will be the father of kings, Macbeth plots to have Banquo and his son, Fleance, killed. Banquo is killed, but Fleance escapes. At a banquet, Banquo's ghost appears, sitting at Macbeth's place. The ghost is visible only to Macbeth, who becomes very upset. Macbeth pledges to kill anyone who stands in his way. Also, he wants to visit the witches again. Meanwhile, Duncan's son Malcolm is living at the English court. Malcolm is raising an army to fight against Macbeth. Macduff has gone to England in order to help Malcolm.

Note-taking Guide

The action comes to a climax in Act III. Use this chart to summarize what happens in Act III and to make predictions about what will happen as the play continues.

Event	Cause	Effect	Prediction
Macbeth arranges Banquo's murder.			
Macbeth vows to keep killing until his place on the throne is secure.			
Macduff goes to England to help raise an army against Macbeth.			

The Tragedy of Macbeth, Act III

1. **Synthesize:** Has the relationship between Macbeth and Lady Macbeth changed? Explain your ideas.

   _____

   _____

2. **Literary Analysis:** Why is Macbeth involved in an **external conflict** with Banquo?

   _____

   _____

3. **Literary Analysis:** Complete this chart to show how the **conflict** increases and moves toward a **climax.**

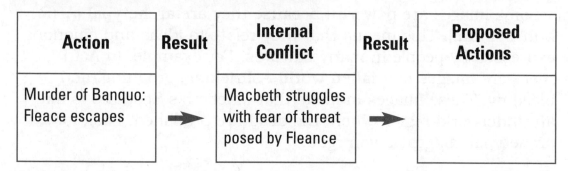

Action	Result	Internal Conflict	Result	Proposed Actions
Murder of Banquo: Fleace escapes	→	Macbeth struggles with fear of threat posed by Fleance	→	

4. **Reading Strategy:** "What man dare, I dare," says Macbeth (III, iv, 100). **Read between the lines** by identifying another remark on manhood earlier in the play.

   _____

   _____

5. **Reading Strategy:** Some critics say that the third murderer is Macbeth himself. By reading between the lines, support or refute this claim.

   _____

   _____

The Tragedy of Macbeth, Act IV

LITERARY ANALYSIS

Imagery (IM ij ree) is the language writers use to appeal to your senses. Imagery helps you to see, hear, feel, smell, and taste what writers describe. It also stirs emotions. Shakespeare often uses related groups of images. In *Macbeth*, he uses groups of images that relate to these things:

- Blood
- Ill-fitting clothes
- Babies and children, sometimes killed by Macbeth; sometimes threatening him

These images relate to important themes in the play. Babies and children represent the future. So these images suggest that Macbeth is warring against the future. As you read, link these groups of images to the play's central ideas.

Some images are powerful because they are **archetypal** [AHR kuh TYP uhl]. This means that they relate to ideas and emotions expressed by people in many cultures. For example, in Act IV, there are **images of a fallen world**—shrieking, groaning, and bleeding. These images indicate that Macbeth's Scotland is like an underworld region where the dead are punished. Look for archetypal images as you read.

READING STRATEGY

You will enjoy a work of literature more if you **use your senses** to experience the imagery it contains. In the chart below, note the images in the lines listed. Then, identify which senses the images appeal to. One image is filled in for you.

Line	Images	Senses
IV, i, 52	"untie the winds"	
IV, i, 53		

The Tragedy of Macbeth, Act IV

William Shakespeare

Summary Macbeth visits the witches, and they show him three spirits. The first warns him to beware of Macduff. The second says that no man "of woman born/Shall harm Macbeth." The third says that Macbeth will not be defeated until the woods themselves come to Dunsinane Hill to fight against him. When Macbeth asks about Banquo's descendants, he is shown "eight Kings and Banquo." This vision disturbs Macbeth. However, the witches vanish before Macbeth can find out what the vision means. Macbeth learns that Macduff has gone to England to join Malcolm. In revenge, Macbeth has Macduff's family killed. In England, Malcolm and Macduff discuss Macbeth. Malcolm agrees to lead a force against Macbeth.

Note-taking Guide

In Act IV, Macbeth sees four images when he visits the witches. Each image gives Macbeth a message. Describe each vision below, and note both its message and how Macbeth reacts to the message.

Description of Image	Message	Macbeth's Reaction

The Tragedy of Macbeth, Act IV

1. **Analyze:** Why does Macbeth readily accept the predictions of the second and third spirits?

   _____

   _____

2. **Literary Analysis:** Use this chart to indicate the emotions that vivid **imagery** expresses. One passage is suggested for you. Write down the imagery it contains. Then, explain the emotions that this imagery expresses.

Passage	Vivid Imagery		Emotions Expressed
IV, iii, 164—173		→	

3. **Literary Analysis:** In Act IV, Scene iii, identify two **archetypal images of a fallen world** that describe Scotland in terms of weeping, bleeding, or both.

   _____

   _____

4. **Reading Strategy:** How does Malcolm's description of Scotland in Act IV, Scene iii, lines 39-41 appeal to the senses of touch, sight, and sound?

   _____

   _____

5. **Reading Strategy:** Why does reading this description of Scotland with your senses make the dialogue between Macduff and Malcolm more dramatic?

   _____

The Tragedy of Macbeth, Act V

LITERARY ANALYSIS

Shakespearean tragedy usually has these elements:

- A main character of high rank and personal quality; the main character also has a **tragic flaw** or weakness
- Closely linked events that lead this character to disaster, partly through his or her flaw
- Lively action • Comic scenes

Viewing a Shakespearean tragedy, the audience sees the destruction of the main character. The audience experiences pity, fear, and awe. These emotions lift people out of their everyday lives. One source of the positive experience the audience has is the **tragic impulse.** This impulse relates to the way the hero meets his or her fate in a noble way.

READING STRATEGY

Great plays reflect the **beliefs** of their time period. Readers can infer, or make educated guesses about, those beliefs by focusing on the ideas the characters express. Then, readers can compare these ideas with modern ideas on the same subject.

Use this chart to compare the idea of the doctor in act inm Act V, Scene i, with those of a modern doctor.

Doctor in Macbeth
Mental problems may produce nighttime disturbances.

↓

Modern Psychiatrist

The Tragedy of Macbeth, Act V

William Shakespeare

Summary Macbeth prepares for battle with the forces of Malcolm and Macduff. Because of the witches' predictions, he feels confident. Meanwhile, Lady Macbeth has been sleepwalking. She feels guilty about the murders. Just before the battle, she dies. Malcolm's soldiers cut down branches of trees to hide their numbers. Disguised in this way, they approach Dunsinane. Malcolm's army defeats Macbeth's army. Then, Macduff kills Macbeth. Malcolm becomes the new king of Scotland.

Note-taking Guide The play ends, or resolves, in Act V. In the chart below, note the outcome for each character.

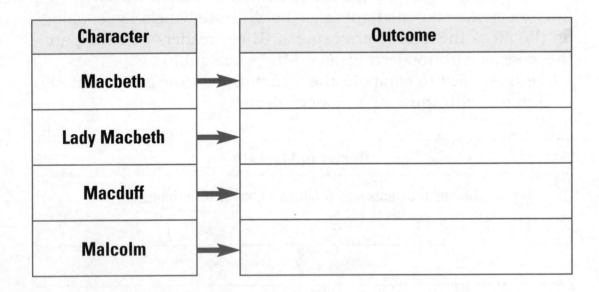

Character	Outcome
Macbeth →	
Lady Macbeth →	
Macduff →	
Malcolm →	

from Macbeth
William Shakespeare

Macbeth, a Scottish nobleman and general, meets three mysterious witches. They predict that he will rule Scotland one day as king. Macbeth's wife urges him to assassinate King Duncan while the king is visiting them. At night, Macbeth prepares for the murder. First he dismisses his servant.

◆ ◆ ◆

MACBETH. Go bid thy mistress, when my drink is ready,
She strike upon the bell. Get thee to bed.
              [*Exit* servant.]
Is this a dagger which I see before me,
The handle toward my hand? Come, let me clutch thee.
5 I have thee not, and yet I see thee still.

◆ ◆ ◆

Macbeth wonders if the dagger is real or imaginary.

◆ ◆ ◆

         I see thee still,
And on thy blade and dudgeon[1] gouts[2] of blood,
Which was not so before. There's no such thing.
It is the bloody business which informs[3]
10 Thus to mine eyes. Now o'er the one half-world
Nature seems dead, and wicked dreams abuse[4]
The curtained sleep; witchcraft celebrates
Pale Hecate's offerings;[5] and withered murder,

---

1. **dudgeon** wooden hilt.
2. **gouts** large drops.
3. **informs** takes shape.
4. **abuse** deceive.
5. **Hecate's** (HEK uh teez) **offerings** offerings to Hecate, the Greek goddess of witchcraft.

from Macbeth **89**

Vocabulary and Pronunciation

Shakespeare often uses the archaic or old-fashioned forms *thy, thee,* and *thou.* If *thy* means "your," what do *thee* and *thou* mean?

thee: _____

thou: _____

Reading Check

Underline the words that show how the dagger's appearance has changed.

When you read **verse for meaning,** how many sentences do you find in the bracketed passage?

_____

_____

_____

In English, writers often use vivid figures of speech, or expressions that are not meant to be taken literally. Shakespeare uses many figures of speech. Here he compares murder to a person. What does this person look like, and how does he move?

_____

_____

_____

What does Macbeth mean by his statement about words and deeds in line 22?

_____

_____

_____

Alarumed[6] by his <u>sentinel</u>, the wolf,
15 Whose howl's his watch, thus with his
        <u>stealthy</u> pace,
With Tarquin's[7] ravishing strides, towards his
        design
Moves like a ghost. Thou sure and firm-set
        earth,
Hear not my steps, which way they walk, for
        fear
Thy very stones prate[8] of my whereabout,
20 And take the present horror from the time,
Which now suits with it.[9] Whiles I threat, he
        lives:
Words to the heat of deeds too cold breath
        gives.
            [*A bell rings.*]
I go, and it is done: the bell invites me.
Hear it not, Duncan, for it is a knell
25 That summons thee to heaven, or to hell.
            [*Exit.*]
                ◆   ◆   ◆

Macbeth murders King Duncan. After Macbeth is crowned king, he and Lady Macbeth cling to power through bloodshed and tyranny. Macbeth has one of his fellow generals murdered. Fearing the nobleman Macduff, Macbeth orders the murders of Macduff's wife and children. Macduff and Malcolm, the rightful heir to the throne, raise a rebel army. The witches tell Macbeth that he does not need to fear until Birnam Wood moves toward the castle at Dunsinane. Also, they say, Macbeth will not be defeated by

---

Vocabulary Development

sentinel (SENT uh nuhl) *n.* guard; watchman
stealthy (STEL thee) *adj.* sly

---

6. **Alarumed** (uh LAR uhmd): urged on to battle.
7. **Tarquin's** of Tarquin, an ancient Roman tyrant.
8. **prate** chatter; talk idly.
9. **and . . . it** remove the horrible silence which suits this moment.

any man "of woman born." At the end of the play, the rebel army meets Macbeth's forces in a life-or-death struggle.

◆   ◆   ◆

[*Enter* MACBETH, SEYTON, *and* SOLDIERS, *with drum and colors.*]

    MACBETH. Hang out our banners on the outward walls.

The cry is still "They come!" Our castle's strength

Will laugh a <u>siege</u> to scorn.

◆   ◆   ◆

    Macbeth says that the enemy army will die of famine and disease during the siege.

◆   ◆   ◆

    [*A cry within of women.*]

What is that noise?

    SEYTON. It is the cry of women, my good lord.

[*Exit.*]

◆   ◆   ◆

    Macbeth reflects that, after so much horror in his life, nothing can terrify him.

◆   ◆   ◆

[*Enter* SEYTON.]

30 **MACBETH.** Wherefore[10] was that cry?

    SEYTON. The queen, my lord, is dead.

    MACBETH. She should[11] have died hereafter;

There would have been a time for such a word.[12]

Tomorrow, and tomorrow, and tomorrow

Creeps in this petty pace from day to day,

35 To the last syllable of recorded time;

And all our yesterdays have lighted fools

English Language Development

In English, writers sometimes use personification, which means that they talk about objects as if they are persons. How does Macbeth personify his castle here?

_____

_____

_____

Reading Check

What has happened to Lady Macbeth?

_____

_____

_____

Vocabulary Development

siege (SEEJ) *n.* attack or blockade against a fortified place

---

10. **Wherefore** for what; why.
11. **should** inevitably would.
12. **word** message.

What have "all our yesterdays" done, according to Macbeth? Underline the words that give the answer.

In a **Shakespearean tragedy,** a tragic flaw or weakness leads the hero to destruction. How does Macbeth's view of life here foreshadow his own downfall?

_____

_____

_____

Why does Macbeth tell Macduff to get back?

_____

_____

_____

What does Macduff mean when he says "my voice is in my sword"?

_____

_____

_____

The way to dusty death. Out, out, brief candle!
Life's but a walking shadow, a poor player
That struts and frets his hour upon the stage
40 And then is heard no more. It is a tale
Told by an idiot, full of sound and fury
Signifying nothing.

♦　♦　♦

    A messenger arrives to tell Macbeth that the forest is moving – Birnam Wood is coming to Dunsinane. It turns out that Malcolm's soldiers are carrying tree branches to hide their approach.

    A battle begins. Macduff pursues Macbeth, eager to face him in single combat. Macbeth vows he will continue to fight against the odds, rather than commit suicide.

♦　♦　♦

[*Enter* MACDUFF.]
MACDUFF. Turn, hell-hound, turn!
MACBETH. Of all men else I have avoided thee.
But get thee back! My soul is too much charged
45 With blood of thine already.[13]
MACDUFF. I have no words:
My voice is in my sword, thou bloodier villain
Than terms[14] can give thee out!
        [*Fight. Alarum.*]
MACBETH. Thou losest labor:
As easy mayst thou the intrenchant[15] air
With thy keen sword impress[16] as make me bleed:
50 Let fall thy blade on vulnerable crests;
I bear a charmèd life, which must not yield
To one of woman born.

13. **blood . . . already** Macbeth had ordered the murders of Macduff's wife and children.
14. **terms . . . out** words can describe you.
15. **intrenchant** incapable of being cut.
16. **impress** make a dent in.

MACDUFF. Despair thy charm,
And let the angel[17] whom thou still hast
served
Tell thee, Macduff was from his mother's
womb
55 Untimely ripped.[18]
MACBETH. Accursèd be that tongue that tells
me so,
For it hath cowed[19] my better part of man![20]
And be these juggling fiends[21] no more
believed,
That palter[22] with us in a double sense;
That keep the word of promise to our ear,
60 And break it to our hope. I'll not fight with
thee.
MACDUFF. Then yield thee, coward.
And live to be the show and gaze o' th' time;[23]
We'll have thee, as our rarer monsters[24] are,
Painted upon a pole,[25] and underwrit,
65 "Here you may see the tyrant."
MACBETH. I will not yield,
To kiss the ground before young Malcolm's
feet,
And to be baited with the rabble's curse.
Though Birnam Wood be come to
Dunsinane,[26]
And thou opposed, being of no woman born,
70 Yet I will try the last. Before my body

TAKE NOTES

Reading Strategy

In lines 52-55, make a slash mark [/] at the ends of lines where you would pause in **reading verse for meaning**.

Stop to Reflect

Why is Macbeth angry now at the witches?

_____

_____

_____

Vocabulary and Pronunciation

The accent mark on the underlined word on page 51 shows that *charmèd* is pronounced as two syllables, not one. This pronunciation is used for the sake of the meter, or the rhythm, in Shakespeare's verse. In line 56 on this page, how many syllables are in the pronunciation of *Accursèd*?

_____

_____

Culture Note

In England during Shakespeare's time, traveling shows and spectator sports like bear-baiting were common. Why do you think Macduff tells Macbeth that he will become part of a traveling show?

_____

_____

_____

17. **angel** fallen angel; fiend.
18. **his . . . ripped** Macduff's mother died before giving birth to him.
19. **cowed** frightened.
20. **better . . . man** courage.
21. **fiends** the three witches.
22. **palter** juggle.
23. **gaze o' th' time** spectacle of the age.
24. **monsters**: freaks.
25. **Painted . . . pole** pictured on a banner stuck on a pole by a showman's booth.
26. **Birnam . . . Dunsinane** Malcolm's soldiers held tree branches in front of themselves when they marched on Dunsinane, Macbeth's castle.

What positive or heroic qualities does Macbeth as **tragic hero** display here?

_____

_____

_____

How does the conclusion of this scene in lines 73-78 illustrate the lively action and vivid spectacle of **Shakespearean tragedy?**

_____

_____

_____

I throw my warlike shield. Lay on, Macduff;
And damned be him that first cries, "Hold,
   enough!"
   [*Exit, fighting. Alarums.*]
   ◆   ◆   ◆

Macduff slays Macbeth. In front of the soldiers, Macduff hails Duncan's son Malcolm as the new king of Scotland.
   ◆   ◆   ◆

[*Enter* MACDUFF, *with* MACBETH'S *head.*]
MACDUFF. Hail, King! For so thou art: behold,
   where stands
Th' usurper's[27] cursèd head. The time is
   free.[28]
75 I see thee compassed with thy kingdom's
   pearl,[29]
That speak my salutation in their minds,
Whose voices I desire aloud with mine:
Hail, King of Scotland!
ALL. Hail, King of Scotland!
   ◆   ◆   ◆

Promising to reward his supporters, Malcolm invites the army to his coronation.

Vocabulary Development

salutation (sal yoo TAY shuhn) *n.*   greeting

---

27. **Th' usurper's . . . head** the head of Macbeth, who had stolen the throne.
28. **The . . free** Our country is liberated.
29. **compassed . . . pearl** surrounded by the noblest people in the kingdom.

The Tragedy of Macbeth, Act V

1. **Literary Analysis:** Use examples from the play to show each element of **Shakespearean tragedy:** a main character with a flaw; closely linked events leading this character to disaster; lively action; and comic scenes.

_____

_____

2. **Literary Analysis:** How does Banquo's response to the witches call attention to Macbeth's **tragic flaw?** Use this chart to show your answer. The witches' predictions have been filled in for you.

Banquo's Response	Witches' Predictions	Macbeth's Response and Flaw
	Macbeth will be Thane of Cawdor and King. Banquo will be the father of kings.	

3. **Reading Strategy:** What do the doctor's remarks lead you to **infer,** or figure out, about Elizabethan concepts of mental illness?

_____

_____

4. **Reading Strategy:** Compare and contrast Elizabethan ideas about mental illness with those of today.

_____

_____

NEWSPAPER ARTICLES

About Newspaper Articles

Newspaper articles are summaries of current events. Sometimes they provide in-depth descriptions or analysis. Other times they simply report the facts. They usually answer such questions as *who, what, when, where,* and *why.*

Newspaper articles often include the quoted words of those interviewed. Articles may provide statistics, names, dates, and firsthand information about the article's topic. Some newspapers have readers from around the world, but most have an audience in a particular town, city, or region.

Reading Strategy

Evaluating Information Newspapers articles should give in-depth, factual, and unprejudiced information. There are steps to follow to **evaluate information** you read in a newspaper article. First, identify the facts and details, the key people, and the events. Then, decide whether this information gives you a complete picture of the subject.

As you read the newspaper article from the *Salisbury Post,* complete the chart shown to evaluate the information.

Title and Subject of the Article	Key Events	Key People	Missing Information
	What? When? Where?	Who?	What else would you like to know?
Conclusion: Do you think this article was clear, concise, and complete? Explain.			

Salisbury Post

Serving historic Rowan County, North Carolina since 1905.

Shakespearean expert brings skills to Rowan County

By Cortney L. Hill

"Hey, Lady Macbeth! Don't stand that way, and uncross your legs," shouted Bob Moyer.

The director of theater arts from the North Carolina School of the Arts was speaking to Salisbury High tenth grader Heather Clayton.

Constantly spewing "Stop," "Do it again," "Louder next time," and "Ugh, I keep forgetting that line," students and teachers responded throughout the morning Saturday.

They filled the Teaching Auditorium at Rowan-Cabarrus County Community College for a dress rehearsal for the Shakespeare Festival performance of "The Tragedy of Macbeth."

Training teachers to breathe life back into the classic works of Shakespeare, Saturday's event was Salisbury's third year hosting the Shakespeare Festival's "Shakespeare Lives!" program.

The program is a collaboration among the International Shakespeare Globe Center in London, the North Carolina School of the Arts, and the Kenan Institute for the Arts, with support from the Robertson Family Foundation of Rowan County.

This year, students and a total of 12 teachers from South Rowan High, Salisbury High, West Rowan High and other high schools and middle schools from Forsyth and Cabarrus counties brought their rendition of the play to the stage by dividing and performing different acts and scenes.

For preparation, students spent three weeks memorizing lines, learning to pronounce the Shakespearean words and understanding the plot of "Macbeth."

The teachers had been preparing for the performance since last spring, including spending two weeks at the International Globe Theater in London in July. They received direction from Patrick Spottiswoode, director of the Globe Theater program, Fiona Banks, assistant director of the Globe Theater, and Gerald Freedman, a Tony Award-winning director of Shakespeare in New York.

"To actually get a feel for Shakespeare's words and meanings, the teachers got to perform scenes from the plays on stage at the Globe Theater in London," Moyer said while sporting a blue and green Bankside London England hat and a Shakespeare face pendant on his shirt.

"Their (teachers') purpose for being there was for them to learn different ways to teach Shakespeare and become energized about it.... That way the students can grasp it and become energized too."

Impressed by the talents of these young student actors (many of them having no acting experience), Moyer sat intensely at the edge of his seat, examining the students' every move and every word. He gasped in relief if their practice went well or shook his head in dissatisfaction if it did not.

"Next time be bigger, make me believe you," Moyer told one student.

Scott Bosch, a Salisbury High English teacher, sat quietly in the front row of the auditorium while he watched his students perform.

"All of my students are tenth graders, and they all volunteered to be a part of this play. It comes from a great interest in theater." Bosch said.

Unlike most of the other students, Kevin Felder and Nicky Blakeley, two of Bosch's students, have a background in theater arts.

"I'm a little nervous today because Shakespeare tends to twist your tongue so," said Felder, who has been in theater arts since the fifth grade. For this performance, Felder played the character "Banquo," whom he described as an envied character who people try to have killed.

"In preparation for this character, I try to think back on other characters I have played and look at it as being no bigger than what I've done before." said Felder, who in the past acted as "Baby John" in a school presentation of "West Side Story."

Felder hopes to someday be as good an actor and as universally known as Martin Lawrence or Eddie Murphy, whom he said he mimics constantly and looks up to.

Nicky Blakeley, who played Macbeth, has been acting since she was in the second grade and was eager to get on stage and perform.

"I am just so excited to be playing the main character," Blakeley said, "and Macbeth, a character normally played by a guy, is just totally awesome to me.... What a challenge!"

Next week, the honors theater student will be performing in a folk tale play at Salisbury High called "Jack Tales", and for the next five weekends she will be starring in other plays

"The most challenging thing for me to do is memorize lines," Blakeley said. "For Macbeth's character, I have to be aggressive. But with much practice and script cramming, I should be fine."

South Rowan English teacher Gerrie Blackwelder sat in tears through her students' practice run through their part of the tragedy. Moyer credits Blackwelder with being a big part of the entire event.

"I am very nervous about today," Blackwelder said. "It's just so emotional and overwhelming to see children do Shakespeare and look as if they are enjoying it.... It's like they've actually morphed themselves into their characters. This is truly wonderful."

As the final groups ran through one last practice before showtime on Saturday, teachers gave pep talks and paced around as if they were trying to memorize their students' lines.

Ingrid Madlock, assistant principal of the Learning Enrichment Acceleration Program (LEAP) Academy in Winston-Salem, is eager to see her students perform because they have never had any exposure to Shakespeare and had a hard time grasping the whole concept.

"I won't be shocked if I'm not in tears by the end of their performance," Madlock said. "When they came to the LEAP Academy, it was to catch up on their academics, but these kids are being challenged doing this.

"I chose the students who I felt needed some help with their self-esteem, because I want them to know that they can do this and that Shakespeare can somehow be a part of their everyday life. I think when this is over, they'll realize that."

The sources for the quotations are identified by their profession or their role in the event.

Background information about the people involved gives the article depth.

Quotation marks call out direct quotations from people interviewed.

THINKING ABOUT THE NEWSPAPER ARTICLE

1. Judging only by the title, what information should the article contain?

   _____

2. What information is missing from this article? Write a question that is not answered by information in the article.

   _____

READING STRATEGY

3. What is one thing the teachers did to prepare for the performance of "Macbeth?"

   _____

4. Describe the program that is featured in this article.

   _____

   _____

TIMED WRITING: EXPLANATION (20 MINUTES)

Summarize why you think this program will or will not interest high-school students in the works of William Shakespeare. Use information from the article to support your opinion.

- List two reasons why you think this program will interest high-school students in Shakespeare.

   _____

- List two reasons why you think this program will not interest high-school students in Shakespeare.

   _____

- Decide which pair of reasons is stronger. Draft a thesis sentence that clearly states your opinion.

   _____

The Works of John Donne

LITERARY ANALYSIS

John Donne and his followers wrote **metaphysical** (MET uh FIZ i kuhl) **poetry**. This type of poetry uses conceits (kuhn SEETS) and **paradoxes** (PAR uh DAHKS ez).

- **Conceits** are extended comparisons. They compare objects or ideas not usually connected. In his poem "A Valediction: Forbidding Mourning," for example, Donne compares two parting lovers to the legs of a drawing compass. The one who stays behind is like the leg of the compass that stays fixed. The one who travels is like the leg of the compass that draws the circle.

- **Paradoxes** are images or descriptions that seem to contradict themselves. For example, in Donne's "Holy Sonnet 10," he writes, "Death, thou shalt die." At first, such a statement seems impossible. However, paradoxes often reveal a deeper truth. Donne is addressing Death as if it were a person. He is saying that Death itself will die. He says this because he believes that when people die and go to heaven, they will live forever.

Look for the conceits and paradoxes in Donne's work. Then, see what they mean.

READING STRATEGY

When you read these poems, imagine the **speaker's situation.** Ask yourself what the speaker is doing and what the speaker wants. Also, try to figure out his **motivation,** or reason, for speaking to another person. As you read "Song," use this chart to note the speaker's words, his situation, and his motivation.

Speaker's Words	Situation	Motivation
"Sweetest love, I do not go, for sweetness of thee,…"		

Song • A Valediction: Forbidding Mourning • Holy Sonnet 10

John Donne

Summaries In "**Song**," the speaker is going away. He asks his beloved not to mourn his absence. In "**A Valediction: Forbidding Mourning**," the speaker also asks a loved one not to mourn his absence. He compares himself and his beloved to the two legs of a drawing compass. Like the legs of a compass, the lovers will be linked even when they are separated.

The speaker talks to Death in "**Holy Sonnet 10**" as if Death were a person. He tells Death not to be so proud. Once people have died and gone to heaven, there will be no more death.

Note-taking Guide

As you read, use this chart. For each poem, fill in the person the speaker is addressing. Also indicate the main idea the speaker is expressing.

Poem	To Whom it is Addressed	Main Idea
Song		
A Valediction		
Holy Sonnet 10		

Meditation 17

John Donne

Summary The speaker hears a church bell ringing. The ringing bell means that someone has died. The speaker realizes that someday he will die, too. Every person adds something to this world. One person's death affects everyone. The death bell rings, then, for everyone.

Note-taking Guide Read the basic arguments from "Meditation 17" in the chart below. Find the comparisons in the poem that support these arguments. Write the comparisons in the ovals to the right.

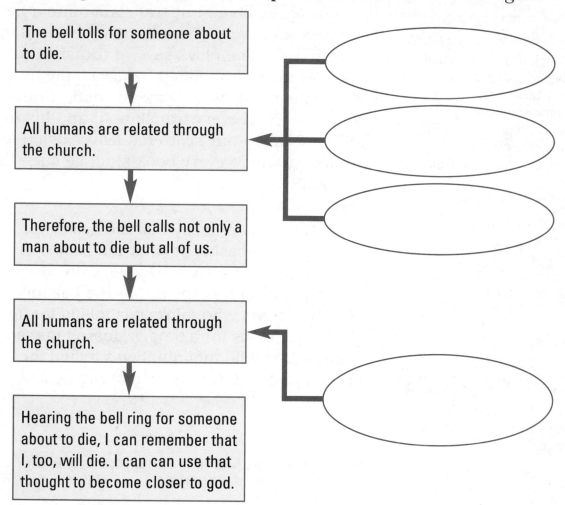

The bell tolls for someone about to die.

All humans are related through the church.

Therefore, the bell calls not only a man about to die but all of us.

All humans are related through the church.

Hearing the bell ring for someone about to die, I can remember that I, too, will die. I can can use that thought to become closer to god.

Many words in English have more than one meaning. For example, the word *volume* can refer to a book or to sound levels. It can also refer to the amount of space within a three-dimensional shape. Which meaning is meant here?

_____

Leaves is another multiple-meaning word. It can refer to pages in a book or parts of a green plant. It is also a verb, meaning "goes away." Which meaning is meant here?

_____

Literary Analysis

Here, Donne uses a feature of **metaphysical poetry** when he does an extended comparison of one thing to another, seemingly unrelated thing. This is called a **conceit**. Read the bracketed passage, and then circle the letter of the correct answer.

In this conceit, Donne compares a person to _____.

(a) a foreign language

(b) a chapter in a book

(c) God

(d) a translator

Reading Strategy

Based on Donne's **situation**, what can you guess about his **motivation**?

_____

_____

Meditation 17
John Donne

Donne talks about a bell that is tolling, or ringing. It is announcing someone's death or coming death. He says that maybe the person doesn't know that the bell is tolling for him. He says it might even be for Donne himself, and he doesn't know it. The church that rings the bell is for all people. So are all the things that the church does.

◆　◆　◆

When she baptizes a child, that action concerns me; for that child is thereby connected to that head which is my head too.[1] . . . And when she buries a man, that action concerns me: all mankind is of one author and one volume; when one man dies, one chapter is not torn out of the book, but translated into a better language; and every chapter must be so translated. God employs several translators; some pieces are translated by age, some by sickness, some by war, some by justice; but God's hand is in every translation, and his hand shall bind up all our scattered leaves again for that library where every book shall lie open to one another.

◆　◆　◆

He goes on to say that the bell is not just for the preacher. It is for the people of the church. It is also for Donne, who is suffering from a sickness. . . . The bell tolls for the person who thinks it is tolling for him. If the bell stops for a time, it doesn't matter. The person who thought it was tolling for him is united to God from that moment.

◆　◆　◆

_____

1. **that head which is my head too** In the Bible, St. Paul calls Jesus the head (spiritual leader) of all the faithful.

No man is an island, entire of itself; every man is a piece of the continent, a part of the main.[2] If a clod be washed away by the sea, Europe is the less, as well as if a <u>promontory</u> were, as well as if a <u>manor</u> of thy friend's or of thine own were. Any man's death <u>diminishes</u> me because I am involved in mankind, and therefore never send to know for whom the bell tolls; it tolls for thee.

◆ ◆ ◆

Donne goes on to say that our troubles are good for us. No one has enough of them. Troubles help us mature. They make us fit for God. We might listen to a bell that tolls for someone else and apply its meaning to ourselves. If we do this, we become closer to God, our only security.

---

2. main (MAYN) *n.* the mainland.

TAKE NOTES

English Language Development

One use of commas is to set off an introductory clause. If you move the clause to the end of the sentence, you don't need the comma. See the chart for an example.

Introductory Clause with Comma	Clause at the End
If the bell stops for a time, it doesn't matter.	It doesn't matter if the bell stops for a time.

Now write your own sentences in the same style. Write one sentence beginning with an introductory clause and a comma. Write the other with the clause at the end.

1. _____

_____

2. _____

_____

Read Fluently

Read aloud the bracketed paragraph. Then circle the part that tells how Donne feels about any other person's death.

Vocabulary Development

promontory (PRAH muhn TAWR ee) *n.* a high point of land or rock jutting out into a body of water

manor (MAN uhr) *n.* the house of an estate

diminishes (di MIN ish uhs) *v.* lessens, reduces

The Works of John Donne

1. **Draw Conclusions:** In "A Valediction: Forbidding Mourning," Donne compares the parting lovers to the legs of a compass. The woman is fixed in place, while the speaker moves. What does the comparison reveal about their relationship?

_____

_____

2. **Literary Analysis:** In "Meditation 17," Donne uses a **conceit,** or extended comparison, to compare suffering and treasure. Think about the forms of treasure he discusses. Then, fill in the chart below. One kind of treasure, for example, is gold. Something else that Donne calls treasure is very surprising.

Main Idea: There are two forms of suffering, just as there are two forms of treasure.		
First Form of Treasure:	**Second Form of Treasure:**	**Relationship Between Forms of Treasure:**

3. **Literary Analysis:** What is the **paradox,** or apparent contradiction, that Donne uses in the fourth stanza of "Song"?

_____

_____

4. **Reading Strategy:** To **recognize a speaker's situation and motivation,** picture the speaker's circumstances and determine his or her reasons for speaking or acting. Choose one of John Donne's poems. Who is the speaker, what is the **speaker's situation,** and what is the speaker's **motivation?**

_____

_____

On My First Son • Still to Be Neat • Song: To Celia

LITERARY ANALYSIS

An **epigram** (E pi GRAM) is a short poem. In an epigram, the writer tries to write something brief, clear, and memorable. These famous lines by Ben Jonson are an epigram: "Drink to me only with thine eyes,/ And I will pledge with mine." Jonson is describing the way that he and his beloved are looking at one another. It is as if they were offering each other a drink.

Epigrams have these features:
- Short lines with memorable rhythms
- Twists of thought, as when Jonson compares looking to drinking
- Similar types of phrases or clauses. For example: "Still to be neat, still to be dressed, . . ."

Look for these features as you read Jonson's poems.

READING STRATEGY

To **hypothesize** (hy PAHTH uh SYZ) means to make an informed guess. When you hypothesize, you
- make a guess about the people, events, or ideas in a work
- then continue reading
- look for new information as you read that confirms your ideas.

Use this chart to help you hypothesize.

Hypothesis	Proved
	Disproved

On My First Son • Still to Be Neat • Song: To Celia

Ben Jonson

Summaries In "**On My First Son**," Jonson says farewell to his young son. The boy died at the age of seven.

In "**Still to Be Neat**," Jonson says that he does not admire women who dress up too much. He prefers beauty that looks more natural.

In "**Song: To Celia**," he expresses his love for a woman. He asks her to give him loving looks, rather than drinks of wine. She has returned a wreath of flowers he sent to her. Now, the wreath grows. It also carries her lovely scent.

Note-taking Guide

Choose a line or two from each poem that tells the main idea. Write the lines on this chart. Then explain the main idea in your own words.

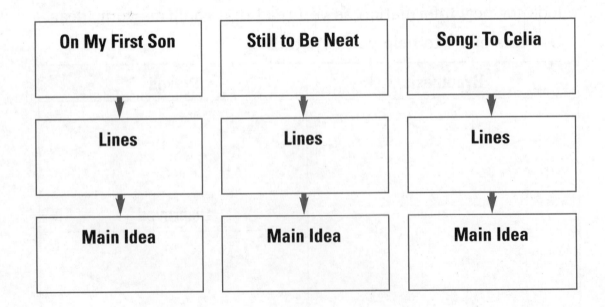

On My First Son	Still to Be Neat	Song: To Celia
Lines	Lines	Lines
Main Idea	Main Idea	Main Idea

On My First Son • Still to Be Neat • Song: To Celia

1. **Evaluate:** Review Jonson's "Still to Be Neat." Does it seem artificial or false by today's standards, or does it capture true feelings?

_____

_____

2. **Literary Analysis:** An **epigram** has these elements: memorable rhythms; parallelism, or similar groups of words; and clever sayings. Using this chart, note such features in "Song: To Celia."

Memorable Rhythms	Parallelism, or Similar Groups of Words	Clever Sayings

3. **Literary Analysis:** The phrase "sweet neglect" in "Still to Be Neat" seems to be impossible or contradictory. Explain how it makes sense.

_____

_____

4. **Reading Strategy:** Using lines 1-4 of "On My First Son" make a **hypothesis**, or informed guess, about the speaker's feelings for his son. Base your guess on these lines only.

_____

_____

5. **Reading Strategy:** Basing your answer on lines 11-12 of "On My First Son," what final hypothesis can you make about the speaker's reaction to his son's death?

_____

To His Coy Mistress • To the Virgins, to Make Much of Time • Song

LITERARY ANALYSIS

Carpe diem (KAR pay DEE em) is Latin for "seize the day." The **theme** of the poems in this grouping is *carpe diem.* In other words, these poems are saying that time is rushing by. Therefore, it is important to enjoy love in the present moment. Herrick expresses this theme in a traditional way. Marvell expresses this theme in an extended way.

Suckling's poem gives the *carpe diem* theme a twist. He does not tell a friend to seize love. Instead, he tells the friend to abandon a lover who is not responding to him.

Look for the *carpe diem* theme as you read these selections.

READING STRATEGY

To understand a poem, you must **infer the speaker's attitude.** This means you must figure out how the speaker feels about the subject of the poem. You must also figure out how the speaker feels about the person he or she is addressing. To recognize the speaker's attitude, you should do the following:

- Focus on the *connotations*, or emotional associations, of the speaker's words.
- Decide which associations are positive and which are negative.
- Use those emotional associations to figure out the speaker's attitude.

Use this chart to note details that convey the speaker's attitude.

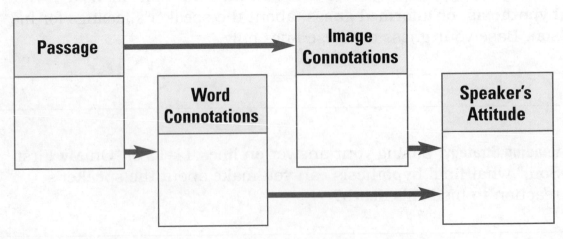

| Passage | Word Connotations | Image Connotations | Speaker's Attitude |

To His Coy Mistress

Andrew Marvell

To the Virgins, to Make Much of Time

Robert Herrick

Song

Sir John Suckling

Summary The speaker in "To His Coy Mistress" explains that time is not limitless. His beloved should return his love now. The speaker in "To the Virgins, to Make Much of Time" also urges young women to look for love now. "Song" tells a young man to forget his beloved if she does not love him.

Note-taking Guide

Use these diagrams to answer questions about each poem.

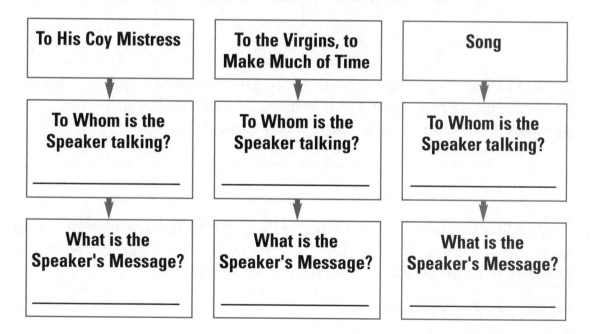

To His Coy Mistress	To the Virgins, to Make Much of Time	Song
To Whom is the Speaker talking?	To Whom is the Speaker talking?	To Whom is the Speaker talking?
What is the Speaker's Message?	What is the Speaker's Message?	What is the Speaker's Message?

To His Coy Mistress
• To the Virgins, to Make Much of Time • Song

1. **Compare and Contrast:** Compare the attitudes toward time at the beginning and end of "To His Coy Mistress."

   _____

   _____

2. **Literary Analysis:** Contrast the *carpe diem* theme in the three poems. Write your ideas in this chart. Find images that express the theme. Explain whether the theme is expressed simply or not. Also, explain whether it is expressed humorously, passionately, or reasonably.

Title	*Carpe Diem* Images	Qualities: Fanciful? Simple?	Humorous? Passionate? Reasonable?
To His Coy Mistress			
To the Virgins, to Make Much of Time			
Song			

3. **Reading Strategy.** Read lines 1–20 of "To His Coy Mistress." The images in these lines are exaggerated. What can you **infer** about the **speaker's attitude** toward his beloved from these lines?

   _____

   _____

4. **Reading Strategy:** Compare the speaker's attitude toward love in "Song" with the speaker's attitude toward love in "To the Virgins." Which speaker is more serious? Which is more casual?

   _____

   _____

Sonnet VII • Sonnet XIX • *from* Paradise Lost

LITERARY ANALYSIS

An **Italian sonnet** is a fourteen-line lyric poem. It is also called a **Petrarchan** (pi TRAHR kuhn) sonnet. The first eight lines are called the octave (AHK tiv). They present a problem or a question. The next six lines are called the sestet (ses TET). They solve the problem or answer the question that appears in the octave.

An **epic** is a long narrative poem about a hero. Milton uses the following features of ancient epics in *Paradise Lost:*

• The story begins in the middle of the action.

• The opening has an invocation (IN voh KAY shuhn). This is a passage in which the poet calls for divine aid in writing.

• The poet uses extended similes (SIM uh LEES). These are long comparisons of unlike things using the words *like* or *as.*

Milton wrote sonnets as well as epics. In his sonnets, he reflects on his ambition to achieve poetic greatness.

READING STRATEGY

You can break down sentences into smaller parts to clarify meaning. First, identify the main clause, which states the main idea of the sentence. The main clause can stand on its own as a sentence. Then, identify the supporting clauses. These clauses add thoughts to the main clause. However, they cannot stand on their own. Use the chart to help you break down long sentences.

Supporting Element		Supporting Element

Main Clause

Supporting Element		Supporting Element

Sonnet VII and Sonnet XIX

John Milton

Summary The speaker in Sonnet VII is 24 years old. He feels he has not yet accomplished much. Whether he does or not will depend on the will of Heaven.

The speaker in Sonnet XIX wonders why he is blind. He still has much of his life to live. First, he asks how God can expect a blind person like himself to accomplish anything. Then, he decides that he can best serve God by patiently waiting.

Note-taking Guide

Use the diagram below to compare Sonnets VII and XIX. In the middle of the diagram, list what the sonnets have in common. List their differences on either side.

Sonnet VII	Have in Common	Sonnet XIX

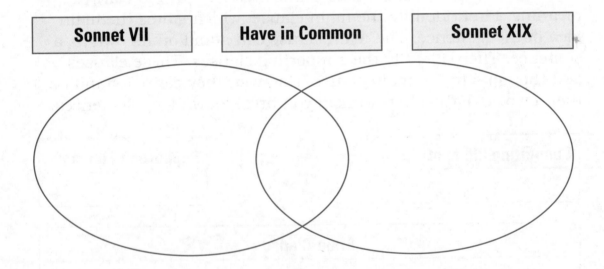

© Pearson Education, Inc., publishing as Pearson Prentice Hall.

from Paradise Lost

John Milton

Summary *Paradis Lost* is a long narrative poem written from a Christian point of view. It tells how Adam and Eve, the first humans according to Jewish and Christian belief, were tempted by the evil angel Satan to disobey God. This disobedience caused them to lose their home in the garden known as Paradise. Instead of living a life of ease forever, they would have to work and, eventually, die.

In this passage from the beginning of the poem, Milton explains what his subject will be. He also calls on Urania (yoo RAY nee uh), goddess of astronomy and poetry, to help him write his poem. Then, he tells how Satan, once a great angel, rebelled against God's rule. In punishment, God hurled Satan and the other rebel angels out of heaven. These angels fell to a place of darkness and fire that God prepared for them. As Satan revives after this fall, his lieutenant Beelzebub (bee EL zuh bub) says that they are defeated. However, Satan is defiant and wants to continue the struggle against God. Satan will seek revenge against God by causing Adam and Eve to lose Paradise.

Note-taking Guide

Use the diagram below to list the epic features in *Paradise Lost*.

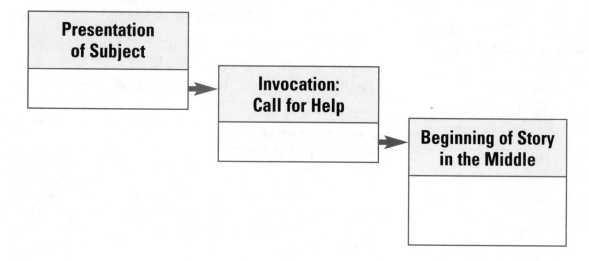

Presentation of Subject

Invocation: Call for Help

Beginning of Story in the Middle

from Paradise Lost
John Milton

Literary Analysis

In the first paragraph, for whose divine aid does the poet ask in writing his **epic poem?** Circle the answer.

Of man's first disobedience, and the fruit
Of that forbidden tree, whose mortal[1] taste
Brought death into the world, and all our woe,
With loss of Eden, till one greater Man[2]
Restore us, and regain the blissful seat,
Sing Heavenly Muse,[3]

♦ ♦ ♦

The speaker of the poem suggests that the Muse is the same spirit that inspired Moses. The speaker asks the Muse to help him finish the epic he is now writing. Then the poet asks the Holy Spirit to help him too.

Literary Analysis

What clues tell you that this is an **epic poem?** List two clues.

1. _____

2. _____

♦ ♦ ♦

. . . what in me is dark
Illumine, what is low raise and support;
That to the height of this great argument[4]
I may assert Eternal Providence,
And justify the ways of God to men.

♦ ♦ ♦

The speaker then asks the Holy Spirit to tell him what made Adam and Eve disobey God's commandment. They were so happy. They were the lords of the world. All they had to do was obey God and avoid eating the fruit of the tree of knowledge.

Vocabulary and Pronunciation

The words *spirit* and *inspired* have the same root. That root is a Latin word, *spiritus,* that means "breathing, breath, air, life, or soul." Underline the root in each of these words:

inspiration   inspirational

spiritual   spirituality

dispirited   inspiring

♦ ♦ ♦

Vocabulary Development

illumine (i LOO muhn) *v.* light up

assert (uh SERT) *v.* declare firmly

justify (JUS tuh FY) *v.* to prove or show to be right

Reading Check

What command of God did Adam and Eve disobey?

_____

_____

_____

1. **mortal** (MOR tuhl) *adj.* deadly.
2. **one greater Man** Jesus Christ.
3. **Heavenly Muse** (MYOOZ) Urania, the muse of astonomy and sacred poetry in Greek mythology. Here, Milton associates Urania with the holy spirit that inspired Moses. Moses received the Ten Commandments from God. He also wrote the first five books of the Bible, including Genesis, the book on which Paradise Lost is based.
4. **argument** (AR gyoo ment) *n.* theme.

Who first seduced them to that foul revolt?
The infernal Serpent; he it was, whose <u>guile</u>
Stirred up with envy and revenge, deceived
The mother of mankind, what time his pride
Had cast him out from Heaven, with all his
    host
Of rebel angels, by whose aid <u>aspiring</u>
To set himself in glory above his peers.

◆ ◆ ◆

The speaker tells more about the fallen angels. Their leader wanted to be equal to God. He waged a war against God. He was very ambitious and fought a brave battle, but he lost. God punished him severely.

◆ ◆ ◆

<u>Him the Almighty Power
Hurled headlong flaming from the ethereal sky
With hideous ruin and combustion down
To bottomless <u>perdition</u>, there to dwell
In adamantine[5] chains and penal fire.</u>

◆ ◆ ◆

Now Satan is tormented by thoughts of lost <u>happiness</u> and lasting pain. He is in a dungeon full of flames. Yet the flames give off no light. He can never find any peace, rest, or hope. The rebel angels are as far from God and the light of Heaven as possible. Soon Satan sees Beelzebub,[6] his main helper in the fight against God. He speaks to Beelzebub about how changed Beelzebub is. Once his own brightness outshone that of the other angels. He joined Satan in the fight against

Vocabulary Development

guile (GYL) *n.* deceitful cunning
aspiring (as PYR ing) *adj.* trying to accomplish a goal
perdition (per DI shun) *n.* complete destruction

---

5. **adamantine** (ad uh MAN teen) *adj.* not able to be broken.
6. **Beelzebub** (bee EL zuh BUHB) Usually, this name refers to the chief devil, or Satan. Here, it refers to Satan's main helper among the fallen angels.

Reading Check

To whom is Satan speaking?

_____

_____

Literary Analysis

What details suggest that Satan has the qualities of an **epic hero?** List two.

1. _____

2. _____

Literary Analysis

Epic poems commonly tell of famous battles. What famous battle is Milton writing about?

_____

_____

Reading Check

What does Satan plan to do in the future?

_____

_____

_____

God, and now misery has joined them both in equal ruin. Satan then tells Beelzebub that he is not sorry for what they did.

◆　◆　◆

What though the field be lost?
All is not lost; the unconquerable will
And study of revenge, immortal hate,
And courage never to submit or yield:
And what is else not to be overcome?
That glory never shall his wrath or might
<u>Extort</u> from me.

◆　◆　◆

Satan tells Beelzebub that he will never give up in his fight against God. He plans to wage eternal war. Then Beelzebub calls Satan a prince, a chief, and a leader of the angels. He says that the mind and spirit are still strong, even though their glory and happiness have changed to endless misery. Then Beelzebub says that it is clear that God is almighty, for how else could he have won against such a mighty force? He wonders what good it is to have eternal life, if all that is in store for them is eternal punishment. Satan answers Beelzebub:

◆　◆　◆

"Fallen cherub, to be weak is miserable,
Doing or suffering:[7] but of this be sure,
To do aught[8] good never will be our task,
But ever to do ill our sole delight,
As being the contrary to his high will
Whom we resist. If then his providence
Out of our evil seek to bring forth good,
Our labor must be to pervert that end,
And out of good still[9] to find means of evil;

◆　◆　◆

Vocabulary Development

extort (ex TORT) _v._ to obtain by force

---

7. **doing or suffering:** whether one is active or passive.
8. **aught** (AWT): anything.
9. **still** always.

Satan goes on to say that their activities will cause God grief and trouble. He sees that God has called his good angels back to Heaven. It looks as if the war is over, at least for now. Satan sees this as an opportunity to rest and gather together their overthrown armies. He wants to think about how they can most offend their Enemy in the future. As Satan talks to Beelzebub, he lies chained on a burning lake of fire. His huge body is as big as any monster from ancient stories.

◆　◆　◆

So stretched out huge in length the Archfiend
　　lay
Chained on the burning lake, nor ever thence
Had risen or heaved his head, but that the will
And high permission of all-ruling Heaven
Left him at large to his own dark <u>designs</u>,
That with <u>reiterated</u> crimes he might
Heap on himself damnation, while he sought
Evil to others, and enraged might see
How all his malice served but to bring forth
Infinite goodness, grace and mercy shown
On man by him seduced, but on himself
Treble confusion, wrath and vengeance poured.

◆　◆　◆

Suddenly Satan gets up from the fiery pool. He opens his wings and flies to dry land. Beelzebub follows him. They are both happy to have escaped on their own strength, rather than by the permission of heavenly power.

◆　◆　◆

In English, a comma is used to separate a long introductory passage from the rest of the sentence. Add the necessary comma in each of these sentences:

For help in writing his epic Milton turns to the Muse and to the Holy Spirit.

To remain lords of the world Adam and Eve had to obey God's commandment.

Because Satan wanted to be equal to God he waged a war against Him.

Reading Strategy

Break down the bracketed passage into two sentences. Write the sentences below in your own words.

_____

_____

_____

Reading Check

What will Heaven bring out of Satan's evil?

_____

_____

_____

Break down the underlined **sentence.** Rewrite it below in your own words.

_____

_____

_____

English Language Development

The word _hath_ is an old-fashioned way of saying "has." Here are some other old-fashioned words:

thee (you)   thy (your)

thine (yours)   thou (you)

Literary Analysis

Reread the bracketed section. In what way are these ideas fitting for the hero of an **epic poem?**

_____

_____

_____

Stop to Reflect

What do you think Satan means by the underlined comment?

_____

_____

_____

"Is this the region, this the soil, the clime,"
Said then the lost Archangel, "this the seat
That we must change for Heaven, this
    mournful gloom
For that celestial light? Be it so, since he
Who now is sovereign can dispose and bid
What shall be right: farthest from him is best,
Whom reason hath equaled, force hath made
    supreme
Above his equals. Farewell happy fields,
Where joy forever dwells. Hail horrors! Hail
Infernal world! and thou, profoundest Hell
Receive thy new possessor, one who brings
A mind not to be changed by place or time.
The mind is its own place, and in itself
Can make a Heaven of Hell, a Hell of Heaven.
What matter where, if I be still the same,
And what I should be, all but less than he
Whom thunder hath made greater? Here at
    least
We shall be free; the Almighty hath not built
Here for his envy, will not drive us hence:
Here we may reign secure, and in my choice
To reign is worth ambition though in Hell:
Better to reign in Hell than serve in Heaven."

◆   ◆   ◆

Satan asks why they should let their fellow fallen angels lie in the fires. Why not call them together again? Together, they can find out what they might regain in Heaven, or what more they might lose in Hell.

Poetry of John Milton

1. **Interpret:** In *Paradise Lost*, what does Milton mean when he says he wants to "justify the ways of God to men" (line 26)?

_____

_____

2. **Literary Analysis:** In **Italian sonnets** VII and XIX, Milton reflects on setbacks to his poetic ambition. Use the chart below to compare the two poems.

Title	Speaker's Situation	Effect on Ambition	Solution and How It Helps
Sonnet VII			
Sonnet XIX			

3. **Literary Analysis:** A main character in an **epic** often has a powerful personality. Does Satan have such a personality? Why or why not?

_____

_____

_____

4. **Reading Strategy: Break down sentences** to identify the main clause in lines 1-8 of Sonnet XIX. Clue: A semicolon separates the main clause from the supporting clauses.

_____

_____

5. **Reading Strategy:** Explain what the supporting clause in lines 1-2 of Sonnet XIX adds to the meaning of the first eight lines.

_____

_____

from Eve's Apology in Defense of Women
• To Lucasta, on Going to the Wars
• To Althea, from Prison

LITERARY ANALYSIS

Tradition and reform may seem to be different. However, they are closely related.

- **Tradition** refers to society's approved values, beliefs, and customs.
- **Reform** is an attempt to change traditional practices and ideas.

Lanier is a reformer. She fights to change traditional ideas about women. Lovelace supports traditional values. He goes to war and then to prison for his king. He values his honor more than his beloved.

As you read, look for the themes of tradition and reform in these poems.

READING STRATEGY

The **historical context** of a work relates to the ideas, customs, and beliefs of its time period. As you read, look for references to these ideas and beliefs. Also, consider which ideas may be responses to events of the period. Complete the chart below to place Lanier's poem and one of Lovelace's poems in their historical context.

Poem	Historical Context	Connection
"Eve's Apology"	Seventeenth-century women's rights were restricted; the story of Eve was used to justify these restrictions	

from Eve's Apology in Defense of Women

Amelia Lanier

To Lucasta, on Going to the Wars • To Althea, from Prison

Richard Lovelace

Summary "Eve's Apology" suggests that Adam rather than Eve bears the greater blame for disobeying God in Eden. The speaker in "Lucasta" asks his beloved not to judge him for leaving to go to war. The speaker in "Althea" has been imprisoned. He is being punished because he fought for his king.

Note-taking Guide

For each poem, consider three questions: Who is the speaker? To whom is he or she addressing the poem? What is his or her main idea or purpose? Record your information in the chart below.

Poem	Speaker	Audience	Main Idea/Purpose
"Eve's Apology"			
"Lucasta"			
"Althea"			

from Eve's Apology. . . • To Lucasta. . . • To Althea. . . **123**

from Eve's Apology in Defense of Women • To Lucasta, on Going to the Wars • To Althea, from Prison

1. **Interpret:** What is the meaning of lines 25-26 of "To Althea, from Prison"? In other words, how can the speaker feel free even though he is in prison?

_____

_____

2. **Literary Analysis: Tradition** refers to approved values, beliefs, roles, and practices. **Reform** refers to attempts to change tradition. In "Eve's Apology," what tradition is Lanier trying to reform? Clue: What traditional argument does she oppose?

_____

_____

3. **Literary Analysis:** In "To Althea," Lovelace plays with two different meanings of the word *freedom.* The usual meaning is the ability to come and go freely. In this chart, record a different meaning that Lovelace uses. Then, explain this new meaning.

Usual Meaning	Other Meaning	Explanation of New Meaning
Ability to come and go freely		

4. **Reading Strategy:** Explain how using the **historical context** helps you understand the third stanza of "To Althea." Why, for example, does the speaker refer to the "glories of my King"?

_____

_____

_____

from The Diary
• *from* A Journal of the Plague Year

LITERARY ANALYSIS

A **diary** or **journal** is a daily account of a writer's experiences. It can include:
- accounts of a writer's day-to-day activities.
- the writer's comments on local events of the day.
- the writer's comments on worldwide events of the time.

Diaries and journals that become literature can give us personal insights into history. As you read, notice how Pepys's *Diary* gives details of public events.

READING STRATEGY

When you **draw conclusions**, you use clues to figure out something that might not be stated directly. For example, Pepys mentions that he had his bags of gold ready to carry away. From this detail, you can draw the conclusion that he had some wealth.

As you read, use the chart below to record details and the conclusions that you draw from them.

Details from *The Diary*	
Pepys hires a boat.	
Conclusion	

Details from *A Journal*	
Conclusion	

from The Diary

Samuel Pepys

Summary These excerpts from *The Diary* of Samuel Pepys (PEEPS) relate to two disasters that struck London: the plague of 1664–1665, an outbreak of disease, and the Great Fire of 1666. Pepys tells how, during the plague, people risk spreading the disease by watching the burial of the dead. However, Pepys and others give orders to ensure that people no longer do this.

    On the first day of the Great Fire, Pepys views it from the Tower of London. He hears that it began earlier in the day at a baker's house. Later, he tells the king and the Duke of York that the only way to stop the fire is to demolish houses around it. The king tells Pepys to order the Lord Mayor of London to put this plan into action.

Note-taking Guide

Use the chart below to record the events of each day in *The Diary*.

Sept. 3, 1665	Sept. 14, 1665	Sept. 2, 1666	Sept. 3, 1666

from The Diary
Samuel Pepys

On September 3, 1665, Pepys writes a diary entry about the plague.[1] He tells how he has a meeting with six men in the church meeting room. There are a few lords and judges in the group. They want to figure out how to stop the plague. They talk about the madness of some people in London. Even though funeral processions are forbidden, many people still have them. They talk about a man in the town who wanted to save his child.

◆　◆　◆

Among other stories, one was very passionate, methought[2] of a complaint brought against a man in the town for taking a child from London from an infected house. Alderman[3] Hooker told us it was the child of a very able citizen in Gracious Street, a saddler,[4] who had buried all the rest of his children of the plague, and himself and wife now being shut up and in despair of escaping, did desire only to save the life of this little child; and so <u>prevailed</u> to have it received stark-naked into the arms of a friend, who brought it (having put it into new fresh clothes) to Greenwich;[5] where upon hearing the story, we did agree it should be permitted to be received and kept in the town.

◆　◆　◆

Vocabulary Development

prevailed (pruh VAYLD) *v.* persuaded (someone) to do something

---

1. the plague (PLAYG) A plague is any contagious disease that affects many people. Here, it refers to the bubonic plague, which devastated London from 1664 to 1666.
2. methought (mee THAWT) an old-fashioned way of saying "I thought."
3. alderman (AWL duhr min) a city official ranking just below mayor.
4. saddler (SAD ler) *n.* a person who makes, sells, and repairs saddles.
5. Greenwich (GREN ich) a section of Greater London.

TAKE NOTES

Vocabulary and Pronunciation

In English, the letter *g* can be pronounced like the *g* in *girl* or like the letter *j,* as in *gem.* Write *g* or *j* to tell how the *g* is pronounced in each of these words:

plague _____   judges _____

figure _____   agree _____

raging _____

Reading Strategy

What **conclusion** can you **draw** about Pepys's position in his community?

_____

_____

_____

Vocabulary and Pronunciation

The letter *u* is sometimes pronounced "yoo," as in *fuel.* It is sometimes pronounced "oo," as in *flu.* Write *yoo* or *oo* to tell how the *u* is pronounced in each of these words:

figure _____   funeral _____

clue _____   endure _____

secured _____

Reading Strategy

Based on the story about the baby, what **conclusion** can you **draw** about the general policy toward people who had been exposed to the plague?

_____

_____

_____

In his entry for September 14, 1665, Pepys says that he found some money and plate[6] that he thought he had lost. He also says that the plague seems to be claiming fewer victims.

He goes on to tell of a tavern and an alehouse that have been closed up. The last time he was at the alehouse, someone was dying of the plague there. He says that his waiter has buried a child and is dying himself. A laborer he hired has died of the plague. The boatman whose boat Pepys used every day has also died. Many other people he knows are sick.

◆ ◆ ◆

To hear that Mr. Lewes hath[7] another daughter sick. And, lastly, that both my servants, W. Hewer and Tom Edwards, have lost their fathers, both in St. Sepulcher's parish, of the plague this week, do put me into great apprehensions of melancholy, and with good reason. But I put off the thoughts of sadness as much as I can, and the rather to keep my wife in good heart and family also.

◆ ◆ ◆

His entry of September 2, 1666, is about the Great Fire of London. He says that some of his maids see a great fire in the city, so they wake Pepys up. The fire seems to be far off, so he goes back to sleep. In the morning, a maid tells him that more than 300 houses were burned down and the fire is spreading. He walks to the Tower of London and gets up on a high spot. The fire has burned down

Stop to Reflect

Do you think Pepys was right to "put off the thoughts of sadness"? Why?

_____

_____

_____

Reading Check

What had Pepys been doing when the fire broke out?

_____

_____

_____

Vocabulary Development

apprehensions (ap ree HEN shuns) *n.* fears
melancholy (MEL uhn KOHL ee) *v.* sadness

6. **plate** (PLAYT) *n.* valuable serving dishes and flatware.
7. **hath** (HATH) an old-fashioned way of saying "has."

St. Magnus's Church and most of Fish Street already. Pepys then takes a boat closer to the fire. He can see people trying to save their goods. Within an hour, the fire is raging in every direction. After the long drought, everything is combustible. Word is brought to the King about the fire.

♦ ♦ ♦

So I was called for, and did tell the King and Duke of York what I saw, and that unless his Majesty did command houses to be pulled down nothing could stop the fire. They seemed much troubled, and the King commanded me to go to my Lord Mayor from him, and command him to spare no houses, but to pull down before the fire every way. The Duke of York bid me tell him that if he would have any more soldiers he shall; and so did my Lord Arlington afterwards, as a great secret.

♦ ♦ ♦

Pepys goes on to describe the streets of London. Everyone is carrying goods that they are trying to save. Then, as the fire progresses, the goods have to be moved again and again. The streets are full of people, horses, and carts carrying goods. Even the boats in the harbor are being filled.

Pepys walks to St. James's Park, where he meets his wife and some friends. They walk to his boat, and they observe the fire from the Thames River. They are as close to the fire as they can get and still avoid the smoke.

♦ ♦ ♦

TAKE NOTES

Read Fluently

Read aloud the bracketed section. Underline the part that tells what the King's command was.

Vocabulary and Pronunciation

Many words have multiple meanings. For example, *rest* can mean "the remainder" or "to nap." Write a sentence of your own in which you use the underlined word in another meaning.

1. The King said to spare no houses.

_____

_____

2. The fire spread quickly.

_____

_____

3. The flames were not like the fine flames of an ordinary fire.

_____

_____

Reading Strategy

What **conclusion** about the fire can you **draw**, based on the way people are moving their belongings?

_____

_____

_____

Where did Pepys go after leaving the river? Circle the answer.

What evidence in this paragraph could lead to the **conclusion** that Pepys was quite wealthy?

_____

_____

_____

Compound words are words that are made up of two other words. For example, the word *sunflower* is made of *sun* and *flower.* For each compound word below, write the two words that it is made of.

highway

_____

alehouse

_____

boatman

_____

firedrops

_____

nightgown

_____

When we could <u>endure</u> no more upon the water, we to a little alehouse on the Bankside, over against the Three Cranes, and there stayed till it was dark almost, and saw the fire grow; and, as it grew darker, appeared more and more, and in corners and upon steeples, and between churches and houses, as far as we could see up the hill of the city, in a most horrid <u>malicious</u> bloody flame, not like the fine flame of an ordinary fire.

◆ ◆ ◆

Pepys goes home "with a sad heart." A friend, Tom Hater, comes over and wants to store some goods at Pepys's house. News comes that the fire is growing. Pepys and his family are forced to start packing up their own goods. By the light of the moon, they carry much of Pepys's goods into the garden. Mr. Hater helps Pepys carry his money and iron chests into the cellar, thinking that is the safest place. Pepys gets his bags of gold ready to carry away. He gets his important papers ready, too. Mr. Hater tries to get some sleep, but he gets very little rest because of all the noise of moving goods out of the house.

◆ ◆ ◆

About four o'clock in the morning, my Lady Batten sent me a cart to carry away all my money, and plate, and best things, to Sir W. Rider's at Bednall Green. Which I did, riding myself in my nightgown in the cart; and, Lord! to see how the streets and the highways are crowded with people running and riding,

---

Vocabulary Development

endure (en DYOOR) *v.* continue in the same state
malicious (muh LISH uhs) *adj.* with evil intentions

---

and getting of carts at any rate to fetch away things. I find Sir W. Rider tired with being called up all night, and receiving things from several friends. His house full of goods, and much of Sir W. Baten's and Sir W. Pen's. I am eased at my heart to have my treasure so well secured. Then home, with much ado to find a way, nor any sleep all this night to me nor my poor wife.

Literary Analysis

What information does the last paragraph include that makes it clear that this is a **diary**?

_____

_____

_____

_____

from A Journal of the Plague Year

Daniel Defoe

Summary The disease known as the plague is killing many people in London. Dead bodies are taken away on carts. Cries of grief are heard on the streets. People are mourning for their loved ones. The narrator sees a terrible pit in Aldgate where bodies are buried daily. He sees a man faint after his dead wife and children are thrown into the pit. What he witnesses is almost too much for him to bear.

Note-taking Guide

Use the chart below to record important details from *A Journal of the Plague Year*.

The Narrator			
What he hears:	**Where he goes:**	**What he sees:**	**How he feels:**

from The Diary • *from* A Journal of the Plague Year

1. **Literary Analysis: Diaries and journals** often provide historical information. Read each question in the chart and decide whether it is answered in Pepys's *Diary*. If so, write the answer in the right-hand column.

Questions about the Great Fire	Answer in *Diary*? Yes/No	Pepys's Answer
What parts of the city were most damaged?		
How many houses were destroyed?		
What was the total monetary damage?		

2. **Literary Analysis: First-person narrators** describe their own experiences and are identified by the pronoun *I*. Find evidence of these two features in Pepys's *Diary* and in Defoe's *Journal*.

_____

_____

3. **Reading Strategy:** When you **draw conclusions,** you make generalizations about the author or subject based on details in a text. Reread the entry in Pepys's *Diary* for Sept. 14, 1665. Draw a conclusion about Pepys's position in society. For example, does he seem to be poor, middle class, or rich?

_____

_____

4. **Reading Strategy:** Draw a conclusion about whether Pepys or Defoe's fictional Narrator is more observant.

_____

_____

from Gulliver's Travels

LITERARY ANALYSIS

Satire is writing that uses humor to poke fun at human error and foolishness. Satire can be good-humored, or it can be bitter.

Writers of satire usually do not name their targets. Instead, they make up imaginary characters and situations to mask their targets. Swift uses masks like these:

- Imaginary lands, like Lilliput, the land of the little people
- Made-up characters, like the Lilliputians and their enemies, the Blefuscudians
- Fictional conflicts, like that between the Big-Endians and the Little-Endians

Satirists often use **irony**, a contradiction between the actual meaning of the words and the meaning intended by the writer. As you read, use this chart to help you understand Swift's use of irony.

What Swift Says	What He Means
"Many . . . volumes have been published" about the best way to break an egg.	People often argue too much about unimportant things.

READING STRATEGY

You will not get the point a satirist is trying to make if you fail to interpret the masks used to hint at their true targets. To **interpret**, or figure out, a satire, follow these tips:
- Read the background before you begin reading the selection.
- Read footnotes as you go along.
- Recognize and figure out ironic meanings.

from Gulliver's Travels

Jonathan Swift

Summary The novel Gulliver's Travels describes four imaginary voyages of Lemuel Gulliver, the narrator. Swift uses these voyages to satirize, or humorously criticize, the customs and institutions of his time. The first voyage takes Gulliver to Lilliput (LIL uh put), the kingdom of the six-inch-tall Lilliputians (LIL uh PYOO shuhnz).

Note-taking Guide

Read each purpose in the first column of the chart below. As you read Gulliver's Travels, find details that achieve these purposes and write them in the second column. plot against him.

Purpose	Details to Achieve This Purpose
• To criticize and make fun of religious disputes between Protestants and Catholics within England. • To criticize and make fun of religious disputes between Protestant England and Catholic France	
• To criticize and make fun of power-hungry rulers in Europe	

In English, the letter w can be either silent, as in *wrinkle*, or voiced, as in *way*. Write *silent* or *voiced* to tell how the w is pronounced in each of these words:

shipwreck _____

war _____

write _____

wakes _____

wades _____

wrong _____

Reading Strategy

How does the footnote help you **interpret** Swift's satire?

_____

_____

_____

Literary Analysis

Swift says that Lilliput and Blefuscu cannot agree on the correct way of breaking eggs. Why do you think he makes this the cause of the conflict between the two countries in his **satire?**

_____

_____

_____

from Gulliver's Travels
Jonathan Swift

Lemuel Gulliver, the narrator, is a doctor on a ship. When he survives a shipwreck, he swims to shore. There, he drifts off to sleep. When he wakes up, he finds that he has been tied down by the Lilliputians. These people are only six inches tall. After a time, Gulliver becomes friendly with the little people. He listens to conversations in the Lilliputian court that remind him of English affairs of state. One day, he talks with the Lilliputian Principal Secretary of Private Affairs. He tells Gulliver that they are at war with the island of Blefuscu.[1] The two countries have been at war for the past three years.

◆ ◆ ◆

It is <u>allowed</u> on all hands, that the primitive way of breaking eggs before we eat them, was upon the larger end; but his present Majesty's grandfather, while he was a boy, going to eat an egg, and breaking it according to the ancient practice, happened to cut one of his fingers. Whereupon the Emperor, his father, published an <u>edict</u>, commanding all his subjects, upon great penalties, to break the smaller end of their eggs. The people so highly resented this law that our histories tell us there have been six rebellions raised on that account; wherein one emperor lost his life, and another his crown.[2]

◆ ◆ ◆

Vocabulary Development

allowed (uh LOWD) *v.* thought
edict (EE dikt) *n.* an official public announcement having the force of law

---

1. **Blefuscu** stands for France.
2. **It is allowed . . . crown** Here, Swift is satirizing the arguments in England between the Catholics (Big-Endians) and the Protestants (Little-Endians). King Henry VIII, who "broke" with the Catholic Church is referred to. So is King Charles I, who "lost his life." And so is King James, who lost his "crown."

The Secretary tells Gulliver that Blefuscu constantly starts these rebellions. He says that eleven thousand persons have died rather than agree to break their eggs at the smaller end.

◆ ◆ ◆

Many hundred large volumes have been published upon this controversy; but the books of the Big-Endians have been long forbidden, and the whole party rendered incapable by law of holding employments.[3]

◆ ◆ ◆

The Secretary then says that the Blefuscudians make accusations against the Lilliputians. They say that the Lilliputians go against an important religious teaching of the great prophet Lustrog. The Secretary then explains the Lilliputians' view.

◆ ◆ ◆

This, however, is thought to be a mere strain upon the text, for the words are these: That all true believers shall break their eggs at the convenient end; and which is the convenient end, seems, in my humble opinion, to be left to every man's conscience, or at least in the power of the chief magistrate[4] to determine.

◆ ◆ ◆

The Secretary then says that the Blefuscudians are preparing to attack with a fleet of fifty war ships. Gulliver says that he will defend Lilliput against all invaders.

A channel 800 yards wide separates the two kingdoms. At high tide, it is about six feet deep. Gulliver orders the strongest cable and iron bars available. The cable is about as thick as thread, and the iron bars are like knitting needles. He triples the cable to make it stronger. He twists three iron bars together to make hooks.

---

3. **holding employments** holding office. (The Test Act of 1673 prevented Catholics from holding public office.)
4. **chief magistrate** (CHEEF MAJ uh strayt): ruler.

from Gulliver's Travels **137**

TAKE NOTES

Stop to Reflect

Do you think the cause of breaking eggs at the smaller end is worth dying for? Write *yes* or *no*. Explain your answer.

_____

_____

Reading Strategy

In this paragraph, Swift is satirizing people who hate other people because of religious differences. Circle two phrases that clearly support this **interpretation.**

English Language Development

In English, there are two ways to show comparisons of adjectives and adverbs. Add *-er* and *-est* to show comparative and superlative degrees, as in *bigger* and *biggest*. Or use the words *more* and *most,* as in *more beautiful* and *most beautiful.* Generally, an adjective or adverb of three or more syllables uses *more* and *most* for comparisons. Also, any adverb that ends in *-ly* uses *more* and *most.* Complete the chart by adding comparative and superlative forms of the words in column 1.

Positive Degree	Comparative Degree	Superlative Degree
Example: strong	*stronger*	*strongest*
tall		
primitive		
highly		
frightened		
great		

Here, Gulliver uses his glasses as a shield in a military operation. What is ironic about this **satire?**

_____

_____

_____

Read aloud the bracketed paragraph. Then underline the part that tells what the Emperor wanted to do.

What does Gulliver say that causes the Emperor to turn against him?

_____

_____

_____

Gulliver wades into the channel and fastens a hook to each of the fifty ships. He holds them all together with cable. Then he cuts the cables that hold the anchors. As he does all this, the enemy shoots thousands of tiny arrows at him. Luckily, his eyes are protected by his glasses. Gulliver wades across the channel with the ships. When he gets to shore, he is made a Nardac on the spot. This is the highest title of honor in Lilliput.

◆　◆　◆

His Majesty desired I would take some other opportunity of bringing all the rest of his enemy's ships into his ports. And so unmeasurable is the ambition of princes, that he seemed to think of nothing less than reducing the whole empire of Blefuscu into a province and governing it by a viceroy; of destroying the Big-Endian exiles and compelling that people to break the smaller end of their eggs, by which he would remain sole monarch of the whole world.

◆　◆　◆

Gulliver thinks this is wrong. He says that he would never help to bring free and brave people into slavery. From then on, there is a campaign against Gulliver. Gulliver comments:

◆　◆　◆

Of so little weight are the greatest services to princes when put into the balance with a refusal to gratify their passions.

from Gulliver's Travels

Jonathan Swift

Summary In this chapter of *Gulliver's Travels*, Gulliver visits Brobdingnag (BRAHB ding NAG). This is a fictional island located near Alaska that is inhabited by giants. Gulliver describes English politics and society to the king of this country. The king reacts to the description with disgust.

Note-taking Guide

Read each purpose in the first column of the chart below. As you read *Gulliver's Travels*, find details that achieve these purposes and write them in the second column.

Purpose	Details to Achieve This Purpose
• To criticize and make fun of religious disputes between Protestants and Catholics within England. • To criticize and make fun of religious disputes between Protestant England and Catholic France	
• To criticize and make fun of power-hungry rulers in Europe	

from Gulliver's Travels

1. **Take a Position:** Do you think that satires like Swift's can ever change people's behavior? Why or why not?

_____

_____

2. **Literary Analysis:** *Gulliver's Travels* is a **satire,** or piece of writing that uses humor to expose human weaknesses. Use the chart below to show three targets of Swift's satire.

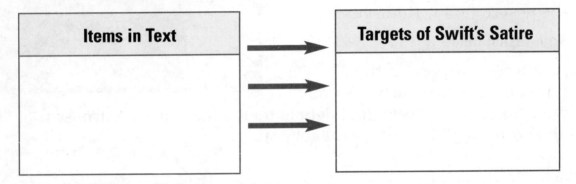

Items in Text	Targets of Swift's Satire

3. **Literary Analysis:** **Irony** is a difference between reality and appearance or between what is said and what is meant. Find an example of irony that depends on a difference between appearance and reality. Explain your choice. Clue: The debate about how to break an egg appears to be serious.

_____

_____

4. **Reading Strategy:** What historical facts do you need to know in order to **interpret,** or figure out the meaning of, the dispute about breaking eggs? Clue: Review the Background and the first three footnotes.

_____

_____

_____

from An Essay on Man
• from The Rape of the Lock

LITERARY ANALYSIS

A **mock epic** is a long, humorous poem that tells a story. Mock epics treat a small, unimportant subject in the grand style of a true epic. For example, in *The Rape of the Lock*, a lock of a woman's hair is stolen. Pope applies these epic elements to this unimportant matter:

- Boasting speeches of heroes and heroines
- Long descriptions of warriors and their weapons
- Involvement of gods and goddesses in the action
- **Epic similes** (SIM uh LEES), or long comparisons in the style of Homer that use the words *like, as,* or *so*

As you read, notice how these epic elements convey Pope's mockery.

An *Essay on Man,* by contrast, is a serious work about human nature. However, in both these poems, Pope uses a figure of speech from **rhetoric,** or public speaking, called antithesis (an TI thuh SIS). **Antithesis** involves the contrast of opposing words, clauses, sentences, or ideas. In the chart below, identify examples of antithesis in both poems. Then, explain what is being contrasted. One example is provided for you.

Poem	Example of Antithesis	What is contrasted
"An Essay on Man"	"Created <u>half to rise</u>, and <u>half to fail</u>; . . ."	
"The Rape of the Lock"		

READING STRATEGY

As you read *The Rape of the Lock,* find evidence of Pope's **purposes,** or reasons for writing. His purposes in this poem were to poke fun at upper-class customs and to entertain.

from An Essay on Man • from The Rape of the Lock

Alexander Pope

Summaries In the excerpt from *An Essay on Man*, the poet attempts to describe human nature. He claims that human beings exist in a middle state between God and beast. Humans are both wise and confused. They are judges of truth, but they also make endless mistakes. That is why he calls humankind "The glory, jest, and riddle of the world!"

This excerpt from *The Rape of the Lock* tells how the baron cuts a lock of hair from Belinda's head. This silly occurrence is described as if it were a major battle in an epic. First, the baron and Belinda engage in a card game. Then, the baron cuts Belinda's hair. There is a fierce battle over the lock of hair.

Note-taking Guide

Use the diagram below to follow the action in *The Rape of the Lock*. Write the events in the order in which they take place.

Setting	
Events	1.
	2.
	3.
End Result:	

from An Essay on Man • from The Rape of the Lock

1. **Connect:** In *An Essay on Man*, Pope says that humankind is "The glory, jest, and riddle of the world." What recent newspaper stories confirm all or part of this description? Explain. A review of the sports pages might give you examples of "glory."

   _____

   _____

2. **Literary Analysis:** *The Rape of the Lock* is a **mock epic**. It is a humorous poem that uses epic elements to poke fun at silly activities. In the chart below, find lines in which the listed epic element appears. Then, briefly describe the action to which this epic element refers. Review III, 161–162 to find one epic element.

Epic Element	Lines in Poem	Action/Activity
Hero's boasts		
Gods and goddesses		
Description of warriors		

3. **Literary Analysis:** An **epic simile** is an elaborate comparison in the manner of Homer that uses the words *like, as,* or *so.* Why are lines 8–16 in Canto V of *The Rape of the Lock* an example of an *epic simile*?

   _____

   _____

4. **Reading Strategy:** Show how in Canto III, lines 105–120 of *The Rape of the Lock*, Pope's **purpose** is to poke fun at social customs and to entertain readers. One clue to the custom is that it involves drinking coffee.

   _____

   _____

from A Dictionary of the English Language
• from The Life of Samuel Johnson

LITERARY ANALYSIS

A **dictionary** is a book that defines words. It may also provide information about a word's pronunciation, history, and usage. Samuel Johnson compiled the first standard dictionary of the English language. As you read, look for features he established. Some of them are still in use today.

A **biography** is an account of someone's life written by another person. James Boswell wrote a biography of Samuel Johnson. It was called the *Life of Samuel Johnson.* Johnson's *Dictionary* helped set the standard for all future dictionaries. In the same way, Boswell's biography helped set the standard for future biographies. As you read it, note how Boswell uses details from his own knowledge to reveal Johnson's character.

Both these works were products of the Enlightenment. The Enlightenment was an eighteenth-century movement that encouraged the pursuit of knowledge. Note how both these works express a respect for knowledge. Compare their **diction,** or choice of words. Also, notice the **tone,** or attitude, that their word choice reveals.

READING STRATEGY

When you **establish a purpose,** you set a goal for reading. For example, two possible goals for reading the *Dictionary* are to learn about Johnson's writing style or to learn about making dictionaries.

To set a purpose, choose a topic related to the selection that you want to know more about. In the chart shown, state what you know about the topic, what you want to know about the topic, and what you learned after reading.

What I Know	What I Want to Know	What I Learned

from A Dictionary of the English Language

Samuel Johnson

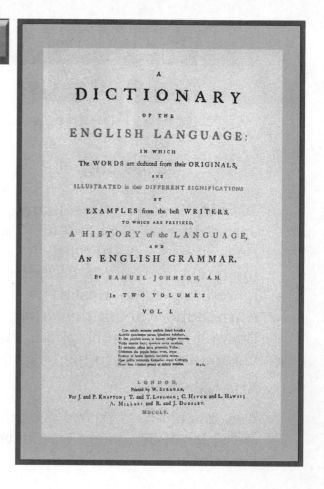

A DICTIONARY OF THE ENGLISH LANGUAGE: IN WHICH The WORDS are deduced from their ORIGINALS, AND ILLUSTRATED in their DIFFERENT SIGNIFICATIONS BY EXAMPLES from the best WRITERS. TO WHICH ARE PREFIXED, A HISTORY of the LANGUAGE, AND AN ENGLISH GRAMMAR. By SAMUEL JOHNSON, A.M. IN TWO VOLUMES VOL. I.

LONDON, Printed by W. STRAHAN, For J. and P. KNAPTON; T. and T. LONGMAN; C. HITCH and L. HAWES; A. MILLAR; and R. and J. DODSLEY. MDCCLV.

Summary In the Preface to his dictionary, Johnson explains that writing a dictionary was not an easy task. Johnson faced many problems and challenges. He had to determine the most accurate and thorough definitions of words without relying on any existing dictionaries. Johnson admits that while his dictionary certainly leaves some words out, he has included a great deal of information nonetheless. The sample entries from Johnson's dictionary range from *athletick* to *youth*.

Note-taking Guide

As you read the selections from Johnson's dictionary, note how the author feels about his undertaking. Use this chart to record what you learn.

Johnson's Feelings About Writers of Dictionaries	Johnson's Feelings About the English Language	Johnson's Feelings About His Own Dictionary	Johnson's Feelings About Himself

from The Life of Samuel Johnson

James Boswell

Summary Samuel Johnson and James Boswell first met in 1763. Boswell was not sure if their meeting had gone well. As he spent more time with Johnson, he learned more about the writer. Boswell reveals much about this fascinating figure in his biography.

Note-taking Guide

Use this chart to record the different sides of Johnson that Boswell describes.

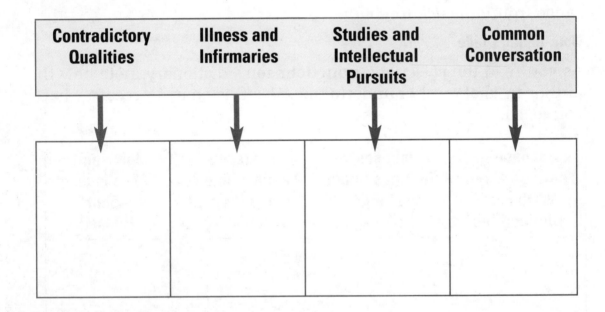

Contradictory Qualities	Illness and Infirmaries	Studies and Intellectual Pursuits	Common Conversation

from A Dictionary of the English Language
• from The Life of Samuel Johnson

1. **Support:** Show how both the Preface to the *Dictionary* and the *Life* use formal **diction,** or word choice. Consider, Johnson's phrase "those who toil at the lower employments." Then, consider Boswell's phrase "to obtain the acquaintance of that extraordinary man.

_____

_____

2. **Literary Analysis:** Use this chart to compare the definition of a word in Johnson's *Dictionary* with the definition of the same word in a modern **dictionary.** The word *patron,* for example, might reveal an interesting contrast.

Johnson's *Dictionary*	Modern Dictionary	Similarities/Differences

3. **Literary Analysis:** Find three examples of facts and three examples of opinions in the **biography** written by Boswell. Remember that you can disprove a fact. You can only disagree with an opinion.

_____

_____

4. **Reading Strategy:** Assume that your **purpose** in reading the Preface to the *Dictionary* is to learn about the history of dictionary-making. What details from the Preface would you record?

_____

_____

Elegy Written in a Country Churchyard
• A Nocturnal Reverie

LITERARY ANALYSIS

Eighteenth-century **Pre-Romantic poetry** shares qualities of two different styles. It shares these qualities with the earlier Neoclassical (NEE oh KLAS i KUHL) poetry of writers like Pope:

- The polished expression of ideas
- The use of balanced phrases and complicated vocabulary

  Pre-Romantic poetry also contains elements that look forward to Romantic poetry:

- A new focus on nature and the life of the common folk
- The expression of feelings

Like the Romantics who come after them, Gray and Finch express strong feelings in their poetry. Gray's stroll through a country churchyard lets him feel the tragedy of life. It also lets him discover life's true value. Finch's nighttime stroll allows her to feel the mind's deep connection with nature.

READING STRATEGY

To help you identify key ideas, **paraphrase** (PAR uh FRAYZ) passages in the poems that follow. To paraphrase is to restate an idea in your own words. Use this chart to help you paraphrase. Record the poet's line or lines under "Original." Then, record your re-wording of the passage under "Paraphrase."

Original

Paraphrase

Elegy Written in a Country Churchyard • A Nocturnal Reverie

Thomas Gray • Anne Finch, Countess of Winchelsea

Summaries In "**Elegy Written in a Country Churchyard**," the speaker walks through a country churchyard as night comes on. He thinks about those who are buried there. They were ordinary village folk, unknown to the outside world. However, they displayed in their daily lives the same traits that famous men and women display. The speaker then imagines that he himself has died. He pictures his own funeral, and he writes his own epitaph.

In "**A Nocturnal Reverie**," the speaker walks through a night land-scape. All her senses are alert. She sees passing clouds and the moon reflected in a river. She smells odors from the plants and trees around her. She hears the sound of falling waters and the cry of birds. Feeling a deep connection with nature, her spirit is content.

Note-taking Guide

Use this chart to list details that Pre-Romantic poetry shares with Neoclassical and Romantic poetry. Illustrate each listed quality with a line or lines from the poems.

Poem	Neoclassical	Romantic
Elegy Written in a Country Churchyard	• polished expression • complicated vocabulary	• nature and simple folk • deep feelings
A Nocturnal Reverie	• polished expression • complicated vocabulary	• nature and simple folk • deep feelings

Elegy Written in a Country Churchyard
• A Nocturnal Reverie

1. **Draw Conclusions:** What message about life does the speaker express in The Epitaph at the end of "Elegy Written in a Country Churchyard"? Focus especially on the last two stanzas.

_____

_____

2. **Literary Analysis: Pre-Romantic poetry** anticipates the Romantic emphasis on mystery and emotion. Reread the lines from the poems that are listed in the chart. Then, for each passage, write the ideas, feelings, and message about life it expresses.

Lines	Stated Ideas	Feelings Expressed	Message About Life
"Elegy" lines 89–92			
"Reverie" lines 39–46			

3. **Reading Strategy: Paraphrase** the key ideas in lines 29–32 of Gray's "Elegy." Restate them in your own words. Remember that "Ambition" and "Grandeur" refer to ambitious and great people.

_____

_____

4. **Reading Strategy:** Paraphrase the wish in lines 47–50 of "A Nocturnal Reverie." Does Finch want to continue walking through the night landscape? Explain.

_____

_____

On Spring • The Aims of *The Spectator*

LITERARY ANALYSIS

An **essay** is a short piece of prose. It explores a topic as if the author were letting you overhear his or her thoughts. The word *essay* means an "attempt" or "test." The term was first applied to writing by the French essayist Michel Montaigne (mee SHEL mahn TAYN).

Johnson's and Addison's essays can be seen as "tests," or experiments. The writers try to connect observations and anecdotes in order to form ideas.

Essays became popular during a time of great change in society. The middle class was growing. This part of society consisted of people like lawyers, shopkeepers, and merchants. As the middle class grew, its members searched for a way to define themselves. The essays of Johnson and Addison helped such readers answer the question, Who am I?

READING STRATEGY

Writers do not always state everything directly. In some cases, you need to **draw inferences** to figure out what the writer does not say directly. Drawing inferences helps you appreciate the writer's attitudes about different topics. Use this chart to make inferences as you read the essays.

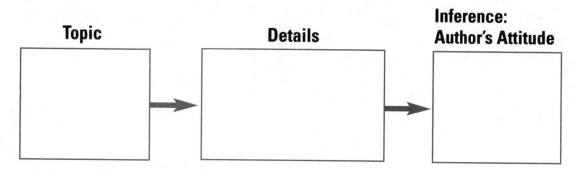

Topic → **Details** → **Inference: Author's Attitude**

On Spring

Samuel Johnson

Summary Johnson recalls a man who always looked forward to the coming of spring. If a particular spring was disappointing, he always looked forward to the next. Johnson himself finds this season very pleasing. He thinks that the rebirth of nature offers many things to observe and think about. He advises younger readers to walk and observe nature during the spring.

Note-taking Guide

Use this chart as you read "On Spring." In the left box, record Johnson's ideas and observations. In the right box, record the advice that he gives readers.

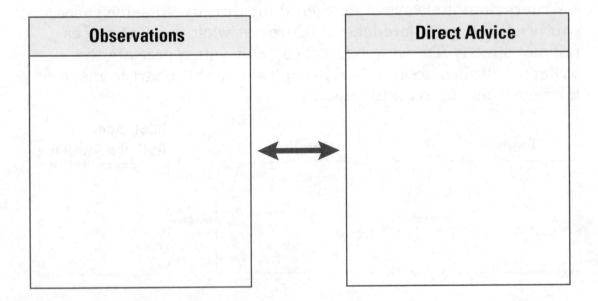

Observations	Direct Advice

The Aims of *The Spectator*

Joseph Addison

Summary Addison discusses the success of his newspaper, *The Spectator.* About 3,000 copies of the paper are distributed each day. He estimates that 20 people read each paper. So he has an audience of 60,000 readers.

He invites four groups of people to read his paper:

- Families, who can enjoy the paper over breakfast
- Curious men with time on their hands, wealthy or lazy men
- The "blanks" of society, people without ideas
- Women looking for innocent entertainment and, perhaps, knowledge

Note-taking Guide

In this chart, note some of the colorful phrases that Addison uses to describe the four groups of people he addresses in his essay.

Families	Gentlemen, My Good Brothers	The Blanks of Society	The Female World

On Spring • The Aims of *The Spectator*

1. **Interpret:** How would you sum up Johnson's idea about happiness in "On Spring"? For example, does he seem to think that happiness comes from studying one's own thoughts and feelings?

_____

2. **Literary Analysis:** Johnson writes that some people "cannot bear their own company." Compare this idea with Addison's portrait of his four types of readers. Use this chart to record your comparison of the two **essays**. In the first column, note whether each author breaks down ideas or describes social types. In the second column, note whether each generalizes about human nature or describes people of a specific time. In the third column, indicate whether each moves logically from idea to idea or writes in a spirit of fun.

Passage	Analytic or Descriptive	General or Of a Specific Era?	Logical or Humorous?
"On Spring" Some "cannot bear their own company"			
"The Aims of *The Spectator*" Portrait of four types of readers			

3. **Literary Analysis:** What attitude does Addison encourage readers to have toward themselves?

_____

4. **Reading Strategy:** Read Addison's description of the "blanks." **Draw inferences** about Addison's attitude toward these people. Does he look down on them? Does he mock them bitterly or affectionately?

_____

_____

A Modest Proposal

LITERARY ANALYSIS

A **satirical essay** is a brief prose work that pokes fun at the flaws and shortcomings of human beings and institutions. Writers of satirical essays want to persuade their readers that reform is urgently necessary. To achieve this purpose, satirical essays use specific tools:

- understatement—describing something as much less than it is
- exaggeration—describing something as much more than it is
- sarcasm—in a mocking way, saying the opposite of what you mean

Style is an author's special way of writing. Many elements contribute to style:

- word choice, for example does the author use words that are formal or informal
- tone, or attitude toward the reader and the subject
- imagery, or words appealing to the senses
- types of sentences, whether they are long or brief, complicated or simple
- figurative language, or comparisons the author makes

READING STRATEGY

An **author's purpose** is his or her reason for writing. In "A Modest Proposal," Swift begins to hint at his purpose in the essay's title. His "proposal" is anything but modest. The outrageous solution Swift proposes to end poverty and hunger is a clue to his deeper purpose: to highlight the social horrors in Ireland. Use the chart to find details within Swift's proposal that reveal this deeper purpose.

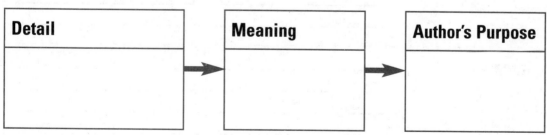

Detail	Meaning	Author's Purpose

A Modest Proposal

Jonathan Swift

Summary This essay is a comment on Irish society during the 18th century. Growing numbers of Irish people suffered in poverty every day. Swift scorns the upper classes as selfish and greedy. He feels they do nothing to end this poverty and often contribute to the problem. Using facts about population, unemployment, and social issues, Swift explains a frightening plan to end poverty: kill poor children and use them for food! Were his plan meant to be taken seriously, it would be truly horrifying. However, Swift does not want his plan to be followed. His purpose is to call attention to social ills.

Note-taking Guide

Use this chart to list two examples of each tool of satire that Swift uses.

Understatement	
	_____ _____ _____ _____
Exaggeration	_____ _____ _____ _____ _____
Sarcasm	_____ _____ _____ _____

A Modest Proposal

1. **Interpret:** In the paragraph beginning, "I do therefore humbly . . .," Swift offers details about cooking young children. In what way do these details make his plan even more shocking?

_____

_____

2. **Literary Analysis:** A **satirical essay** attacks social problems or wrongs. What is the main target of Swift's **satire** in "A Modest Proposal"?

_____

_____

3. **Literary Analysis:** Use the chart below to list four examples of Swift's **style,** his special way of writing. Then, indicate the way these examples contribute to the satire. Word choice refers to the types of word he uses, whether formal or informal, technical or conversational. Imagery refers to the ways in which his writing appeals to the senses. Figurative language refers to his use of comparisons. Tone refers to his attitude toward his subject.

Examples	Contribution to the Satire
Word choice: Imagery: Figurative language: Tone:	

4. **Reading Strategy:** Swift claims that his **purpose** is to offer a "modest proposal" for preventing poor children from being a burden. Which details in Swift's proposal reveal his deeper purpose in writing it?

_____

_____

ONLINE SEARCH ENGINES

About Online Search Engines

An **online search engine** is a tool for finding information on the World Wide Web. Some search engines track and locate information on the entire Web. Others search only within a given Web site.

Most of the major search engines conduct searches using keywords. Keywords are important terms related to a subject. When you provide general keywords, a search engine will return many pages. Specific keywords are more useful because they will result in fewer pages, which are more closely related to your topic.

For example, suppose you are looking for information on Britain's Cavalier poets. The search term *poetry* calls up many pages, or hits, about all kinds of poetry. A search using the keywords *Cavalier poets* locates information about only the poets fitting that category. In addition to text articles, most search engines provide links to other media, additional Web sites, and more.

Reading Strategy

Certain sources of information work best for certain research topics. For example, articles are probably the most useful source for a research paper on Cavalier poets. Keep in mind the best sources for your topic as you **evaluate the appropriateness of a search result.**

For a focused search, avoid Web sites that do not reflect the topic or the type of information you need. In addition, avoid sites that are not recognized by experts or sponsored by noteworthy institutions. You may need to modify your keywords to broaden or narrow the focus of your search.

Complete the chart below to illustrate how you would organize a search.

Research Topic	Search Keywords	Useful Types of Information	Information to Avoid
• British Cavalier Poets	• • •	• • •	• • •

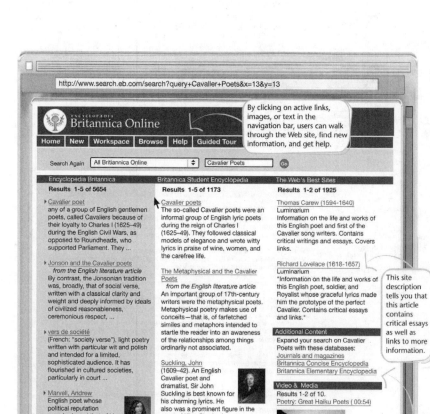

Reading Online Search Engins

Circle the numbers that tell how many results were found on the Encyclopedia Britannica. How many results are there on the Britannica Student Encyclopedia?

_____

Reading Strategy

Look at the headers showing Web sites with keyword information. Many search engines find information other than articles. What other type of media source for Cavalier poets appears on this page?

_____

Is this result useful for a report on Cavalier poets? Explain.

_____

Reading Check

Why was this group of poets called the "Cavaliers"?

_____

Circle the entry where you found your answer.

Reading Strategy

Evaluate the appropriateness of these search results. Would it be appropriate to use these results for research? Explain.

_____

Reading Check

What were opponents of King Charles I called? Why did the king's opponents have this nickname?

_____

_____

Underline the nickname where it first appears in the entry.

Reading Strategy

What information does the box at the bottom of the page provide? Why is this information important?

_____

_____

_____

Stop to Reflect

Read the information in this entry. What other keywords might you use to find more information about the Cavalier poets and their time period? Why would these be useful search terms?

_____

_____

_____

Reading Informational Materials

List two advantages and two disadvantages to doing research online. Explain your answer.

_____

_____

_____

_____

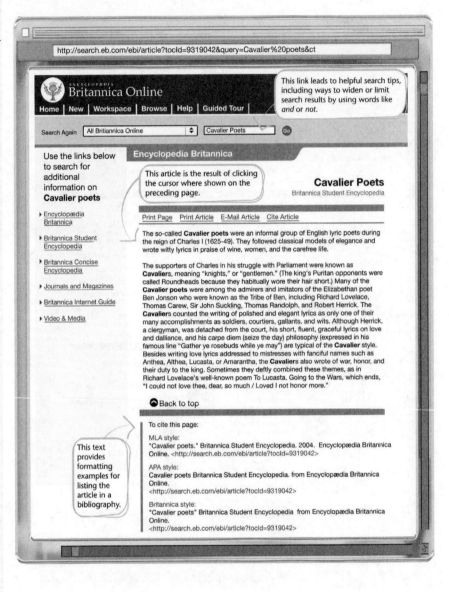

http://search.eb.com/ebi/article?tocId=9319042&query=Cavalier%20poets&ct

Britannica Online

Home | New | Workspace | Browse | Help | Guided Tour

This link leads to helpful search tips, including ways to widen or limit search results by using words like *and* or *not*.

Search Again | All Britiannica Online | Cavalier Poets | Go

Encyclopedia Britannica

This article is the result of clicking the cursor where shown on the preceding page.

Use the links below to search for additional information on **Cavalier poets**

▸ Encyclopædia Britannica
▸ Britannica Student Encyclopedia
▸ Britannica Concise Encyclopedia
▸ Journals and Magazines
▸ Britannica Internet Guide
▸ Video & Media

Cavalier Poets
Britannica Student Encyclopedia

Print Page   Print Article   E-Mail Article   Cite Article

The so-called **Cavalier poets** were an informal group of English lyric poets during the reign of Charles I (1625-49). They followed classical models of elegance and wrote witty lyrics in praise of wine, women, and the carefree life.

The supporters of Charles in his struggle with Parliament were known as **Cavaliers**, meaning "knights," or "gentlemen." (The king's Puritan opponents were called Roundheads because they habitually wore their hair short.) Many of the **Cavalier poets** were among the admirers and imitators of the Elizabethan poet Ben Jonson who were known as the Tribe of Ben, including Richard Lovelace, Thomas Carew, Sir John Suckling, Thomas Randolph, and Robert Herrick. The **Cavaliers** counted the writing of polished and elegant lyrics as only one of their many accomplishments as soldiers, courtiers, gallants, and wits. Although Herrick, a clergyman, was detached from the court, his short, fluent, graceful lyrics on love and dalliance, and his carpe diem (seize the day) philosophy (expressed in his famous line "Gather ye rosebuds while ye may") are typical of the **Cavalier** style. Besides writing love lyrics addressed to mistresses with fanciful names such as Anthea, Althea, Lucasta, or Amarantha, the **Cavaliers** also wrote of war, honor, and their duty to the king. Sometimes they deftly combined these themes, as in Richard Lovelace's well-known poem To Lucasta, Going to the Wars, which ends, "I could not love thee, dear, so much / Loved I not honor more."

⬤ Back to top

This text provides formatting examples for listing the article in a bibliography.

To cite this page:

MLA style:
"Cavalier poets." Britannica Student Encyclopedia. 2004. Encyclopædia Britannica Online. <http://search.eb.com/ebi/article?tocId=9319042>

APA style:
Cavalier poets Britannica Student Encyclopedia. from Encyclopædia Britannica Online. <http://search.eb.com/ebi/article?tocId=9319042>

Britannica style:
"Cavalier poets" Britannica Student Encyclopedia from Encyclopædia Britannica Online. <http://search.eb.com/ebi/article?tocId=9319042>

THINKING ABOUT ONLINE SEARCH ENGINES

1. Review the search engine results. Which source of information works best for writing a paper on the Cavalier poets? Why?

_____

_____

2. Other than an encyclopedia Web site, what other types of Web sites might provide useful information about the Cavalier poets?

_____

_____

READING STRATEGY

3. What might you learn about Cavalier poets, in general, by reading a few of the biographies in the search results?

_____

4. Suppose you searched for information on a specific Cavalier poet. How might your search results differ from the results of this search?

_____

TIMED WRITING: EXPLANATION (25 MINUTES)

Create a chart for a new research topic related to British literature. Use the chart from the Reading Informational Materials page as a model. Explain why you chose each search keyword. Also explain why some types of Web sites and information would be best for your topic.

List three possible research topics. Think about stories, poems, or plays you have read in class to help you think of ideas for a topic.

_____

_____

_____

Circle the topic you would like to research. Choose three keywords for the search. Be as specific as possible. Use these notes as you begin to complete your chart.

To a Mouse • To a Louse • Woo'd and Married and A'

LITERARY ANALYSIS

Dialect is the way that people of a region, class, or group actually speak. It is common, everyday spoken language. Dialect includes different pronunciation, grammar, and expressions than those that are found in the standard written form of a language. Robert Burns and Joanna Baillie use Scottish dialect in their poems. This is the common language of the people of Scotland. Using dialect helps the poets achieve these goals:

• Establishing character, mood, and setting
• Adding charm for readers who do not speak the dialect

READING STRATEGY

As you read, **translate the dialect.** You can do this two ways. First, use the footnotes. Second, look for similarities between English words and the words you read in dialect. Use these similarities together with context clues. For example, in "thou need na start awa" *na* is "not" and *awa* is "away." Use the chart below to help you translate some words of the dialect.

Footnotes	*Sleekit*[3]
	3.
Context	*saunt an' sinner*
Word Similarities	*dinna*
Missing Letters	*woo'd, a'*

To a Mouse • To a Louse

Robert Burns

Woo'd and Married and A'

Joanna Baillie

Summaries In Robert Burns's poems, the speaker addresses small animals. In "To a Mouse," the speaker sympathizes with the mouse whose home he has plowed up. He concludes that the plans of both "mice and men" often go wrong. In "To a Louse," Burns talks to a louse he sees on a finely dressed lady. (Louse is the singular form of lice.) The lady's ignorance of the louse shows her foolish pride. In Joanna Baillie's "Woo'd and Married and A'," a bride is upset because she is poor. Her parents tell her she should not be upset, but that does not help. Then her husband-to-be flatters her and comforts her.

Note-taking Guide

Use this chart to record details about "To a Mouse" and "To a Louse."

	How the Speaker Finds His Topic	Whom/What the Speaker Addresses	Speaker's Main Message
"To a Mouse"	The speaker is plowing a field and plows up the mouse's home.		
"To a Louse"			

To a Mouse • To a Louse • Woo'd and Married and A'

1. **Analyze Cause and Effect:** In "Woo'd and Married and A,'" what effect do the words of the bridegroom have on the bride?

   _____

   _____

2. **Literary Analysis:** What does the use of **dialect** in the poems by Burns suggest about the speaker's social standing?

   _____

   _____

3. **Literary Analysis:** Use the chart below to analyze the poems.

Poem	Subject	Message
"To a Mouse"		
"To a Louse"		
"Woo'd and Married and A'"		

4. **Reading Strategy:** Choose four lines from one of the poems and translate them into standard English.

   _____

   _____

   _____

   _____

The Lamb • The Tyger • The Chimney Sweeper • Infant Sorrow

LITERARY ANALYSIS

A **symbol** is a word, image, or idea that stands for something else. Often, a symbol is something that can be seen, heard, or touched. It stands for something that cannot be seen, heard, or touched. This may be a feeling or an idea. In this line, river" and "Sun" are symbols:

> And wash in a river and shine in the Sun.

Washing "in a river" symbolizes baptism in the Christian church. For Christians, when someone is baptized, he or she is washed of sin. The Sun symbolizes the light of holiness.

Blake uses symbols to express his **poetic vision.** This is his way of seeing life. As you read "The Lamb," use the chart below to help you understand Blake's symbols.

Association		Association
	Symbol	
Association		**Association**

READING STRATEGY

When you read literature that has pictures, **use the visuals as a key to meaning.** Look closely at the details of the illustrations that go with these poems. Think about how they support or add to the author's words.

The Lamb • The Tyger • The Chimney Sweeper • Infant Sorrow

William Blake

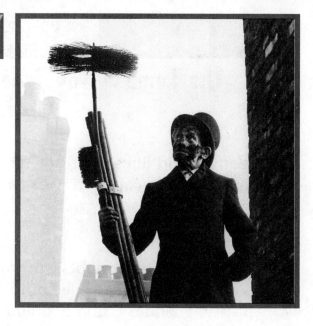

Summary In **"The Lamb,"** the speaker of the poem is a child. The child asks questions of a lamb. The speaker explains that the Creator made them both. An adult speaker in **"The Tyger"** wonders who could have made such a frightening creature. In **"The Chimney Sweeper,"** a child named Tom has a dream that gives him a new attitude toward life. In **"Infant Sorrow"** the speaker is a baby who describes life as a kind of trap.

Note-taking Guide

Use this chart to record the important words and ideas in each poem.

Poem	Key Words	Key Ideas
The Lamb		
The Tyger		
The Chimney Sweeper		
Infant Sorrow		

The Lamb • The Tyger • The Chimney Sweeper • Infant Sorrow

1. **Infer:** Reread lines 15-18 of "The Lamb." What do the speaker and the lamb have in common with the lamb's creator?

_____

2. **Literary Analysis: Symbols** are words, images, or ideas that represent something else. In "The Lamb," the lamb reminds the reader of purity, goodness, and gentleness. What might the lamb symbolize?

_____

_____

3. **Literary Analysis:** "The Chimney Sweeper" is partly about suffering. Use the chart below to show how suffering is shown in the poem.

Who Suffers?	Why?	Is Suffering Fair?	Suggested Solution	Is the Solution Fair?

4. **Reading Strategy:** When a literary work has pictures, **use the visuals as a key to meaning.** Compare Blake's picture of a tiger to the tiger in the poem.

_____

_____

Introduction to *Frankenstein*

LITERARY ANALYSIS

Gothic literature is concerned with the supernatural. Gothic writers use their imaginations to create worlds that are beyond the everyday world of reason. This type of writing became popular in the late eighteenth and early nineteenth centuries. Gothic stories were set in scary places, such as dark, mysterious castles, towers, and underground passages. *Frankenstein* is an example of Gothic literature because it takes the reader out of the world of reason into an imaginary world of horror.

The Gothic novel became popular in the late 1700s and was part of the new **Romantic Movement** in literature. The Romantics rejected the idea that reason could explain everything. Instead, they believed in the powers of nature and the imagination.

READING STRATEGY

One way to be an active reader is to **predict,** or make guesses about what will happen next. Good readers revise, or change, their predictions as they learn more abut characters and events. Use the chart below to make predictions, check them, and change them as you read.

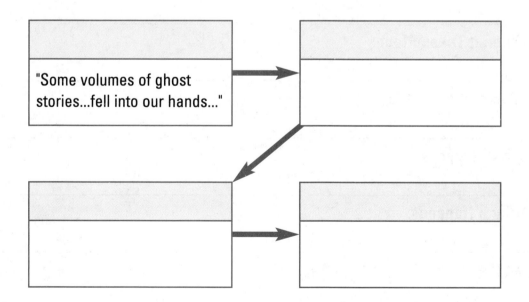

"Some volumes of ghost stories...fell into our hands..."

Introduction to *Frankenstein*

Mary Wollstonecraft Shelley

Summary In this introduction, Mary Shelley tells how she got the idea for *Frankenstein.* While visiting Lord Byron, a group of friends told ghost stories. At first, Shelley couldn't think of one. One night, the friends discussed experiments that involved creating life. Later that night, Shelley began to imagine an awful sight. She pictured someone kneeling over a thing he had put together, a thing that showed signs of life. Once created, the living creation could not be stopped. Shelley knew she had her story. All she had to do was describe the terror she felt in her imagination.

Note-taking Guide

Use this chart to record details about the Introduction to *Frankenstein.*

Who is Involved:
When it Takes Place:
Where it Takes Place:
What Happens:
How it Happens:

Introduction to *Frankenstein*

1. **Connect:** Shelley gets the idea for *Frankenstein* from a discussion about the possibility of creating life. After hearing this discussion, she has a strange vision. What does this vision suggest about her reaction to Dr. Darwin's experiments?

_____

_____

2. **Literary Analysis:** Literature in the **Gothic tradition** contains supernatural elements. In her third paragraph, Shelley recalls reading ghost stories. Which characteristics of the **Gothic tradition** do these ghost stories share? List examples in the chart.

Gothic Characteristic	Example in Shelley

3. **Literary Analysis:** What idea does Shelley's imagined vision suggest about the dangerous possibilities of science?

_____

_____

4. **Reading Strategy:** When you **predict,** you use clues in the text to guess what will happen next. Were you able to predict how Shelley would react to the discussion of Darwin's experiments? Explain.

_____

_____

Lines Composed a Few Miles Above Tintern Abbey • *from* The Prelude • The World Is Too Much With Us • London, 1802

LITERARY ANALYSIS

Romanticism was a literary movement that took place in late-eighteenth-century Europe. Earlier writers, such as Pope and Jonson, used fancy language to discuss themes that had little to do with everyday life and feelings. Unlike those earlier writers, the works of many Romantic poets include

- Simple or direct language
- The expression of strong, personal feelings
- Deeply felt and thoughtful responses to nature

English Romanticism began with William Wordsworth. His poetic form was the **lyric,** a poem in which a single speaker expresses personal emotions and observations.

Diction, or word choice, was freer and simpler in Romantic poetry. Wordsworth used many simple words. Nevertheless, the poet also relied on abstract terms such as *a sense sublime* to convey his less concrete ideas.

READING STRATEGY

Literary context is the term used to describe the ideas that people of a particular time period have about what literature is and what it should do. Wordsworth brought about a change in the literary context. Use the chart to identify details and qualities in his work that were new.

Setting	
Characters	
Main Events	
High Point of Story	
Conclusion	

Lines Composed a Few Miles Above Tintern Abbey

William Wordsworth

Summary The poet revisits a country place near Tintern Abbey in Wales after five years. He addresses this poem to his sister, Dorothy. He explains that the memory of this place had a soothing effect on him during his absence. He recalls his childhood relationship to nature. By contrast, the adult poet now feels a great spirit in nature. He calls upon his sister to share his feelings for this place and to remember his devotion to nature.

Note-taking Guide

Use this chart to record main ideas about the poem.

Who	
When	
Where	
What	
Why	

Lines Composed a Few Miles Above Tintern Abbey
William Wordsworth

In English, the suffixes –sion and –tion often mean "the state of." If the adjective secluded in line 6 means "isolated" or "hidden away," what does the noun seclusion mean?

_____

_____

In the bracketed passage, circle two features of the scene that the speaker notices with his senses of hearing and vision.

An apostrophe may either show possession, as in the phrase the poet's sister, or it may stand for a missing letter. The word 'mid is short for amid, meaning "in the middle of." What letters do you think are missing in the word o'clock, used to tell time?

_____

_____

Reread lines 13–15 and underline the answers to these questions.

(1) Where was the speaker located when he felt "sensations sweet"?

(2) In what parts of his body did he have these feelings?

Five years have passed since Wordsworth last visited the valley of the River Wye and the ruins of Tintern Abbey in Wales. On a second visit, he has brought his sister Dorothy with him to share the experience.

◆ ◆ ◆

Five years have passed; five summers, with the length
Of five long winters! and again I hear
These waters, rolling from their mountain springs
With a soft inland murmur. Once again
5 Do I <u>behold</u> these steep and lofty cliffs,
That on a wild <u>secluded</u> scene impress
Thoughts of more deep seclusion; and connect
The landscape with the quiet of the sky.

◆ ◆ ◆

The poet lies under a sycamore tree. He observes the silent, peaceful orchards and farms around him.

◆ ◆ ◆

These beauteous[1] forms,
10 Through a long absence, have not been to me
As is a landscape to a blind man's eye:
But oft,[2] in lonely rooms, and 'mid the <u>din</u>
Of towns and cities, I have owed to them
In hours of weariness, sensations sweet,
15 Felt in the blood, and felt along the heart.

Vocabulary Development

behold (bee HOHLD) v. see
secluded (suh KLOOD uhd) adj. isolated
din (DIN) n. loud noise

_____

1. **beauteous** (BYOO tee uhs) adj. beautiful.
2. **oft** adv. often.

♦ ♦ ♦

Memories of peaceful nature are precious to the poet. They make him a kinder, better person. They also inspire his soul. In moments of distress, memories of the Wye valley have consoled his spirit.

♦ ♦ ♦

And now, with gleams of half-extinguished[3]
    thought,
With many recognitions dim and faint,
And somewhat[4] of a sad <u>perplexity</u>,
The picture of the mind revives again;
20 While here I stand, not only with the sense
Of present pleasure, but with pleasing
    thoughts
That in this moment there is life and food
For future years.

♦ ♦ ♦

The speaker remembers how he felt about nature on his first visit five years ago. Then he was younger and more passionate. Now he is more mature and reflective.

♦ ♦ ♦

For I have learned
To look on nature, not as in the hour
25 Of thoughtless youth; but hearing
    oftentimes
The still, sad music of humanity,
Nor harsh nor <u>grating</u>, though of ample
    power
To chasten[5] and subdue. And I have felt
A presence that disturbs me with the joy

Read Fluently

Read the bracketed passage aloud. How does the speaker relate the present to the future in this passage?

_____

_____

_____

Reading Check

What has caused the speaker to look differently at nature?

_____

_____

_____

_____

Vocabulary Development

perplexity (puhr PLEK suh tee) *n.* confusion; bewilderment

grating (GRAYT ing) *adj.* annoying; irritating

---

3. **half-extinguished** *adj.* half-destroyed.
4. **somewhat** *adv.* something.
5. **chasten** (CHAY suhn) *v.* punish in order to correct.

In **Romanticism**, a deeply felt response to nature is an important theme. In the underlined passage, what feeling about all creation does nature inspire in the speaker?

_____

_____

_____

Literary context is the group of assumptions that influence a writer. How do the bracketed lines reflect the literary context of Romanticism?

_____

_____

_____

30 Of <u>elevated</u> thoughts; a sense <u>sublime</u>
Of something far more deeply interfused,[6]
Whose dwelling is the light of setting suns,
And the round ocean and the living air,
And the blue sky, and in the mind of man;
35 <u>A motion and a spirit, that impels</u>
<u>All thinking things, all objects of all</u>
<u>thought, And rolls through all things.</u>
Therefore am I still
A lover of the meadows and the woods
And mountains; and of all that we behold
40 From this green earth; of all the mighty
world
Of eye, and ear—both what they half create
And what perceive; well pleased to
recognize
In nature and the language of the sense,
The anchor of my purest thoughts, the
nurse,
45 The guide, the guardian of my heart, and
soul
Of all my moral being.

◆   ◆   ◆

The speaker prays that his sister will also experience the joy that nature offers. The quietness and beauty of nature have the power to comfort us in all the troubles of life. The poet predicts that his sister will cherish precious memories of their visit together.

Vocabulary Development

elevated (EL uh vay tuhd) *adj.*   noble; inspiring
sublime (suh BLYM) *adj.*   noble and thrilling; majestic
impels (im PELZ) *v.*   pushes; moves forward

---

6. **interfused** (in tuhr FYOOZD) *adj.* closely linked together.

                                    ◆ ◆ ◆
                        Nor, perchance—
        If I should be where I no more can hear
        Thy voice, nor catch from thy wild eyes
            these gleams
50 Of past existence—wilt thou then forget
        That on the banks of this delightful stream
        We stood together; and that I, so long
        A worshipper of Nature, hither came
        Unwearied in that service: rather say
55 With warmer love—oh! with far deeper zeal
        Of holier love. Nor wilt thou then forget,
        That after many wanderings, many years
        Of absence, these steep woods and lofty
            cliffs,
60 And this green <u>pastoral</u> landscape, were to
            me
        More dear, both for themselves and for thy
            sake!

Vocabulary Development

pastoral (PAS tuh ruhl) *adj.* rural

---

from The Prelude •
The World Is Too Much
With Us • London, 1802

William Wordsworth

Summary In *The Prelude*, the speaker contrasts the promise of freedom at the start of the French Revolution with the terrible reality that followed. In **"The World Is Too Much With Us,"** the speaker says people waste their lives by going after material things instead of appreciating Nature. In **"London, 1802,"** the speaker expresses worry about the present time. He calls on the great poet Milton to return England to its former values of passion and freedom.

Note-taking Guide

Use this chart to record the main message of each poem.

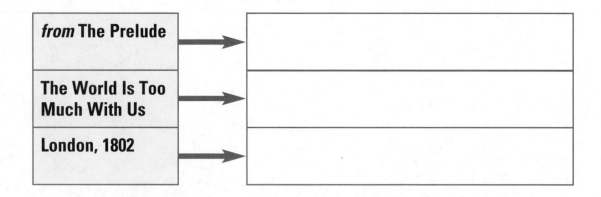

from The Prelude	
The World Is Too Much With Us	
London, 1802	

Lines Composed a Few Miles Above Tintern Abbey • *from* The Prelude • The World Is Too Much With Us • London, 1802

1. **Infer:** Explain the difference in the poet's attitude from his first to his second visit to Tintern Abbey.

   _____

2. **Compare and Contrast:** The poems "London, 1802" and "The World Is Too Much With Us" identify problems in society. How are the problems the same in both poems? How are they different?

   _____

3. **Literary Analysis:** Find examples in the poems of **diction** that is specific and simple, abstract but simple, or abstract and difficult. List one example for each heading in the chart below.

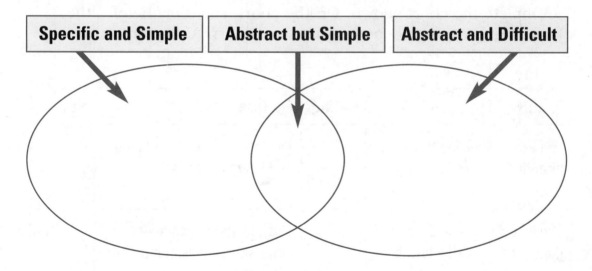

| Specific and Simple | Abstract but Simple | Abstract and Difficult |

4. **Reading Skill:** What do the hopes described in *The Prelude* tell you about the Romantic **literary context**?

   _____

   _____

GUIDEBOOKS

About Guidebooks

Guidebooks are written for tourists who are traveling. They give directions to a location. They also give the location's history and information about ways to see the attractions. Guidebooks list hours, admission costs, and parking information. They may use the following to clearly explain information to their readers:

- diagrams of the location and how to see its attractions
- photos that show important details
- descriptions with subheads dividing the information
- historical and practical information for visitors

Reading Strategy

A **diagram** is a drawing that breaks down a larger topic. It shows all of the parts of something and how the parts fit together. **To interpret and use a diagram**, you need to look at the layout and smaller parts. Then, you use the key to see how the parts are related.

Complete the chart shown. On the chart, rate how helpful the diagram and each guidebook entry for Tintern Abbey are to you.

Feature	Rating	Feature	Rating
The arrow showing the direction		The labeled map of buildings and how they are laid out	
The incusion of the location of the river and nearby towns		The scale showing how large one thing is compared to another	
The key that shows the ages of the buildings		The arrow that shows the entrance to the abbey	
The parking symbols		The parking symbols	

from The Green Guide to Wales, a Michelin Travel Publications guide

TINTERN ABBEY
Monmouthshire

The Cistercians[1] came to this remote and lovely location amid the woods of the winding Wye[2] in 1131, and the picturesque ruins of their great abbey still stands, a magnet for visitors ever since the first tourists floated down the river in search of sublime and romantic scenery in the late 18th century.

Its roof gone, its glass smashed, its walls obliterated by ivy, the abbey church nevertheless remains essentially intact and, although the greater part of its extensive buildings have been reduced to stubs of walls, Tintern still conveys a powerful impression of the architectural splendor which accompanied the severities of monastic life.

Norman Foundation Tintern was the first Cistercian abbey to be established in Wales, a daughter house of the abbey at L'Aumone in Normandy, whose monks were invited here by Walter Fitz Richard de Clare of Chepstow Castle. The lords of Chepstow were to continue as benefactors of the abbey, the greatest of them being Roger Bigod III who was responsible for the lavish rebuilding of the abbey church in the late 13th century. By the time of the Dissolution[3], Tintern was the wealthiest abbey in Wales, a complex of buildings extending over much of the narrow strip of flat land between the river and the steep wooded slopes.

Romantic Tintern In the mid-eighteenth century the abbey ruins were taken in hand by the Duke of Beaufort, who tidied and turfed the interior, thus making it ready for the tourists who were soon to arrive. The elegiac atmosphere sought by such visitors was captured by the artist J. M. W. Turner (1755-1851) who made a number of studies of the ruins in the course of the 1790s. Tintern occupied a special place in the heart of William Wordsworth (1770-1850), who came here twice, in 1793 and again in 1798, composing his famous "Lines Written a Few Miles Above Tintern Abbey" which recall:

...these steep and lofty cliffs,
Which on a wild secluded scene impress
Thoughts of more deep seclusion...

---

1. Cistercian (si STER shuhn) A monastic order that follows a strict interpretation of religious life based on the teachings of saint Benedict.
2. Wye (WY) river in Southeast Wales.
3. Dissolution In 1536, Henry VIII began dissolving the Catholic monasteries, including Tintern Abbey, in part to pour their riches into the royal treasuries, but also to reinforce his position as the apex of power in England. The Dissolution was an early but decisive step towards the Reformation, which aimed to reform the Catholic Church and initiate Protestantism as the official religion of England.

TINTERN ABBEY

Abbey Ruins Souvenir shops and car and coach parks attest to Tintern's longstanding popularity. Entry is via discreetly designed modern buildings flanking the riverside car park, and most visitors will be drawn first to the majestic abbey church, built, unusually, to the south of the cloister and its surrounding buildings. With its high walls crowned by the four great gables of nave, transepts, and sanctuary[1], this is the structure raised by the munificence of Roger Bigod between 1269 and 1301 to replace the far more modest 12th century Norman church whose outline is marked on the floor of the nave.

All the screens and subdivisions which reflected the complexities of monastic ritual have long since disappeared, and the eye is led directly to the far end of the building, where the **east window (1)**, bare of all tracery and with but a single central mullion[2], links the abbey with its gloriously wooded setting. Columns, shafts and pointed arches in Decorated style[3] still evoke something of the confidence and expansiveness of the late 13th century, but it is the great, seven-light **west window (2)** which is the most splendid surviving single feature.

Along the north side are substantial remains of the monks' dining hall, flanked by kitchen to the west and **warming house** to the east.

The abbey precinct extended over an area larger than that of most medieval Welsh towns. To the east of the main cloister, a secondary cloister developed, dominated by the infirmary and by the **abbots' quarters (4)**, both of which were added to and improved in the course of the 14th and 15th centuries.

---

1. nave, transept, and sanctuary three sections of a church. A nave is the main, and longest, section that runs between the side aisles from main door to the altar. The transept intersects the nave at a right angle and creates the shape of a cross. The sanctuary is any place of high religious importance in a church, such as the altar.
2. tracery... mullion In ornamental windows, such as Gothic or stained glass windows, tracery is delicate branching lines that separate panels of glass. A mullion is a stronger bar that divides windows into smaller portions.
3. Decorated style a style of English Gothic architecture dating from the late 13th century to the mid-14th century.

Thinking About the Guidebook

1. Use the historical key to the diagram. Then, tell what parts of the abbey were built in the late thirteenth and early fourteenth centuries.

   _____

2. Why are the reference numbers on the diagram helpful to the reader?

   _____

Reading Skill: Interpreting and Using Diagram Features

3. Look at the key and the text. What part of the abbey ruins are the oldest?

   _____

4. Imagine that you are standing at the exhibition and ticket office. In which direction must you walk to get to the chapter house and the north transept?

   _____

Timed Writing: Description (25 minutes)

   Write a short description of the abbey in your own words. Take notes on the following as you reread the guidebook entry:

• List the names and ages of three of the buildings.

   _____

   _____

• List the abbey's overall size.

   _____

• List three facts about its history.

   _____

   _____

Use your notes to write your description.

The Rime of the Ancient Mariner • Kubla Khan

LITERARY ANALYSIS

Romantic poetry uses **poetic sound devices** to create music, beauty, and emotion. These devices including the following:

- **Alliteration** is the repetition of a consonant sound at the beginnings of words: "The fair <u>br</u>eeze <u>bl</u>ew, the white <u>f</u>oam <u>fl</u>ew..."

- **Consonance** is the repetition of consonant sounds at the end of stressed syllables that have different vowel sounds: "A frightful fie<u>nd</u> / Doth close behi<u>nd</u> ..."

- **Assonance** is the repetition of a vowel sound in stressed syllables that have different consonant sounds: "The western w<u>a</u>ve was all afl<u>a</u>me."

- **Internal Rhyme** is the use of rhymes within a line of poetry: "With heavy th<u>ump</u>, a lifeless l<u>ump</u> ..."

READING STRATEGY

Analyzing poetic effects, such as those discussed above, will help you appreciate poetry. As you read, use a chart like the one shown. Find examples of alliteration, consonance, assonance, and internal rhyme. Note how these devices affect the poem.

Passage

The ship drove fast, loud roared the blast, / And southward aye we fled.

→

Sound Device	Image	Effect of Sound on Image
1.		1.
2.		2.

The Rime of the Ancient Mariner

Kubla Khan

Samuel Taylor Coleridge

Summary In "The Rime of the Ancient Mariner," an old sailor, or mariner, stops a guest on his way to a wedding. The Mariner tells the guest of a voyage through strange seas during which he killed a bird called an albatross. The albatross is a symbol of good luck. A curse falls on the ship, and all die except the Ancient Mariner. When the Mariner finds love for nature in his heart, the curse is partially lifted. The dead crew begins to steer the ship. Still, the Mariner is doomed to retell the tale.

"Kubla Khan" is an unfinished poem. The first part describes a "pleasure dome" built by Kubla Khan. Near the pleasure dome is a deep pit from which negative things arise. The second part of the poem describes a dream vision of a "damsel," or young woman, with a musical instrument called a dulcimer. The speaker says he would build the dome in the air if he could bring back her song. Yet those who heard the song would cry "Beware!" and close their eyes.

Note-taking Guide

Use this chart to record details of the setting—the time and place of the action—in each poem.

Poem	Details of the Setting
The Rime of the Ancient Mariner	
Kubla Khan	

Circle two phrases in the first stanza that describe the mariner.

An **idiom** is an expression that is unique to a particular language. If *kin* means "blood relative," what does the idiom *next of kin* mean?

_____

_____

_____

Underline the line in the bracketed stanza that explains how the mariner is able to make the wedding guest listen to his story.

The Rime of the Ancient Mariner
Samuel Taylor Coleridge

It is an ancient <u>Mariner,</u>
And he stoppeth one of three.
"By thy long gray beard and glittering eye,
Now <u>wherefore</u> stopp'st thou me?"

5 "The Bridegroom's doors are opened wide,
And I am next of kin;
The guests are met, the feast is set:
May'st hear the merry <u>din</u>."

He holds him with his skinny hand,
10 "There was a ship," quoth[1] he.
"Hold off! unhand[2] me, graybeard loon!"
Eftsoons[3] his hand dropped he.

He holds him with his glittering eye—
The Wedding Guest stood still,
15 And listens like a three years' child:
The Mariner hath his will.

♦ ♦ ♦

The mariner tells how his ship sails south until it crosses the equator. A storm then drives the ship to the South Pole.

♦ ♦ ♦

"The ice was here, the ice was there,
The ice was all around;
It cracked and growled, and roared and howled,
20 Like noises in a swound!"[4]

Vocabulary Development

mariner (MAR uh nuhr) *n.* sailor
wherefore (HWAHR fawr) *adv.* why?
din (DIN) *n.* loud noise

---

1. quoth (KWOHTH) *v.* said.
2. unhand *v.* release.
3. Eftsoons *adv.* immediately.
4. swound *n.* swoon; fainting spell.

"At length did cross an Albatross,
Thorough[5] the fog it came;
As if it had been a Christian soul,
We hailed it in God's name.

25 "It ate the food it ne'er had eat,[6]
And round and round it flew.
The ice did split with a thunder-fit;
The <u>helmsman</u> steered us through!

"And a good south wind sprung up behind;
30 The Albatross did follow,
And every day, for food or play,
Came to the mariner's hollo!

"In mist or cloud, on mast or shroud,[7]
It perched for vespers[8] nine;
35 Whiles all the night, through fog-smoke
     white,
Glimmered the white Moonshine."

<u>"God save thee, ancient Mariner!</u>
<u>From the <u>fiends</u>, that plague thee thus!—</u>
<u>Why look'st thou so?"[9] "With my crossbow</u>
40 <u>I shot the Albatross!"</u>

◆ ◆ ◆

The breeze drops and the ship is becalmed. The crew runs out of water. The mariner's shipmates condemn him for killing the albatross.

◆ ◆ ◆

Vocabulary Development

helmsman (HELMZ muhn) *n.* steersman of a ship
fiends (FEENDZ) *n.* devils

---

5. **thorough** *prep.* through.
6. **eat** (ET) old form of *eaten.*
7. **shroud** (SHROWD) *n.* ropes stretching from the ship's side to the masthead.
8. **vespers** *n.* evenings.
9. **God . . . so** spoken by the Wedding Guest.

TAKE NOTES

Literary Analysis

Which line from lines 21–24 contains an example of **internal rhyme**? Circle the rhyming words.

English Language Development

An apostrophe may indicate possession, as in the phrase *the ship's crew.* An apostrophe may also indicate a missing letter. What letter is missing in *ne'er in line 25?*

_____

Stop to Reflect

In the bracketed lines, which events are connected to the presence of the albatross around the ship?

_____

_____

_____

Reading Check

There are two speakers in the underlined stanza. Who speaks which lines?

_____

_____

Culture Note

Wearing a cross on a chain around the neck is still a custom for many Christians. Why do you think the mariner refers to the cross when he tells about the albatross being hung around his neck to punish him for his deed?

_____

_____

_____

Literary Analysis

Circle two words in the underlined lines that illustrate the **poetic effect** of **alliteration**.

Stop to Reflect

At the moment of the crewmen's death, how does the speaker remind us of the albatross?

_____

_____

_____

"Ah, well a-day! What evil looks
Had I from old and young!
Instead of the cross, the Albatross
About my neck was hung!"

❖   ❖   ❖

A mysterious, ghostly ship approaches. Aboard the ship are Death and his mate, the lady Life-in-Death. The mariner's shipmates die, one by one.

❖   ❖   ❖

45 "One after one, by the star-dogged Moon,[10]
Too quick for groan or sigh,
Each turned his face with a <u>ghastly</u> pang,
And cursed me with his eye.

"Four times fifty living men,
50 (And I heard nor sigh nor groan)
<u>With heavy thump, a lifeless lump,</u>
<u>They dropped down one by one.</u>

"The souls did from their bodies fly—
They fled to <u>bliss</u> or woe!
55 And every soul, it passed me by,
Like the whizz of my crossbow!"

❖   ❖   ❖

The mariner realizes he is cursed. He suffers spiritual torture. He is the only one alive on the ship. He tries to pray, but he cannot.

❖   ❖   ❖

Vocabulary Development

ghastly (GAST lee) *adj.* horrible
bliss (BLIS) *n.* great joy or happiness

---

10. **star-dogged Moon** omen of impending evil to sailors.

"Beyond the shadow of the ship,
I watched the water snakes:
They moved in tracks of shining white,
60 And when they reared, the elfish[11] light
Fell off in hoary[12] flakes.

"Within the shadow of the ship
I watched their rich <u>attire</u>:
<u>Blue, glossy green, and velvet black,</u>
65 <u>They coiled and swam; and every track</u>
<u>Was a flash of golden fire.</u>

"O happy living things! no tongue
Their beauty might declare:
A spring of love gushed from my heart,
70 And I blessed them unaware;
Sure my kind saint took pity on me,
And I blessed them unaware.

"The selfsame moment I could pray;
And from my neck so free
75 The Albatross fell off, and sank
Like lead into the sea."

♦ ♦ ♦

The spirits of angels guide the ship
onward. Two spirits discuss the mariner's
crime of killing the harmless albatross. The
mariner's suffering and prayers break the
spell of the curse. He returns to his native
country. A saintly hermit absolves the
mariner from sin. Ever since his journey, the
mariner must tell his tale to listeners like the
wedding guest. He bids the guest farewell.

♦ ♦ ♦

Reading Strategy

(1) Which words in the underlined section illustrate **assonance?**

_____

_____

(2) Which words illustrate **alliteration?**

_____

_____

(3) What mood does the vivid description in these lines create?

_____

_____

Read Fluently

Read the bracketed stanza aloud. What do you think is the symbolic significance of the albatross finally dropping from the mariner's neck into the sea? (*Hint:* What does the mariner do just before that happens?)

_____

_____

_____

Vocabulary Development

attire (uh TYR) *n.* fine clothing

---

11. **elfish** *adj.* like an elf, or mischievous spirit.
12. **hoary** *adj.* white.

According to the mariner, what kind of person prays well? Circle the words in this stanza that give the answer.

Stop to Reflect

(1) Why do you think the wedding guest is sadder?

_____

_____

_____

(2) Why is he wiser?

_____

_____

_____

"Farewell, farewell! but this I tell
To thee, thou Wedding Guest!
He prayeth well, who loveth well
80 Both man and bird and beast.

"He prayeth best, who loveth best
All things both great and small:
For the dear God who loveth us,
He made and loveth all."

85 The Mariner, whose eye is bright,
Whose beard with age is hoar,
Is gone; and now the Wedding Guest
Turned from the bridegroom's door.

He went like one that hath been stunned
90 And is of sense forlorn;
A sadder and a wiser man,
He rose the morrow morn.

The Rime of the Ancient Mariner • Kubla Khan

1. **Interpret:** What do you think the Albatross stands for? Explain.

_____

_____

2. **Literary Analysis:** What **sound device** does Coleridge use in the line "It cracked and growled, and roared and howled ..."?

_____

3. **Literary Analysis:** Choose a poem by Coleridge. In the first column of the chart below, list two of the subjects in that poem. In the second column, tell the setting for each subject. In the third column, list an event associated with each subject. In the fourth column, copy the exact words Coleridge uses to describe the subject. In the last column, explain why or how the language suits the subject, setting, or event.

Subject	Setting	Events	Language	Why Suitable?

4. **Reading Strategy:** In "Kubla Khan," how do poetic devices, such as repetition, contribute to the **poetic effect** of lines 45–54?

_____

_____

She Walks in Beauty • Apostrophe to the Ocean • *from* Don Juan

LITERARY ANALYSIS

Poetry usually contains **figurative language.** This is language that is meant to be understood imaginatively, rather than literally. Poets use figurative language to help readers see things in new ways. Here are some common types of figurative language:

- **Similes**—direct comparisons of things that are not alike using the words *like* or *as*
- **Metaphors**—comparisons of unalike things in which something is described as though it were something else.
- **Personifications**—language in which a nonhuman subject is given human characteristics

In these three poems, Byron uses figurative language to express the sense of power in nature that escapes human understanding. Compare the observations that Byron makes about the power of nature, human beauty, and aging.

READING STRATEGY

By asking **questions** as you read, you can focus your understanding of poetry. Begin with *who, what, where, when,* and *why* questions. Use the chart below to record and answer your questions as you read.

Passage	Questions
She walks in beauty, like the night Of cloudless climes and starry skies;	1. Who is she? 2. What is her relationship to the speaker? 3. To what does the speaker compare her?

She Walks in Beauty • Apostrophe to the Ocean • from Don Juan

George Gordon, Lord Byron

Summaries In these three poems, Lord Byron expresses the Romantic spirit. The speaker of **"She Walks in Beauty"** declares his admiration for the outer and inner beauty of a woman. In **"Apostrophe to the Ocean,"** the speaker celebrates the power and beauty of nature. In *Don Juan,* the title character thinks about his youth. Although he regrets missed opportunities, he reaches at an interesting conclusion about life and death.

Note-taking Guide

Use the chart below to help you understand the poems. For each poem, write the poem's subject—who or what the poem is about. Then write lines from the poem that describe the subject. Finally, think about the way the speakers describe each subject. Based on the descriptions, decide how each speaker feels about the subject of the poem.

	Subject of Poem	Description in Poem	Speaker's Feelings
She Walks in Beauty			
Apostrophe to the Ocean			
Don Juan			

She Walks in Beauty • Apostrophe to the Ocean • *from* Don Juan

1. **Analyze:** In "Don Juan," the speaker thinks about his age and how much of his life has passed by. How would you describe his mood?

_____

_____

2. **Literary Analysis:** All three poems use **figurative language** to help make meaning clear. Find at least one example each of **simile, metaphor,** and **personification** in the three poems by Lord Byron. Use the chart below to show how each example suggests the poet's idea.

Figurative Language	What Is Being Described	Associations Suggested
Simile		
Metaphor		
Personification		

3. **Literary Analysis: Personification** involves making nonhuman things seem human. In "Apostrophe to the Ocean," how does the personification of the ocean affect the poem and its message?

_____

_____

4. **Reading Strategy:** When you **question** a text, you ask questions about *who, what, where, when,* and *why,* and answer these as you read. Did questioning help you understand the poems? Explain.

_____

_____

Ozymandias • Ode to the West Wind • To a Skylark

LITERARY ANALYSIS

Imagery is descriptive language. Poetic imagery has certain characteristics:

- It appeals to any or all of the five senses: sight, hearing, smell, taste, and touch.

- It often creates patterns supporting a poem's theme.

By creating the powerful images of the West Wind or of a skylark, Shelley links these natural beings to the desires of his own spirit. In the **Romantic philosophy** of the imagination, an image connects what is "outside" the mind with what is "inside" the mind, linking nature and spirit. Identify the specific ideas Shelley expresses through images. Then, judge how well his images capture both the thing being described and the needs of his spirit.

READING STRATEGY

You **can respond to imagery** in a poem even before you fully understand the meaning of the work. Get the most from poetic images by noting their sensory "texture"—dark or light, rough or smooth. What sorts of feelings and ideas, or associations, does each image bring to mind? Use the chart below to note the sensory "texture" and associations of the given image.

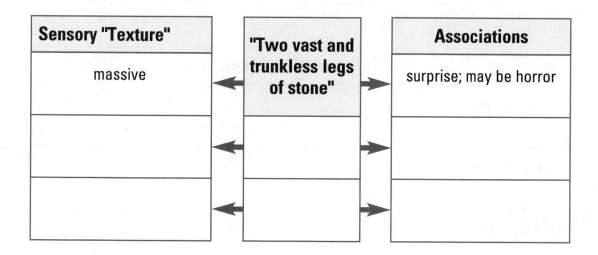

Sensory "Texture"	"Two vast and trunkless legs of stone"	Associations
massive		surprise; may be horror

The Poetry of Shelley **195**

Ozymandias • Ode to the West Wind • To a Skylark

Percy Bysshe Shelley

Summaries "Ozymandias" is about human pride and ambition. In the poem, a traveler describes the ruins of an ancient statue. On the base is writing that says, "Look on my works, ye Mighty, and despair!" However, what is left of the statue stands in an empty desert. The works of Ozymandias have been destroyed by time and nature.

The speaker in **"Ode to the West Wind"** describes the force of the West wind as it blows dead leaves, stirs up the ocean, destroys plants, and tells of winter's arrival. The speaker is amazed by the wind's strength. The poet wants the wind to make him new again.

"To a Skylark" is addressed to a bird. The poem describes its soaring music. The speaker wishes he could express himself as delightfully as the skylark does so that the world would listen to him.

Note-taking Guide

In the chart below, record words used to describe the subjects of each of the poems.

Poem	Words used to describe it
Ozymandias	
Ode to the West Wind	
To a Skylark	

Ozymandias • Ode to the West Wind • To a Skylark

1. **Infer:** The expression on the face of Ozymandias includes a frown, a wrinkled lip, and a sneer. What does his expression suggest about the kind of ruler he was?

_____

2. **Literary Analysis:** In "Ode to the West Wind," find three **images** that show the wind's power. Explain to which senses each image appeals.

_____

3. **Literary Analysis:** In **Romantic philosophy,** the imagination connects nature and spirit. Choose two images from Shelley's poems that connect the speaker and nature. Note the details of the image and its associations in the chart below.

Image	How Vivid?	Associated Ideas	Link: Nature and Spirit

4. **Reading Strategy:** Select a passage from one of the poems that contains images that you find striking. Explain your **response** to it.

_____

_____

Poetry of John Keats

LITERARY ANALYSIS

An **ode** is a lyric poem that is very emotional. Odes pay respect to a person or thing. The speaker of the poem addresses that person or thing directly.

John Keats created his own type of ode, using ten-line stanzas. Each line in Keats's odes contains ten beats with a repeated pattern of weak syllable/strong syllable, known as iambic pentameter. Often those stanzas begin with four lines rhymed *abab* followed by six rhymed lines.

In his odes, Keats follows the tradition of paying respect to something. Yet his odes tell as much about him as they do about his topics. In "Ode to a Nightingale," for instance, Keats longs for an ideal beauty he cannot find in real life. As you read, compare how each work describes a conflict in the speaker.

READING STRATEGY

Paraphrasing, or restating text in your own words, is a useful way to understand a difficult work. Use the chart below to paraphrase difficult parts of Keats's poems.

Original Words	Paraphrase
"When I have fears that I may cease to be. . ."	

On First Looking into Chapman's Homer • When I Have Fears That I May Cease to Be • Ode to a Nightingale

John Keats

Summaries In these poems, the poet looks across time, into both the past and the future. In **"On First Looking into Chapman's Homer,"** the speaker shows his delight in discovering the works of the ancient Greek poet Homer. In **"When I Have Fears That I May Cease to Be,"** the poet writes about his fear of dying young. Ultimately, he learns that neither love nor fame is important. In **"Ode to a Nightingale,"** the speaker writes about his desire to join with the bird in its world of beauty, joy, and imagination.

Note-taking Guide

Use the chart below to list the subjects, major points, and speaker's attitudes in each poem.

Poem	Subject	What the Poem Shows	Speaker's Attitude
"Homer"	Classical poetry	Admiration for the past	
"Fears"			
"Nightingale"			

Ode on a Grecian Urn

John Keats

Summary Keats's poem is addressed to an ancient Grecian urn and contains thoughts about beauty and truth inspired by the urn. The urn is decorated with the following scenes and details: men or gods chasing young women, a musician, trees, a priest leading a young cow to be sacrificed, and the empty town from which the priest and others have come. Keats reflects that those who are depicted pursuing the women will never catch them. However, they will also never grow old. Keats uses the urn to draw a conclusion about the human experience.

Note-taking Guide

Use the chart below to analyze the images and meaning of each stanza.

Stanza	Images	Speaker's Observation
I	Men, women, and gods playing musical instruments and chasing one another	
II		
III		
IV		
IV		

Ode on a Grecian Urn

John Keats

Thou still unravished[1] bride of quietness
Thou foster child of silence and slow time,
Sylvan[2] historian, who canst thus express
A flowery tale more sweetly than our rhyme:
5 What leaf-fringed legend haunts about thy
    shape
  Of <u>deities</u> or mortals, or of both,
  In Tempe[3] or the <u>dales</u> of Arcady?[4]
  What men or gods are these? What maidens
    loath?[5]
  What mad pursuit? What struggle to escape?
10 What pipes and timbrels?[6] What wild
    <u>ecstasy</u>?

❖ ❖ ❖

On the urn there is a picture of a young man. He seems to be singing of his love for a young woman. Unlike love in the real world, their love will last forever. Another picture on the urn shows a procession and a sacrifice in an ancient little town. The speaker wonders about the occasion for the ceremony. But the urn will not reveal the secret.

❖ ❖ ❖

Vocabulary and Pronunciation

Many words in English have different meanings, depending on their part of speech.

(1) What does *still* mean as an adjective?

_____

(2) What does the same word mean as an adverb?

_____

Stop to Reflect

Personification gives human qualities to something nonhuman. Circle three words or phrases that the speaker uses to personify the urn.

Reading Check

The **setting** is the time and place of an event or a work.

(1) In what region of the world does the scene on the urn take place?

_____

_____

(2) At what period in history does this scene occur?

_____

_____

Vocabulary Development

deities (DEE uh teez) *n.* gods
dales (DAYLZ) *n.* valleys
ecstasy (EK stuh see) *n.* great joy

---

1. **unravished** *adj.* pure.
2. **Sylvan** (SIL vuhn) *adj.* rustic; representing the woods or forest.
3. **Tempe** (TEM pee) valley in Greece that has become a symbol of supreme rural beauty.
4. **Arcady** (AR kuh dee) region in Greece that has come to represent the peace and contentment of countryside surroundings.
5. **loath** (LOHTH) *adj.* unwilling.
6. **timbrels** (TIM bruhlz) *n.* tambourines.

In a **paraphrase,** you use your own words to restate a passage. Paraphrase the bracketed lines.

_____

_____

_____

_____

_____

_____

An **ode** honors a person or thing. Why do you think the speaker calls the urn a "friend to man" in the final lines?

_____

_____

_____

O Attic[7] shape! Fair attitude! With brede[8]
Of marble men and maidens overwrought,[9]
With forest branches and the trodden[10] weed;
Thou, silent form, dost tease us out of
    thought
15 As doth eternity: Cold Pastoral![11]
When old age shall this generation waste,
Thou shalt remain, in midst of other woe
Than ours, a friend to man, to whom thou
    say'st
"Beauty is truth, truth beauty,"—that is all
20 Ye know on earth, and all ye need to know.

_____

7. Attic Attica was the region of Greece in which Athens was located; the art of the region was characterized by grace and simplicity.

8. brede *n.* interwoven pattern.

9. overwrought *adj.* adorned with.

10. trodden *v.* trampled.

11. Cold Pastoral unchanging rural scene.

Poetry of John Keats

1. **Compare and Contrast:** In "Ode to a Nightingale," the speaker wishes to leave the world behind and join the nightingale. What differences does he see between the bird's life and his own that cause him to wish this?

_____

2. **Literary Analysis:** An **ode** is a lyric poem that pays respect to a person or thing. In what ways does Keats honor his subjects? Explain, using examples from the poems.

_____

3. **Literary Analysis:** Review the characteristics of a Keats ode on the Build Skills page. Using one of the poems in this grouping, explain how it fits the form of a Keats ode.

_____

4. **Reading Strategy:** To **paraphrase** a literary work, put lines or passages into your own words. Using a chart like the one shown, paraphrase the following lines.

Poem	Lines	Paraphrase
"Homer"	9–10	
"Nightingale"	71–72	
"Grecian Urn"	31–34	

5. **Reading Strategy:** Paraphrase one line that you find difficult in "Ode to Nightingale."

_____

_____

Speech to Parliament: In Defense of the Lower Classes • A Song: "Men of England" • On the Passing of the Reform Bill

LITERARY ANALYSIS

Political commentary offers opinions on political issues. In order to be persuasive, writers build their arguments or positions by making assumptions. Assumptions are ideas or statements accepted as true. Evaluate both the evidence and the assumptions that each writer uses. Shelley, for example, makes this argument, based on the assumption below it:

Argument: The common people of England should rebel because those they work for oppress them.

Assumption: Duty is not a one-way street; workers and employers are bound together by mutual obligations.

Though each of these commentators works in a different form—speech, poem, and letter—they all want to persuade. Each writers uses persuasive techniques, including

- **Rhetorical questions**—questions with an obvious answer that are asked for dramatic effect

- **Balanced clauses**—two or more clauses in the same sentence that share a similar structure

READING STRATEGY

You will often get more from your reading if you first **set a purpose,** or choose a reason for reading. Think about what you already know about the subject and use the graphic organizer shown to set a purpose for reading each of these selections.

Prior Knowledge	Reading Purpose	Evidence for Answer
Byron was thought of as a "bad boy."	How serious and well informed were his political positions?	

In Defense of the Lower Classes

George Gordon, Lord Byron

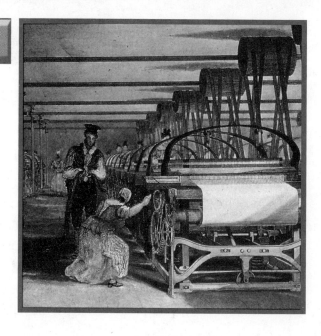

Summary In this speech to Parliament, Lord Byron aks the members to reconsider their plan to punish rebellious workers with death.

Note-taking Guide

Use this chart to keep track of Lord Byron's arguments as he attempts to change the minds of members of Parliament.

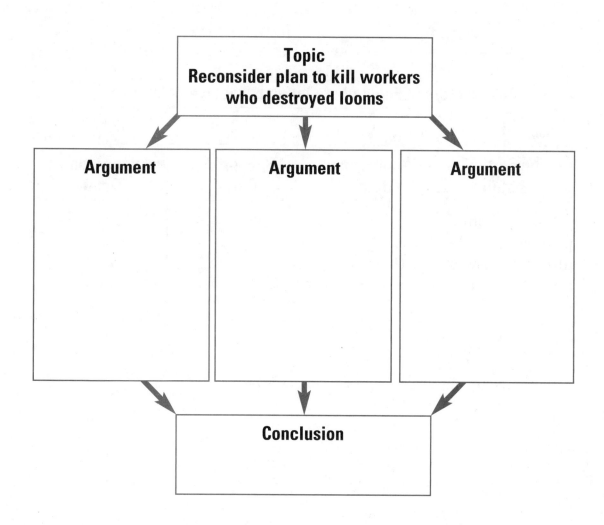

Topic
Reconsider plan to kill workers who destroyed looms

Argument	Argument	Argument

Conclusion

A Song: "Men of England"

Percy Bysshe Shelley

Summary Shelley's poem encourages workers to stop plowing the fields and weaving the robes of the rich. In a series of questions and commands, he urges them to revolt before England forces them to weave their own shrouds, or burial cloths.

Note-taking Guide

In the chart below, write down details from the poem that support the main idea given.

Main Idea **The workers in England are taken advantage of by the rich**			
Supporting Detail	**Supporting Detail**	**Supporting Detail**	**Supporting Detail**

On the Passing of the Reform Bill

Thomas Babington Macaulay

Summary "On the Passing of the Reform Bill" is a letter Macaulay wrote to his friend Ellis in celebration. He describes the uncertain and disorganized counting of the vote that resulted in the passage of an important bill in the House of Commons. The bill was important in making Britain more democratic.

Note-taking Guide

Use the sequence of events chart to examine how the Reform Bill passed the House of Commons.

Beginning Event:

↓

↓

↓

↓

Final Outcome:

Speech to Parliament: In Defense of the Lower Classes
• A Song: "Men of England"
• On the Passing of the Reform Bill

1. **Analyze:** In "On the Passing of the Reform Bill," Macaulay builds suspense, or tension, as he tells a story in his letter. List two ways in which Macaulay makes his telling more suspenseful and exciting.

_____

_____

2. **Evaluate:** Summarize Shelley's argument in "A Song: 'Men of England.'" Evaluate the argument using the chart.

Evidence		Assumptions
	Argument	
Evaluation		**Evaluation**

3. **Literary Analysis:** Find two examples of **balanced clauses** in Shelley's "A Song: 'Men of England.'" What effect does this device have on the reader?

_____

_____

4. **Reading Strategy** List three details on which you would focus if your **purpose in reading** Byron's speech was to learn more about his life.

_____

On Making an Agreeable Marriage • *from* A Vindication of the Rights of Woman

LITERARY ANALYSIS

Social commentary is writing or speech that offers criticisms about society. Social commentary can be *unconscious* or *conscious.* In *unconscious* social commentary, a writer reveals a problem caused by social customs without directly challenging those customs. The commentary is *conscious* when a writer points out a direct link between a problem and a social custom. As you read these selections, pay attention to the assumptions about women that they reveal, consciously or unconsciously.

Both authors use **persuasive techniques** such as the following:

- appeals to logic based on sound reasoning
- appeals to readers' sense of morality or ethics
- appeals to emotion, addressing readers' feelings

READING STRATEGY

When reading, **determine the writer's purpose** by using background knowledge and clues such as the title of the work. Use the chart below to help you determine the author's meaning.

Selection	Background	Clues in Title	Direct Statements	Writer's Tone	Writer's Purpose
"On Making an Agreeable Marriage"	Author writes about the manners and morals of society during the early 1800s				
"A Vindication of the Rights of Woman"	Author supported rights for women				

On Making an Agreeable Marriage

Jane Austen

Summary In a letter, Jane Austen responds to her niece's doubts about marriage. The author provides advice to the young woman, Fanny Knight. She also offers a glimpse into what society considered a desirable marriage in one social class during the early 1800s.

Note-taking Guide

As you read Jane Austen's letter, consider the persuasive techniques she uses. Use the chart shown to record examples of each kind of appeal that the author uses.

Appeals to Logic	Appeals to Morality	Appeals to Emotions

from A Vindication of the Rights of Woman

Mary Wollstonecraft

Summary In her essay, Wollstonecraft explains that women's education has been neglected. Because women are brought up to be admired, they are silly and vain rather than strong and useful. The only way for a woman to advance in the world is through marriage. Wollstonecraft attacks society for the limits it places on women, who in some cases clearly show more sense than their male relatives.

Note-taking Guide

As you read Mary Wollstonecraft's essay, consider the persuasive techniques she uses. Use the chart shown to record examples of each kind of persuasive appeal.

Appeals to Logic	Appeals to Morality	Appeals to Emotions

from A <u>Vindication</u> of the Rights of Woman

Mary Wollstonecraft

Wollstonecraft has studied history and the world. She concludes that either people are very different from one another or civilization has been unfair.

◆ ◆ ◆

I have turned over various books written on the subject of education, and patiently observed the conduct of parents and the management of schools; but what has been the result?—a profound conviction that the neglected education of my fellow creatures is the grand source of the misery I deplore, and that women, in particular, are rendered weak and wretched by a variety of concurring[1] causes, originating from one hasty conclusion. The conduct and manners of women, in fact, evidently prove that their minds are not in a healthy state; for, like the flowers which are planted in too rich a soil, strength and usefulness are sacrificed to beauty; and the flaunting leaves, after having pleased a <u>fastidious</u> eye, fade, disregarded on the stalk, long before the season when they ought to have arrived at maturity.

◆ ◆ ◆

Women are the victims of poor education and of false social expectations. They should have nobler ambition. They should demand respect.

◆ ◆ ◆

Reading Strategy

How do the words *misery* and *deplore* give clues to the **author's purpose?**

_____

_____

_____

Read Fluently

Read the bracketed passage aloud. What unfortunate fact about the position of women does the author's comparison help to express?

_____

_____

_____

Vocabulary Development

vindication (vin duh KAY shun) *n.* act of providing justification or support for

fastidious (fa STID ee uhs) *adj.* particular; difficult to please

---

1. **concurring** *adj.* joining together.

Indeed the word masculine is only a bugbear;[2] there is little reason to fear that women will acquire too much courage or <u>fortitude</u>, for their apparent inferiority with respect to bodily strength must render them in some degree dependent on men in the various relations of life; but why should it be increased by prejudices that give a sex to virtue, and confound[3] simple truths with sensual <u>reveries</u>?

◆   ◆   ◆

Mistaken ideas about women deprive them of a good education and of equality. These ideas also cause some women to act slyly and childishly. Many individual women, however, have more sense than their male relatives and husbands.

Literary Analysis

Besides their dependence on men, what additional problems do women face, according to the author's **social commentary** here? Circle the words that give the answer.

English Language Development

If you break down a long sentence, you can often discover the author's main idea. Reread the bracketed sentence word by word. Now write the meaning of the sentence in your own words.

_____

_____

_____

_____

_____

_____

Vocabulary Development

fortitude (FORT uh tood) *n.* courage; strength to endure

reveries (REV uh reez) *n.* daydreams

---

2. bugbear *n.* frightening imaginary creature, especially one that frightens children.

3. confound *v.* confuse by mixing together.

On Making an Agreeable Marriage
• *from* A Vindication of the Rights of Woman

1. **Make a Judgment:** Based on her letter to her niece, would you say Jane Austen is a good judge of human nature? Why or why not?

   _____

2. **Literary Analysis:** According to Wollstonecraft's **social commentary,** how are women's personalities affected by society's notions of the ideal woman?

   _____

3. **Literary Analysis:** Reread Austen's letter. Then, use the chart shown to analyze the importance Austen's society placed on the elements of marriage.

	Love	Suitability for Each Other	Money	Respectability
Examples				
Importance				

4. **Reading Strategy:** Compare Wollstonecraft's and Austen's purposes in writing. Explain the clues you use to **determine the purpose** of each author.

   _____

   _____

from In Memoriam, A.H.H.
• from The Princess: Tears, Idle Tears
• Ulysses • The Lady of Shalott

LITERARY ANALYSIS

The **speaker** is the person who says the words of a poem. The poet is not necessarily the same person as the speaker. In a narrative poem, or one that tells a story, the speaker is sometimes a character in the story and sometimes a narrator who stands outside the story. In either case, the speaker provides details about events, characters, and settings as well as his or her feelings about them.

The speakers in Tennyson's poems show different experiences of time. Typical in these poems are

• present, in which nothing changes.

• future, which is unknown.

• past, which is lost.

Compare the views of time in each poem you read.

READING STRATEGY

Most poems convey messages about life. When you **judge a poet's message**, you decide how true and useful the message is. First, use the details in the poem to determine the poet's message about life. Next, compare that message to your own experiences in life. Last, make a judgment about whether the poet's message is true and valuable.

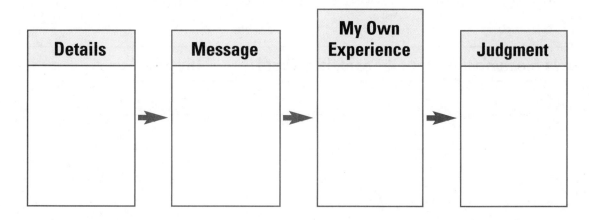

Details	Message	My Own Experience	Judgment

from In Memoriam, A.H.H. • from The Princess: Tears, Idle Tears • Ulysses

Alfred, Lord Tennyson

Summary In *In Memoriam*, Tennyson is both the poet and the speaker. In this poem he is mourning the death of his friend, Arthur Henry Hallam. Hallam died at the age of twenty-two. Tennyson is angry because his friend is no longer in a place where they can sit and talk and be together. Tennyson comes to accept the death of his friend. His sense of loss is softened by his memories of his friend.

"Tears, Idle Tears" and *"Ulysses"* have different speakers. The speaker in "Tears, Idle Tears" cries when he thinks of friends who have died and love that was lost a long time ago. The speaker in the poem "Ulysses," is the hero named in the title—Ulysses. The poem takes place after Ulysses has returned home from being away at war. He is the king, but no one knows him anymore. He is facing old age, and he is tired of staying at home. He thinks about another journey to exotic lands.

Note-taking Guide
In each poem, the speaker deals with feelings of loss. Use this chart to record details about each speaker's feelings.

In Memoriam	Tears, Idle Tears	Ulysses

The Lady of Shalott

Alfred, Lord Tennyson

Summary The Lady of Shalott lives on an island in a river. This river flows down to Camelot, the town where King Arthur has his court. She is a weaver and has heard that she will be cursed if she looks "down to Camelot." She views the world through the mirror hung before her loom, or weaving machine. Often she likes to weave into her cloth the scenes from outdoors that she sees reflected in the mirror. One day she sees in her mirror Sir Lancelot, King Arthur's greatest knight, as he rides by on the way to Camelot. She is disturbed by the sight, the mirror cracks, and she realizes that the curse is taking effect. She leaves her home, finds a boat, and paints on it The Lady of Shalott. Then she gets in the boat and begins drifting toward Camelot. Singing, she dies before the boat reaches the town. The residents of Camelot come out and wonder who the dead woman is. Lancelot says to himself, "She has a lovely face; . . ."

Note-taking Guide
Use this chart to record the events of the poem.

The Lady of Shalott lives on an island on a river flowing toward Camelot.	The Lady weaves a magic web.	Sir Lancelot comes riding by.	The Lady finds a boat.

Put letters at the ends of lines of the first stanza that have the same rhyming sound. Use *A* for the first rhyme, *B* for the second rhyme, and so forth. How does the poem's music make the setting seem?

(a) dreamy and attractive

(b) noisy and unpleasant

(c) dull and singsong

(d) dark and gloomy

(1) What does the Lady of Shalott do all the time? Circle the answer in the underlined stanza, and label it *What?*

(2) Why does she never look directly at Camelot? Circle the answer and label it *Why?*

The poem uses forms of verbs that were already out of date in Tennyson's day, such as *weaveth.* Circle another out-of-date verb in the next line. Why do you think Tennyson used these old verb forms?

The Lady of Shalott
Alfred, Lord Tennyson

According to legend, King Arthur ruled England from a place called Camelot (KAM uh lot). There he invited all the great knights of the day. The Shalott (shuh LOT) of this poem is an island in the river that flows to Camelot.

◆ ◆ ◆

On either side the river lie
Long fields of barley and of rye,
That clothe the wold[1] and meet the sky;
And through the field the road runs by
   To many-towered Camelot,
And up and down the people go,
Gazing where the lilies blow
Round an island there below,
   The island of Shalott.

◆ ◆ ◆

The Lady of Shalott lives in a gray-towered castle on the island. No one ever sees her. They do hear her singing. She sits at a loom, a device for weaving yarn into fabric. The loom has a mirror over it.

◆ ◆ ◆

There she weaves by night and day
A magic web with colors gay.
She has heard a whisper say,
A curse is on her if she stay
   To look down to Camelot.
She knows not what the curse may be,
And so she weaveth steadily,
And little other care hath she,
   The Lady of Shalott.

---

1. **wold** *n.* rolling land.

And moving through a mirror clear
That hangs before her all the year,
Shadows of the world appear.
There she sees the highway near
  Winding down to Camelot:

◆ ◆ ◆

The Lady of Shalott sees all of life, from
weddings to funerals, in her mirror.

◆ ◆ ◆

And sometimes through the mirror blue
The knights come riding two and two:
She hath no loyal knight and true,
  The Lady of Shalott.

◆ ◆ ◆

The Lady of Shalott grows tired of looking at a shadow world. One day she sees the
knight Sir Lancelot in her mirror.

◆ ◆ ◆

His broad clear brow in sunlight glowed;
On burnish'd[2] hooves his war horse trode;[3]
From underneath his helmet flowed
His coal-black curls as on he rode,
  As he rode down to Camelot.
From the bank and from the river
He flashed into the crystal mirror,
"Tirra lirra,"[4] by the river
  Sang Sir Lancelot.

She left the web, she left the loom,
She made three paces through the room,
She saw the waterlily bloom,
She saw the helmet and the plume,[5]
  She looked down to Camelot.

Vocabulary Development

paces (PAY suhz) *n.* steps made walking back and forth

---

2. **burnish'd** *adj.* polished; shining.
3. **trode** *v.* trod; walked.
4. **Tirra lirra** a meaningless sound for singing, like "Tra-la-la."
5. **plume** *n.* the feather on Lancelot's helmet.

TAKE NOTES

English Language Development

Poets often use unusual word order different from that of regular speech. Rewrite the underlined sentence in natural word order.

_____

_____

_____

Literary Analysis

What impression does the **speaker** give of Sir Lancelot? Circle the letter of the best answer below.

(a) young and foolish

(b) handsome and cheerful

(c) strange and mysterious

(d) dark and gloomy

Now, circle details in the bracketed stanza that help convey this impression.

(1) Why do you think the Lady of Shalott risks the curse and does what is forbidden?

_____

_____

(2) Based on the Lady's behavior, what do you think the **poet's message** is?

_____

_____

(3) Do you agree with the message? Why, or why not?

_____

_____

Culture Note

A **superstition** is a belief that is not reasonable. Instead it relies on magic or the idea of good and bad luck. For instance, many cultures have a superstition that breaking a mirror brings bad luck. What other superstitions can you think of?

_____

Read Fluently

Read the five bracketed lines aloud. Try to capture the music.

(1) Give one example of _alliteration,_ or repeated consonant sounds at the start of words.

_____

(2) Give one example of _rhyme_ at the end of lines.

_____

(3) Give one example of a _repeated word._

_____

Out flew the web and floated wide;
The mirror cracked from side to side;
"The curse is come upon me," cried
   The Lady of Shalott.

      ♦   ♦   ♦

     The Lady of Shalott goes down to the river. She finds a boat, unties it, and lies down in it. The river carries the boat downstream.

      ♦   ♦   ♦

Lying, robed in snowy white
That loosely flew to left and right—
The leaves upon her falling light—
Through the noises of the night
   She floated down to Camelot:
And as the boathead[6] wound along
The willowy hills and fields among,
They heard her singing her last song,
   The Lady of Shalott.

Heard a <u>carol</u>, mournful, holy,
Chanted loudly, chanted lowly,
Till her blood was frozen slowly,
And her eyes were darkened wholly,
   Turned to towered Camelot.
For ere[7] she reached upon the tide
The first house by the waterside,
Singing in her song she died,
   The Lady of Shalott.

      ♦   ♦   ♦

6. **boathead** _n._ the front of the boat.
7. **ere** (AYR) _adv._ before.

As the boat drifts into Camelot, the knights and ladies come to see who is inside. On the prow, or front, of the boat, they read the name, *The Lady of Shalott*.

◆　◆　◆

Who is this? and what is here?
And in the lighted palace near
Died the sound of royal cheer;
And they crossed themselves for fear,
　　All the knights at Camelot:
But Lancelot <u>mused</u> a little space;[8]
He said, "She has a lovely face;
God in his mercy lend her grace,[9]
　　The Lady of Shalott."

Vocabulary and Pronunciation

Lowly usually means "of low rank or little importance." What is the meaning here? How do you know?

lowly:

_____

Explanation:

_____

_____

English Language Development

As you know, poetry sometimes uses inverted, or switched, word order. Rewrite the underlined clause in natural word order.

_____

_____

Vocabulary Development

mused (MYOOZD) *v.* thought about; considered

---

8. **a little space** some; a bit.
9. **grace** *n.* divine love and protection.

1. **Assess:** Which of these poems seems to be the most hopeful?

_____

Explain.

_____

2. **Literary Analysis:** How does the loss of the **speaker's** friend affect the scene in *In Memoriam?*

_____

3. **Literary Analysis:** What inner argument does the speaker face in the poem "Ulysses"?

_____

_____

4. **Literary Analysis:** Use this chart to compare Ulysses' view of time with the Lady of Shalott's view.

	Past	**Present**	**Future**
Ulysses			
The Lady of Shalott			

5. **Reading Strategy:** Choose one poem and summarize the **poet's message.**

_____

_____

My Last Duchess • Life in a Love • Love Among the Ruins • Sonnet 43

LITERARY ANALYSIS

A **dramatic monologue** is a long speech by one character. Though dramatic monologues are often parts of plays or other longer works, Robert Browning specialized in short poems that are dramatic monologues all on their own. Browning's dramatic monologues have these elements:

- A speaker whose remarks reveal his or her situation and character.
- A silent listener that the speaker talks to.

Look for these elements as you read "My Last Duchess."

READING STRATEGY

An **inference** is a reasonable guess that you make from the details you are given. When you read a dramatic monologue, you use the speaker's words and actions to make inferences about the speaker's personality, attitudes, and situation.

As you read "My Last Duchess," fill out this chart. Use the speaker's words and actions to make inferences about his character and situation.

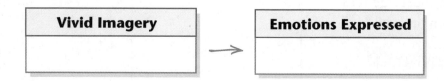

Vivid Imagery		Emotions Expressed
	→	

My Last Dutchess

Robert Browning

Summary As the poem begins, the Duke is showing a man a painting of the Duke's first wife, who is now dead. The man is an agent representing the father of the woman the Duke hopes to marry. The Duke tells the man that his first wife was "Too easily impressed" by whatever she saw or by whatever anyone did for her. He did not like the way she seemed to rank his "gift" of a great family "name" as equal to "anybody's gift." The Duke "gave commands;/Then all smiles stopped together." The two men begin to leave. The Duke tells the agent that he knows his demands for an adequate dowry, property due to him as the groom, will be met by the new bride's father.

Note-taking Guide
Fill in the timeline below with events that take place in the poem. Place each event in either the "Present" or "Past" tense.

Words/Action of Speaker	Meaning	Inferences
"That's my last Duchess painted on the wall, . . ."		

My Last Duchess
Robert Browning

> The Duke of Ferrara is an Italian noble-man in the 1500s. He has lost his first wife after just three years of marriage. Now he hopes to wed the daughter of another noble-man, a Count. He is speaking to the Count's representative about the planned marriage.

◆ ◆ ◆

That's my last Duchess painted on the wall,
Looking as if she were alive. I call
That piece a wonder, now: Frà Pandolf's[1]
    hands
Worked busily a day, and there she stands.

◆ ◆ ◆

> The Duke explains that the joy on the Duchess's face did not only come from her husband's presence.

◆ ◆ ◆

                        She had
A heart—how shall I say?—too soon made
    glad,
Too easily impressed; she liked <u>whate'er</u>
She looked on, and her looks went every-
    where.

◆ ◆ ◆

> Everything pleased her—the Duke's love, the setting sun, a small gift, even the mule she rode.

◆ ◆ ◆

She thanked men—good! but thanked
Somehow—I know not how—<u>as if she ranked</u>
<u>My gift of a nine-hundred-years-old name</u>
<u>With anybody's gift</u>.

◆ ◆ ◆

---

1. **Frà Pandolf's** work of Brother Pandolf, an imaginary painter.

Literary Analysis

(1) Who is the speaker of this **dramatic monologue?**

_____

(2) Who is the person spoken to?

_____

(3) Explain the situation that brings the two together.

_____

_____

Vocabulary and Pronunciation

A *Duchess* (DUCH uhs) is the wife of a *Duke.* What do you think the wife of a *Count* is called?

_____

English Language Development

Poets sometimes leave out letters to create a certain rhyme. For example, they say *o'er* instead of *over* in order to have a one-syllable word instead of two. The **apostrophe** (') shows where one or more letters have been left out. Squeeze in the missing letter in the underlined word.

Reading Strategy

Based on the underlined remark, what **inferences** do you make about the Duke's personality? Circle the word below that best describes him.

modest   proud   democratic

Reading Strategy

What **inference** do you make about the Duke from the way he moves on to discuss another piece of art? Answer by completing this sentence:

The Duke cares more about

_____

_____

_____

than he does about

_____

_____

_____ .

Her attitude disgusted the Duke. But he would not lower himself to correct something so small. He is a man who never stoops.

◆   ◆   ◆

Oh sir, she smiled, no doubt,
Whene'er I passed her; but who passed without
Much the same smile? <u>This grew; I gave commands;</u>
<u>Then all smiles stopped together</u>. There she stands
As if alive. Will 't please you rise?

◆   ◆   ◆

As they head downstairs, the Duke mentions the Count's daughter's fine dowry, or property she will bring to the marriage. He also points out a bronze statue of the Roman sea god Neptune.

◆   ◆   ◆

Notice Neptune, though,
Taming a sea horse, thought a <u>rarity</u>,
Which Claus of Innsbruck[2] cast in bronze for me!

Vocabulary Development

rarity (RAYR uh tee) *n.* something unusual and valuable

---

2. **Claus of Innsbruck** an imaginary Austrian sculptor.

Life in a Love
• Love Among the Ruins

Robert Browning

Sonnet 43

Elizabeth Barrett Browning

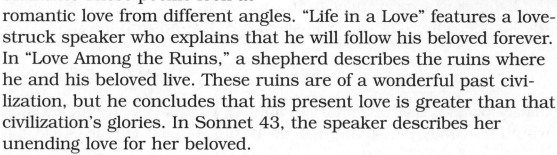

Summaries These poems look at romantic love from different angles. "Life in a Love" features a love-struck speaker who explains that he will follow his beloved forever. In "Love Among the Ruins," a shepherd describes the ruins where he and his beloved live. These ruins are of a wonderful past civilization, but he concludes that his present love is greater than that civilization's glories. In Sonnet 43, the speaker describes her unending love for her beloved.

Note-taking Guide
Use this chart to record your ideas about how each speaker feels about love. Put a checkmark (✔) in the boxes that apply to that speaker. Categories may apply to more than one poem.

Speaker	Believes in love forever	Believes in love that will continue after death	Believes that his love is greater than even a great civilization	Believes that love hurts those who love
"Life in a Love"				
"Love Among the Ruins"				
Sonnet 43				

My Last Duchess • Life in a Love • Love Among the Ruins • Sonnet 43

1. **Relate:** Name a popular song that praises love. Compare the song's language, attitude, and images to those of one of the poems.

_____

_____

2. **Literary Analysis:** In "My Last Duchess," the speaker is the duke, and the listener is a messenger from the count. How can you tell when the listener interacts with the speaker? Give an example.

_____

3. **Literary Analysis:** Use this chart to analyze the places at which a speaker would naturally pause in lines 14–16 of "My Last Duchess."

Line 14	Her hus-	-band's pre-	-sence on-	-ly, called	that spot
Natural pauses					
Line 15	Of joy	into	the Duch	-ess' cheek;	perhaps
Natural pauses					
Line 16	Frà Pan	-dolf chanced	to say	"Her man-	-tle laps
Natural pauses					

4. **Reading Strategy:** To **make inferences about the speaker** of a poem, make guesses based on his or her words and actions. In "Love Among the Ruins," what can you **infer** about the speaker's attitude toward the ancient past?

_____

_____

from Hard Times • *from* Jane Eyre

LITERARY ANALYSIS

A **novel** is a long work of fiction that has some or all of these features:

- A fairly complicated **plot**, or sequence of events
- Many **settings** in which events occur
- Main **characters** and less important, or **minor**, ones
- One or more **themes** expressing general ideas about life

Though, like all fiction, novels have imaginary characters and events, they also may include some real history as part of their setting. When they do, they may make **social criticism**, calling attention to problems in society. As you read, notice how each author criticizes society.

READING STRATEGY

All forms of writing have a purpose. For example, an author may write to entertain, to describe a scene, to poke fun at human behavior, or to reveal a truth about life. **Recognizing the writer's purpose** can help you understand a novel better. Look for clues about the writer's purpose in the events, characters' conversations, the writer's comments about characters, and other details. Keep track of them on this diagram.

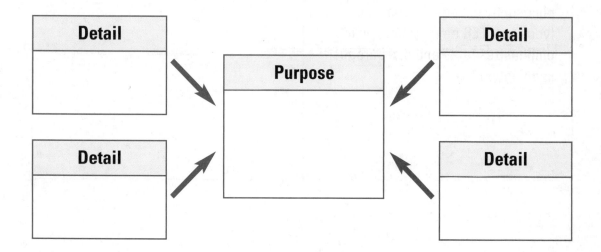

from Hard Times

Charles Dickens

Summary Mr. Gradgrind, who runs a school, lectures its students on the importance of facts. He calls on a girl named Sissy Jupe and, learning her name, tells her to change it to Cecilia. On hearing her father works with horses, he asks her to define a horse. She cannot do so. Then, a boy drily defines a horse as "Quadruped. Graminivorous. Forty teeth . . ." and wins Gradgrind's approval. A teacher named M'Choakumchild teaches the students in such a way as to discourage the exercise of imagination.

Note-taking Guide
Read the purpose in the chart below. Then find details in the text that support that purpose. Write the details in the right-hand column.

Purpose	Details That Support Purpose
• To humorously critcize the philosophy called utilitarianism (yoo til uh TER ee un iz um), which emphasizes facts and discourages imagination	

from Hard Times

Charles Dickens

In the industrial city of Coketown, England, a rich retired businessman named Gradgrind has started a school for poor children. Gradgrind believes that facts and logic must rule all activities. He feels that everything can be weighed and measured and that material things will make people happy. He explains his ideas when he meets with a government official and the teacher he has hired, Mr. M'Choakumchild.

♦ ♦ ♦

"Now, what I want is, Facts. Teach these boys and girls nothing but Facts. Facts alone are wanted in life. Plant nothing else, and root out everything else. You can only form the minds of reasoning animals upon Facts: nothing else will ever be of any service to them. This is the <u>principle</u> on which I bring up my own children, and this is the principle on which I bring up these children. Stick to Facts, sir!"

<u>The scene was a plain, bare, monotonous vault of a schoolroom.</u>

♦ ♦ ♦

The children are seated in number order. Mr. Gradgrind thinks of them as little pitchers, waiting to have facts poured into them. Now he addresses the class.

♦ ♦ ♦

"Girl number twenty," said Mr. Gradgrind, squarely pointing with his square forefinger, "I don't know that girl. Who is that girl?"

"Sissy Jupe, sir," explained number twenty, blushing, standing up, and curtseying.

"Sissy is not a name," said Mr. Gradgrind. "Don't call yourself Sissy. Call yourself Cecilia."

"It's father as calls me Sissy, sir," returned the young girl in a trembling voice, and with

Literary Analysis

Coke is a coal product used as a fuel in industry or left over when other fuels burn.

What **social criticism** is Dickens making by calling the city Coketown?

_____

_____

Vocabulary and Pronunciation

Homophones are words with the same sound but different spellings and meanings. A *principle* is a basic rule. A *principal* is the head of a school; it can also mean "main" or "most important."

In the underlined sentence, circle three words that have homophones. Write them and their homophones below. Then write the meanings of each word and its homophone below.

(1) Word _____

Meaning _____

Homophone _____

Meaning _____

(2) Word _____

Meaning _____

Homophone _____

Meaning _____

(3) Word _____

Meaning _____

Homophone _____

Meaning _____

"Then he has no business to do it," said Mr. Gradgrind. "Tell him he mustn't. Cecilia Jupe. Let me see. What is your father?"

"He belongs to the horse-riding, if you please, sir."

◆   ◆   ◆

Sissy's father rides horses in the circus. Mr. Gradgrind does not approve of this job. He tells Sissy to say that her father trains and shoes horses and treats them when they are ill. He continues:

◆   ◆   ◆

"Give me your definition of a horse."

(Sissy Jupe thrown into the greatest alarm by this demand.)

Girl number twenty unable to define a horse!" said Mr. Gradgrind, for the general behoof[1] of all the little pitchers. "Girl number twenty possessed of no facts, in reference to one of the commonest of animals! Some boy's definition of a horse. Bitzer, yours."

◆   ◆   ◆

Bitzer is the sort of "pitcher" Mr. Gradgrind likes. He has an excellent memory and has absorbed many facts. He is a pale, freckled boy with cold eyes.

◆   ◆   ◆

"Quadruped.[2] Graminivorous.[3] Forty teeth, namely twenty-four grinders, four eye-teeth, and twelve incisive. Sheds coat in the spring; in marshy countries, sheds hoofs, too. Hoofs hard, but requiring to be shod with iron.[4] Age known by marks in mouth." Thus (and much more) Bitzer.

"Now girl number twenty," said Mr. Gradgrind. "You know what a horse is."

◆   ◆   ◆

---

1. **behoof** (bi HUF) *n.* behalf; benefit.
2. **Quadruped** (KAWD ruh ped) *n.* an animal with four legs.
3. **Graminivorous** (gram uh NIV uh ruhs) *adj.* grass-eating.
4. **shod with iron** shoed with iron horseshoes to protect the horses' feet.

The other visitor now steps forward. He is a government official who has spent his life following petty rules and dull routine.

◆ ◆ ◆

"Now, let me ask you girls and boys. Would you paper a room with <u>representations</u> of a horse?"

After a pause, one half of the children cried in chorus, "Yes, sir!" Upon which the other half, seeing in the gentleman's face that Yes was wrong, cried out in chorus, "No, sir!"—as the custom is, in these examinations.

"Of course, No. Why wouldn't you?"

◆ ◆ ◆

The children have no idea. The visitor points out that horses never walk up and down rooms in reality. So it makes no sense to have them do it on wallpaper. Then he asks if the students would get a carpet with pictures of flowers on it. By now, most of the children know they should answer "No." A few still say "Yes," including Sissy Jupe.

◆ ◆ ◆

Sissy blushed, and stood up.

"So you would carpet your room—or your husband's room, if you were a grown woman, and had a husband—with representations of flowers, would you," said the gentleman. "Why would you?"

"If you please, sir, I am very fond of flowers," returned the girl.

"And is that why you would put tables and chairs upon them, and have people walking over them with heavy boots?"

English Language Development

Children is the plural of *child:*

1 *child*   2 or more *children*

Most English words form their plurals by adding *s* or *es.* But a few, like *child,* are irregular. Write the irregular plural form of each word listed below. Then say all the words aloud.

(1) 1 foot, 2 or more

_____

(2) 1 gentleman, 2 or more

_____

(3) 1 mouse, 2 or more

_____

(4) 1 woman, 2 or more

_____

Reading Check

What is Sissy's reason for wanting a carpet with pictures of flowers?

_____

_____

_____

_____

Vocabulary Development

representations (rep ruh zen TAY shuhnz) *n.*   pictures; illustrations

Literary Analysis

The *M'* in the teacher's name is an old way of writing *Mc.*

(1) What does the rest of the teacher's name suggest? Explain below.

Choakumchild:

_____

_____

(2) What **social criticism** is Dickens making about Mr. M'Choakumchild and the way he was taught to teach?

_____

_____

_____

Reading Check

Explain what the underlined statement means by completing the sentence below.

If Mr. M'Choakumchild only

_____

_____

he would be

_____

_____

.

"It wouldn't hurt them, sir. They wouldn't crush and <u>wither</u> if you please, sir. They would be the pictures of what was very pretty and pleasant, and I would fancy—"

"Ay, ay, ay! but you mustn't fancy," cried the gentleman, quite <u>elated</u> by coming so happily to his point. "That's it! You are never to fancy."

"You are not, Cecilia Jupe," Thomas Gradgrind solemnly repeated, "to do anything of that kind."

"Fact, fact, fact!" said the gentleman. And "Fact, fact, fact!" repeated Thomas Gradgrind.

◆ ◆ ◆

The official tells Sissy to forget the word *fancy,* for it is the very opposite of *fact.* Then he asks Mr. M'Choakumchild to begin teaching the first lesson.

◆ ◆ ◆

So, Mr. M'Choakumchild began in his best manner. He and some one hundred and forty other schoolmasters, had been lately turned at the same time, in the same factory, on the same principles, like so many pianoforte[5] legs.

◆ ◆ ◆

Mr. M'Choakumchild has learned the facts in a long list of subjects. He knows all about language, geography, and science.

◆ ◆ ◆

<u>If he had only learnt a little less, how infinitely better he might have taught much more!</u>

Vocabulary Development

wither (WITH uhr) *v.* shrivel up; dry out, wrinkle, and die
elated (i LAY tid) *adj.* excited

---

5. **pianoforte** (PYAN oh fawrt) *n.* an old term for a piano.

from Jane Eyre

Charlotte Brontë

Summary In this chapter of the novel, Jane is at a boarding school for orphan girls called Lowood. She describes the harsh physical conditions, the lack of sufficient food for the girls, and the cruel way in which one of the teachers, Miss Scatcherd, treats a girl named Helen Burns. Later, Jane has the opportunity to speak with Helen in private. Jane is surprised by Helen's acceptance of the wrongs done to her.

Note-taking Guide

Use the chart below to compare and contrast the characters of Jane Eyre and Helen Burns

	Jane Eyre	Helen Burns
Similarities		
Differences		

On the list below, check the **social criticisms**, or negative comments, made here about schools like Lowood. Circle the details that help make this criticism.

___ Lighting is poor.

___ Heating is poor.

___ Food portions are skimpy.

___ Clothing is falling apart.

Why is it impossible for the girls to wash on this morning?

_____

_____

_____

from Jane Eyre
Charlotte Brontë

After Jane Eyre's parents die, her selfish aunt sends her to a school for poor girls called Lowood. The school is a grim place with a strict routine that Jane does not like. Little money is spent on the girls' food or comfort. Though it is January, there is almost no heat. Jane, who is telling the story, has been at Lowood for two days.

◆　◆　◆

The next day <u>commenced</u> as before, getting up and dressing by rushlight;[1] but this morning we were <u>obliged</u> to <u>dispense</u> with the ceremony of washing: the water in the pitchers was frozen. . . . Before the long hour and a half of prayers and Bible reading was over, I felt ready to <u>perish</u> with cold. Breakfast time came at last. . . . How small my portion seemed! I wished it had been double.

◆　◆　◆

Jane is unfamiliar with the school routine. She is glad when her lessons end at three o'clock and she is given a hem to sew. But some older girls are still reading with Miss Scatcherd, the history teacher. The girls are seated with the best reader first. The best reader is a girl who spoke kindly to Jane the day before. Jane is surprised when the teacher suddenly sends this girl from first to last place for no very good reason.

Vocabulary Development

commenced (kuh MENST) *v.* began

obliged (uh BLYJD) *v.* forced

dispense (dis PENS) *v.* give up

perish (PER ish) *v.* die

---

1. **rushlight** cheap, smelly, smoky lighting obtained from burning rushes, or reeds, twisted together and dipped in wax.

Miss Scatcherd continued to make her an object of constant notice: she was continually <u>addressing</u> to her such phrases as the following:—

"Burns" (such it seems was her name: the girls here, were all called by their surnames,[2] as boys are elsewhere), "Burns, you are standing on the side of your shoe, turn your toes out immediately." "Burns, you poke your chin most unpleasantly, draw it in." "Burns, I insist on your holding your head up: I will not have you before me in that attitude," etc. etc.

A chapter having been read through twice, the books were closed and the girls examined. . . . every little difficulty was solved instantly when it reached Burns: her memory seemed to have retained the substance of the whole lesson, and she was ready with answers on every point. I kept expecting that Miss Scatcherd would praise her attention; but, instead of that, she suddenly cried out:—

"You dirty, disagreeable girl! you have never cleaned your nails this morning!"

Burns made no answer: I wondered at her silence.

"Why," thought I, "does she not explain that she could neither clean her nails nor wash her face, as the water was frozen?"

◆ ◆ ◆

Jane is called away by another teacher. That teacher needs help winding thread for sewing. When Jane returns to her seat, Miss Scatcherd has just sent Burns to get a bundle of twigs to be used as a punishment rod.

◆ ◆ ◆

Vocabulary Development

addressing (uh DRES ing) *v.*   talking to

---

2. **surnames** (SUR naymz) last names; family names.

TAKE NOTES

Culture Note

A surname is a family name, which in English comes last. For example, in *Jane Eyre*, *Eyre* is Jane's family name. In many Asian cultures, however, the family name comes first. What is the style used in your native land? To answer, write your name as it is written in your native land, and circle the family name:

_____

Reading Strategy

Circle the letter of the choice that states the **writer's purpose** here. Then, on the lines below, explain how you know this is the purpose.

The writer wants to show

(a) an English history lesson.

(b) Jane's dislike for school.

(c) the importance of good manners.

(d) the unfair treatment of Burns.

_____

_____

_____

Reading Check

Who seems to be Miss Scatcherd's brightest student? Write your answer here:

_____

Then circle the details that tell you.

English Language Development

The suffix -ly is some-
times added to
adjectives to turn
them to adverbs of manner. For
example,

quiet + ly = quietly,

which means "in a quiet, or soft-
spoken, manner." Circle two
more adverbs of manner in this
sentence. Then, on the lines
below, explain their meanings.

(1)

_____

_____

(2)

_____

_____

Reading Strategy

What can you learn about Jane
from her conversation with
Burns? Circle the correct
answer.

(a) She is unfriendly.

(b) She is curious and friendly.

(c) She is rude and impolite.

(d) She hopes Burns will be her
best friend.

. . . then she quietly, and without being told, unloosed her pinafore,[3] and the teacher instantly and sharply inflicted on her neck a dozen strokes with the bunch of twigs. Not a tear rose to Burns's eye; and, while I paused from my sewing, because my fingers quivered at this spectacle with a sentiment of unavailing and impotent anger, not a feature of her pensive face altered its ordinary expression.

"Hardened girl!" exclaimed Miss Scatcherd, "nothing can correct you of your slatternly habits: carry the rod away."

Burns obeyed: I looked at her narrowly as she emerged from the book closet; she was just putting back her handkerchief into her pocket, and the trace of a tear glistened on her thin cheek.

◆ ◆ ◆

Soon it is evening play hour. This time is Jane's favorite time at school so far. Still hungry, she is glad to have a bit of bread and coffee. She then looks for Burns and finds her reading by the fireplace.

◆ ◆ ◆

I sat down by her on the floor.
"What is your name besides Burns?"
"Helen."
"Do you come a long way from here?"
"I come from a place further north; quite on the borders of Scotland."
"Will you ever go back?"
"I hope so; but nobody can be sure of the future."

Vocabulary Development

pensive (PEN siv) adj.   serious; thoughtful
slatternly (SLAT ern lee) adj.   like a slob; very sloppy

3. **pinafore** (PIN uh for) n. an overdress of light fabric resembling an apron and bib.

"You must wish to leave Lowood?"

"No: why should I? I was sent to Lowood to get an education; and it would be of no use going away until I have attained that object."

"But that teacher, Miss Scatcherd, is so cruel to you?"

"Cruel? Not at all! She is severe: she dislikes my faults."

"And if I were in your place I should dislike her: I should resist her; if she struck me with that rod, I should get it from her hand; I should break it under her nose."

"Probably you would do nothing of the sort: but if you did, Mr. Brocklehurst[4] would expel you from the school; that would be a great grief to your relations. It is far better to endure patiently a smart[5] which nobody feels but your-self, than to commit a hasty action whose evil consequences will extend to all connected with you—and, besides, the Bible bids us return good for evil."

◆ ◆ ◆

Jane does not really understand Helen's views. She feels it makes no sense to reward mean people with kindness and good behav-ior, for then they will never change. Yet she deeply admires Helen for holding such noble views.

◆ ◆ ◆

"You say you have faults, Helen: what are they? To me you seem very good."

"Then learn from me, not to judge by appear-ances: I am, as Miss Scatcherd said, slatternly; I seldom put, and never keep, things in order; I am careless; I forget rules; I read when I should learn my lessons; I have no method; and sometimes I say, like you, I cannot bear to be subjected to systematic arrangements.

---

4. **Mr. Brocklehurst** the man who runs the school.
5. **smart** pain; sting.

from Jane Eyre **239**

TAKE NOTES

Literary Analysis

Put a check in front of any **social criticism** you think this passage helps make.

____ Poor girls often put up with bad treatment to get an education.

____ Family pressure forced the girls to compete to see who was smart.

____ The girls were not treat-ed with the religious ideals they were taught.

____ The schools were so crowded that girls were expelled for no reason.

Reading Check

Number the seven faults that Helen says she has.

(1) Why do you think the monitor is mean to Helen?

She is mean because _____

_____

(2) What **social criticism** about schools does her behavior show?

Her behavior shows that in schools _____

_____

This is all very <u>provoking</u> to Miss Scatcherd, who is naturally neat, punctual, and particular."

"And <u>cross</u> and cruel," I added; but Helen Burns would not admit my addition: she kept silence. . . .

She was not allowed much time for <u>meditation</u>: a monitor, a great rough girl, presently came up, exclaiming in a strong Cumberland[6] accent—

"Helen Burns, if you don't go and put your drawer in order, and fold up your work this minute, I'll tell Miss Scatcherd to come and look at it!"

Vocabulary Development

provoking (pruh VOH king) *adj.* irritating
cross (KRAWS) *adj.* easily irritated; angry
meditation (med i TAY shun) *n.* deep thought

---

6. **Cumberland** (KUM ber lind) *n.* a county in northern England.

from Hard Times • *from* Jane Eyre

1. **Make a Judgment:** Do you believe that schools have a responsibility for the types of adults that children become? Explain.

_____

_____

2. **Literary Analysis:** In *Hard Times,* the setting is a "plain, bare, monotonous vault of a schoolroom." How does this description contribute to a **criticism of society**?

_____

3. **Literary Analysis:** Choose a passage from one of the selections and complete the chart below.

Passage	Intended Effect on Reader	Intended Message

4. **Reading Strategy:** To **recognize a writer's purpose,** look at details and think about why the writer chose them. In *Hard Times,* what is the **writer's purpose** in naming the instructor Mr. M'Choakumchild?

_____

5. **Reading Strategy:** Based on the descriptions in Jane Eyre, how did Bronte probably feel about schools such as Lowood?

_____

Dover Beach • Recessional
• The Widow at Windsor

LITERARY ANALYSIS

The thoughts and emotions in poems create the **mood.** The mood is the feeling a poem calls up. It is closely related to the poem's central idea, or **theme.** Read poetry with your feelings. Respond to the emotionally charged words, and you will find your way to the poem's ideas.

The mood of these poems is about the problems of the Victorian Period:

- Scientific progress caused people to doubt their faith.
- Wealth meant some people grew richer and other poorer.
- Ruling much of the world meant great responsibility for the Empire.

Compare the ways these poems look at the issues.

READING STRATEGY

When you read, you **draw conclusions** about what you read. You draw conclusions when you look at the evidence and then make generalizations. For example, in "The Widow at Windsor," it may not be clear why a "widow" had a "gold crown." You may also wonder why she has "ships on the foam." Later in the poem, you read about "Misses Victorier's sons." These seem like unrelated things, but you can put them together. You would then draw the conclusion that the widow is Queen Victoria.

Use this chart to draw more conclusions about the poems.

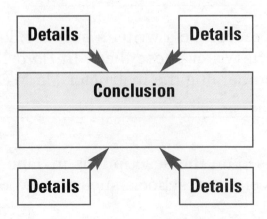

Dover Beach

Matthew Arnold

The Widow at Windsor

Rudyard Kipling

Summaries "Dover Beach" is about the British Empire in the Victorian Period. The speaker in "Dover Beach" looks out a window from the white chalk cliffs of Dover. He describes the moonlit beach to his love. He tells her to think about the ocean. It reminds him of the sadness of the times. He decides that lovers have only each other in the modern world, which has neither faith, happiness, love, nor hope.

"The Widow at Windsor" is also about the Victorian Period. The poem describes Queen Victoria. The speaker is a soldier. The speaker is proud of the queen's wealth, power, and military strength. At the same time, he understands the suffering of the soldiers. They must fight for the queen. The speaker reminds the people of Britain that their rule over much of the world comes at a high price.

Note-taking Guide

In the chart, record images from each poem that illustrate the world the speaker describes.

Dover Beach	The Widow at Wndsor

Recessional

Rudyard Kipling

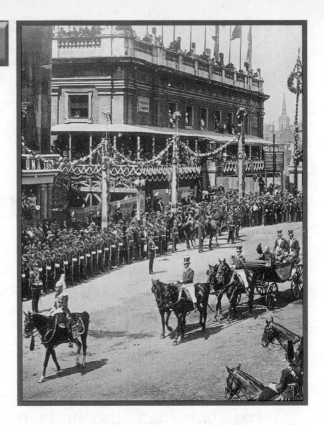

Summary This poems is also about the Victorian Period. The title, "Recessional," means the end of a religious service. It also means the end of the British Empire. The speaker warns the people of England that things change over time. He tells them that today's glories can go disappear. He says that the people should still be humble, and depend on God.

Note-taking Guide

Use this chart to record the main idea of each stanza in the poem. Then, write the main idea of the entire poem.

Stanza 1	Stanza 2	Stanza 3	Stanza 4	Stanza 5

Main Idea of Poem:

1. **Assess:** Which of these poems presents the most positive view of the British Empire? Explain.

_____

_____

Which poem presents the most negative view? Explain.

_____

_____

2. **Literary Analysis:** Fill in this chart with images in "Dover Beach." In the second column, record where the image is in the poem. In the third column, write about the **mood** the images suggest. On the line under the chart, write the **theme** of the poem.

Image	Where It Appears	Mood It Evokes

Theme of poem: _____

3. **Reading Strategy:** Why does Kipling describe the Empire from the perspective of a common soldier in "The Widow at Windsor"?

_____

4. **Reading Strategy:** Basing your answer on the last two lines of each stanza in "Recessional," what **conclusion** can you draw about Kipling's message?

_____

Condition of Ireland •
Progress in Personal Comfort

LITERARY ANALYSIS

Journalistic essays are short pieces of writing about things that are in the news. An essayist is someone who writes essays. Some essayists write about the world around them. Journalistic essayists write about what they think and feel about current events.

- Some essayists write as though they know everything. This is the way the essay "Condition of Ireland" is written.

- Some essayists write about their own thoughts and feelings about an issue. The essay "Progress in Personal Comfort" is written this way.

Writers write in different ways for different readers. "Conditions of Ireland," is addressed to people who care about the way other people must live. It talks about what is right and wrong. "Progress in Personal Comfort" is about things the writer has experienced. It uses humor and exaggeration to make its point. Compare and contrast the two essays.

READING STRATEGY

Emotive language uses words, phrases, and examples for emotional effect. **Informative language** conveys facts. As an aid to understanding these authors' opinions, use this chart to tell the difference between emotive and informative language.

	Condition of Ireland	Progress in Personal Comfort
Emotive language		
Informative language		

Condition of Ireland

The Illustrated London News

Summary This essay talks about the British Empire. It discusses the causes of the famine in Ireland. A famine is when there is not enough food, and people starve. At least a million people died in Ireland from the famine. Many people said the famine was caused by a failed potato crop. The writer says it was caused by "ignorant and vicious legislation." He writes about laws that were unfair to the common people. The land was rich and good for growing crops, but the people were not allowed to farm the land. The land belonged to a few rich people.

Note-taking Guide

Use the chart below to show the cause and effect of the Irish potato famine.

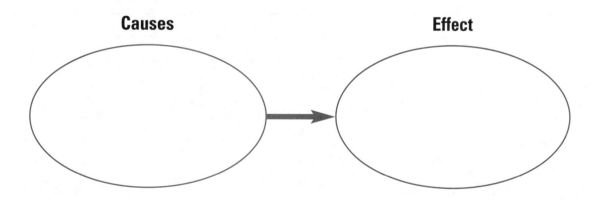

Causes   Effect

Progress in Personal Comfort

Sydney Smith

Summary This essay comments on the British Empire of its time. The essay describes all the social improvements that occurred during the author's lifetime. He writes about advances in science and technology. Important changes include gas street lamps, the steamboat, railroads, savings banks, and the postal service.

Note-taking Guide
Use the chart below to record improvements mentioned in the essay. Then, write what life was probably like before the improvement, and how the improvement changed life.

Invention	Life Before the Invention	Life After the Invention

Condition of Ireland • Progress in Personal Comfort

1. **Generalize:** Think about the inventions in the essay "Progress in Personal Comfort." What inventions do you think are also a sign of progress? Explain your answer.

   _____

   _____

2. **Literary Analysis:** In the **journalistic essay** "Condition of Ireland," the author writes as a judge. He writes, "we . . . exonerate the parties . . . " Find another place where the author writes as a judge. Explain your choice.

   _____

   _____

3. **Literary Analysis:** Fill in this chart with examples that show the writer's approach in each essay.

Exaggeration	Humor	Moral Drama: Good vs. Evil
_____	_____	_____
_____	_____	_____
_____	_____	_____
_____	_____	_____

4. **Reading Strategy:** Distinguish **emotive and informative language** in the sentence beginning, "In their terrible distress, . . . " This is in the first paragraph of "Condition of Ireland."

   _____

   _____

WEB SITES

About Web Sites

Web sites are specific places on the Internet. Each Web site has its own address or URL (Universal Resource Locator). Most Web sites have many pages. You can move from one page to another by clicking your mouse on a picture or a "button." You can also click your mouse on a highlighted or underlined phrase called a *link.*

The Web site may have a *site map.* This lists all the major Web pages on the site. The site map may also have a page that tells who is responsible for the site and why the site was made.

Reading Strategy

Evaluating Credibility of Sources When you look at a Web site, you must **evaluate its credibility.** This means that you must decide if the author can be trusted to give correct information. Ask who the author is. Then ask why the author has set up the site. Some authors try to sell something or persuade readers. Their sites may not provide fair information. Also, check to see if the author is an expert on that topic. Experts are far more trustworthy than those who are not experts. Use the checklist to evaluate the credibility of Web sites.

Web site's author or sponsor:
- If an author, what makes him or her an expert?
- If a sponsor, is it well established and well known?

Purpose of the Web site:
- Does it have a clear purpose?
- Does the purpose help you answer your research?

Credibility of information:
- Is the information documented, or is there a list of souces?
- Is the information supported by research?
- Does another source, like the encyclopedia, agree with the information given?

Relationship of the Web site to other sites:
- Does the site provide links to other good research and educational sources?
- Do these links make the Web site more believable, or are they questionable?

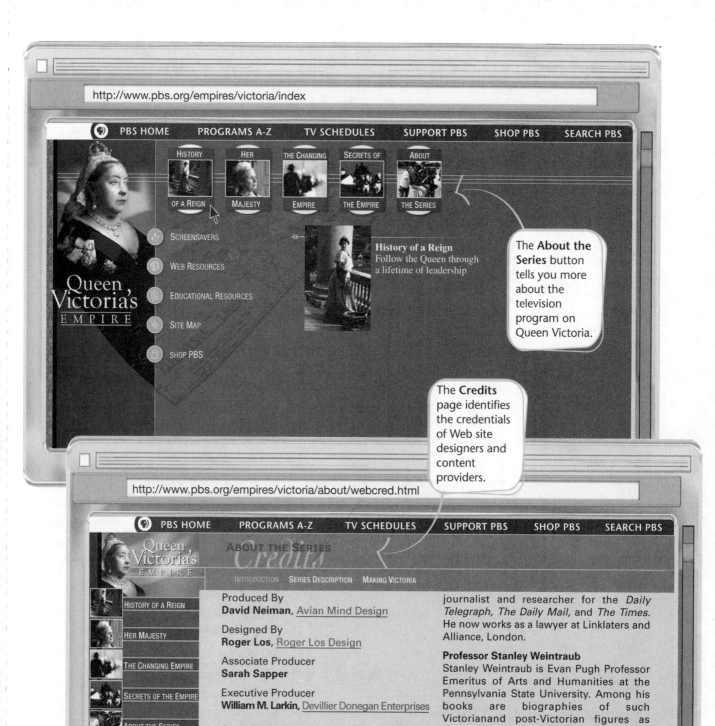

http://www.pbs.org/empires/victoria/index

PBS HOME   PROGRAMS A-Z   TV SCHEDULES   SUPPORT PBS   SHOP PBS   SEARCH PBS

HISTORY OF A REIGN   HER MAJESTY   THE CHANGING EMPIRE   SECRETS OF THE EMPIRE   ABOUT THE SERIES

SCREENSAVERS

WEB RESOURCES

EDUCATIONAL RESOURCES

SITE MAP

SHOP PBS

Queen Victoria's EMPIRE

History of a Reign
Follow the Queen through a lifetime of leadership

The **About the Series** button tells you more about the television program on Queen Victoria.

The **Credits** page identifies the credentials of Web site designers and content providers.

http://www.pbs.org/empires/victoria/about/webcred.html

PBS HOME   PROGRAMS A-Z   TV SCHEDULES   SUPPORT PBS   SHOP PBS   SEARCH PBS

Queen Victoria's EMPIRE

ABOUT THE SERIES
Credits

INTRODUCTION   SERIES DESCRIPTION   MAKING VICTORIA

HISTORY OF A REIGN

HER MAJESTY

THE CHANGING EMPIRE

SECRETS OF THE EMPIRE

ABOUT THE SERIES

SCREENSAVERS

WEB RESOURCES

EDUCATIONAL RESOURCES

SITE MAP

SHOP PBS

Produced By
David Neiman, Avian Mind Design

Designed By
Roger Los, Roger Los Design

Associate Producer
Sarah Sapper

Executive Producer
William M. Larkin, Devillier Donegan Enterprises

Content Providers:
Edward James
Edward James studied history as an undergraduate at Christ Church, Oxford, and then continued his education at St. Andrews University, where he studied International Security Studies as a postgraduate. He has worked as a

journalist and researcher for the *Daily Telegraph, The Daily Mail,* and *The Times.* He now works as a lawyer at Linklaters and Alliance, London.

Professor Stanley Weintraub
Stanley Weintraub is Evan Pugh Professor Emeritus of Arts and Humanities at the Pennsylvania State University. Among his books are biographies of such Victorianand post-Victorian figures as Victoria herself, Prince Albert, Edward VII (asthe Prince of Wales), Disraeli, the Rossettis, Whistler, Beardsley, Shaw, andLawrence of Arabia. His newest book from this group is *Edward the Caresser* (on Edward VII). His next book, out in November, will be *Silent Night: The Remarkable Christmas Truce of 1914.*

http://www.pbs.org/empires/victoria/history/index.html

PBS HOME   PROGRAMS A-Z   TV SCHEDULES   SUPPORT PBS

Queen Victoria's EMPIRE

HISTORY OF A REIGN

Engines of Change

ENGINES OF CHANGE   PASSAGE TO INDIA   THE MORAL CRUSADE   THE SCRAMBLE FOR AFRICA

HISTORY OF A REIGN

HER MAJESTY

THE CHANGING EMPIRE

SECRETS OF THE EMPIRE

ABOUT THE SERIES

SCREENSAVERS

WEB RESOURCES

EDUCATIONAL RESOURCES

SITE MAP

SHOP PBS

The author of this article is clearly identified.

This head indicates the link you clicked on to get to the Web page.

For ease of navigation, these links are the same as those on the first page of this site. Use them to link directly to more information without returning to the Home page

by Stanley Weintraub

As a teenager, Princess Victoria -- aware, as was the English public, that she was heir to the throne of her childless uncle, William IV -- was taken by her mother, the Duchess of Kent, on a royal progress -- by carriage -- through the rain-drenched Midlands into North Wales. For Victoria, it was a horrifying introduction to the Britain that kept the elegant society of the great houses at which they would stay comfortable and prosperous. "The men, women, children, country and houses are all black...," she wrote in her diary. "The grass is quite blasted and black." A blast furnace the entourage passed in their carriages was "an extraordinary building flaming with fire," after which everything continued to be "black, engines flaming, coals, in abundance; everywhere, smoking and burning coal heaps, intermingled with wretched huts and carts and little ragged children." Yet despite the grim conditions, at every stopping place, enthusiastic crowds shouted greetings, lengthy addresses by local officials promised future devotion, choirs sang patriotic anthems, and salutes were fired by happy celebrants, unaware that such anticipations of his death made old King William more than unhappy. At the great country houses, the princess dined from gold plates and drank from gilt cups, unaware that the industrial progress she had witnessed had left her future subjects behind in an abject misery concealed by their loyalty.

Before the industrial revolution

In February 1837, the year of her accession, she again saw the future. At Hersham in Surrey, on a visit to Claremont, the country home of her uncle, King Leopold of the Belgians, she encountered her first railway train, and "saw the steam carriage pass with surprising quickness, striking sparks as it flew along the railroad, enveloped in clouds of smoke & making a loud noise. It was a curious thing indeed!" The invention would transform Victoria's world and way of life.

The new age of technology suggested to Albert in the later 1840s a grand world's fair to display the arts and manufactures of all nations, and he tirelessly promoted funds for its fulfilment. On May 1, 1851 the Great Exhibition opened at the Crystal Palace, an engineering marvel itself, on the southeastern edge of Hyde Park. A wonder of iron and glass, it was the first substantial prefabricated building, and housed a staggering sampling of the new developments in engineering, manufactures and the arts. Its impetus in fostering change would be enormous, and the setting, with light streaming through its 293,655 panes of glass, awesome. Six million visitors were recorded, equal to a third of the kingdom. Charlotte Brontë wrote to her father, "Whatever human industry has created, you will find there." It would be another thrust by the Crown into modernity....

The steam engine changed England forever

Look for specific information in Web site articles, such as names and dates. Double-checking those facts can help you to confirm the Web site's credibility.

BACK TO THE TOP

THINKING ABOUT THE WEB SITE

1. You might want to know more about the television series and how it was made. What major section of the Web site could give you that information?

_____

2. Four major parts of Queen Victoria's history and empire are found on this Web site. List them.

_____

_____

READING STRATEGY

3. PBS is known for its educational programs. What is one of the main reasons PBS created this Web site?

_____

_____

4. Who wrote the information about Queen Victoria contained in this Web Site?

_____

TIMED WRITING: DESCRIPTION (25 MINUTES)

Write a brief description of Queen Victoria's Empire Web site. Follow these steps:

• Name the sponsoring organization.

_____

• List people who might use this Web site.

_____

• List the kinds of information given on the Web site.

_____

Use your notes to write your description.

Remembrance • The Darkling Thrush • Ah, Are You Digging on My Grave?

LITERARY ANALYSIS

Stanzas are a number of lines that form a unit within a poem. Stanzas are like paragraphs in prose. Stanzas may be repeated groups of two or more verse lines that make up a pattern. Patterns can be based on length, rhythm, frequency, and rhyme. The stanza structure of a poem is the pattern of stanzas. Readers usually expect a regular pattern when they read a poem.

Irony occurs when what is said is different from what is meant. Irony can provide a source of humor, but it can also show that things are not what they seem.

Both stanza structure and irony relate to what the reader expects in the poem. The first stanza leads you to think all the stanzas should be the same. Irony surprises you. It is different from what you expected.

READING STRATEGY

Reading Stanzas as Units of Meaning

Many poetic stanzas express a single main idea, as paragraphs do in prose. **Read stanzas as units of meaning**, noticing how each stanza builds on the one before. Reading this way gives you a better understanding of what the poet is saying. Use this chart to understand how each stanza leads to the next in the first three stanzas in "Remembrance.

"Remembrance"

Stanza 1	Stanza 2	Stanza 3
Speaker may be forgetting her true love, who died.		

Remembrance

Emily Brontë

The Darkling Thrush • Ah, Are You Digging on My Grave?

Thomas Hardy

Summaries The speaker in "Remembrance" is a woman addressing her love, who died fifteen years before. She asks him to forgive her if she forgets him. Although her joy died with him, her mind is now on other desires and hopes. In "The Darkling Thrush," the speaker describes a bleak winter day that is suddenly brightened by a bird called a thrush. The bird's song gives the speaker hope. The speaker in "Ah, Are You Digging on My Grave?" is a dead woman wondering who is digging on her grave. Is it her loved one, her family, or an enemy?

Note-taking Guide

Use this chart to record feelings of sadness and hope that are described in each poem. Record the stanzas in which you find each emotion.

Poem	Sadness	Stanza	Hope	Stanza
Remem-brance				
"The Darkling Thrush"				
"Ah, Are You Digging on My Grave?"				

Remembrance • The Darkling Thrush • Ah, Are You Digging on My Grave?

1. **Make a Judgment:** Which poet presents the most sympathetic speaker? Explain.

   _____

   _____

2. **Literary Analysis:** Use this chart to compare the first and last **stanzas** of each poem.

Number of lines	Number of lines	Rhyme scheme	Meter
Remembrance	First Stanza:		
	Last Stanza:		
"The Darkling Thrush"	First Stanza:		
	Last Stanza:		
"Ah, Are You Digging on My Grave?"	First Stanza:		
	Last Stanza:		

3. **Literary Analysis:** What is **ironic** about the last stanza of "Ah, Are You Digging on My Grave?"

   _____

   _____

4. **Reading Strategy:** Read **stanzas as units of meaning** in "Remembrance." How does the speaker gradually work out an answer to the question in the first stanza?

   _____

   _____

God's Grandeur • Spring and Fall: To a Young Child • To an Athlete Dying Young • When I Was One-and-Twenty

LITERARY ANALYSIS

Some poetry has a regular **rhythm**. Rhythm is the pattern of stressed and unstressed syllables. Poetry with regular rhythm is called **metrical verse**. Metrical verse is made up of different groups of syllables called **feet**. Following are some samples of feet and the pattern of stressed (´) and unstressed (˘) syllables in them:

- **Iambic:** unstressed, stressed; as in *the time*
- **Trochaic:** stressed, unstressed, as in *grandeur*
- **Anapestic:** unstressed, unstressed, stressed, as in *to the low*

Lines with three feet are called **trimeter**. Lines with four feet are called **tetrameter**. Lines with five feet are called **pentameter**. Iambic pentameter is a five-foot line with iambic feet. Trochaic tetrameter is a four-foot line with trochaic feet. Housman uses iambic and trochaic tetrameter. Hopkins uses these rhythms:

- **Counterpoint rhythm**—two different rhythms are used, for example, two trochaic feet in an iambic line.
- **Sprung rhythm**—all feet begin with a stressed syllable (sometimes marked with an accent); they have a different number of unstressed syllables.

READING STRATEGY

Applying biography means that you should learn about the poets' lives. Then you can use what you have learned to help you understand their poems. Read the information on page 978 in your textbook. Use this chart to apply biography to these poems.

	Gerard Manley Hopkins	A. E. Housman
Fact about poet		
Poet's beliefs		
Insight into poetry		

God's Grandeur • Spring and Fall: To a Young Child

Gerard Manley Hopkins

Summaries Both of these poems talk about nature. In **"God's Grandeur,"** the speaker asks why people hurt nature. He says that nature always shows the grandeur, or greatness, of God. Nature remains fresh no matter what people do to it. In **"Spring and Fall: To a Young Child,"** the speaker talks about a girl's sadness. The girl is sad because the autumn leaves are falling. The speaker says that everything dies. He says the girl is really sad over her own mortality, or the knowledge that she too will one day die.

Note-taking Guide
Use this chart to record lines from each poem that talk about beauty or about the fact that things die.

Poem	Beauty	Line	Morality	Line
"God's Grandeur"	_____ _____ _____		_____ _____ _____	
"Spring and Fall: To a Young Child"	_____ _____ _____		_____ _____ _____	

To an Athlete Dying Young • When I Was One-and-Twenty

A.E. Housman

Summary The speaker in **"To an Athlete Dying Young"** watches as people carry home the body of a young athlete. The speaker says that the glories of youth do not last. He also says that disappointment comes with age and experience. The speaker thinks that perhaps the athlete was lucky to have died young. That way, he did not have to live past his glory.

In **"When I Was One-and-Twenty,"** the speaker talks about advice he received when he was a young man. The advice was to give young women gifts, but not his heart. The theme of this poem is similar to that of "To an Athlete Dying Young." The theme is that the glories of youth do not last, and that disappointment comes with age and experience.

Note-taking Guide

Use this chart to record lines from each poem that talk about beauty or about the fact that things die.

Image	Words/Phrases	Line Number
To an Athlete Dying Young		
When I Was One-and-Twenty		

1. **Make a Judgment:** Which poem presents the most caring view of human mortality, or the fact that people die? Explain.

_____

_____

2. **Literary Analysis:** Use this chart to record the scansion symbols (˘ ˊ)that show the pattern of stressed and unstressed syllables in line 5 of "God's Grandeur."

| Generations have trod, have trod, have trod, . . . |
| _____   _____ |

3. **Literary Analysis:** In lines 1-8 of "To an Athlete," the **meter** includes five **iambic tetrameter** lines and three **trochaic tetrameter** lines. How do the trochaic lines strengthen the idea of a "stiller town"?

_____

_____

_____

4. **Reading Strategy: Apply the author's biography** to a passage in "God's Grandeur" that shows Hopkins's love of nature. Explain your choice.

_____

_____

_____

5. **Reading Strategy:** Find lines in "To An Athlete Dying Young" that reflect Housman's sadness. Explain your choice.

_____

_____

_____

When You Are Old • The Lake Isle of Innisfree • The Wild Swans at Coole • The Second Coming • Sailing to Byzantium

LITERARY ANALYSIS

In literature, a **symbol** is an image, character, objéct, or action that serves the following purposes:

- It stands for something beyond itself.
- It triggers a number of related thoughts, or associations.
- It makes readers' feelings stronger and adds deeper meaning.

The swans in "The Wild Swans at Coole" combine associations of beauty (they are graceful and attractive), pureness (they are white), freedom (they are wild), and the eternal (they return year after year). Like other strong symbols, the swans have multiple meanings: They can stand for the cycle of nature and the speaker's earlier life.

Yeats builds multiple meanings in "The Wild Swans at Coole" by contrasting two encounters with the swans, one past and one present. He creates his symbol from personal experiences. In other poems, though, he builds multiple meanings by turning to more common symbols, such as the Sphinx in "The Second Coming."

READING STRATEGY

A writer's experiences, beliefs, and knowledge shape his or her works. As you read, **apply literary background**—information about history, literature, and the writer's life—to help you understand. Use the chart below.

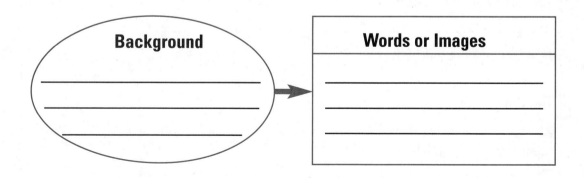

When You Are Old • The Lake Isle of Innisfree • The Wild Swans at Coole • The Second Coming • Sailing to Byzantium

William Butler Yeats

Summaries Yeats uses themes of aging, loss, and change in these poems. "**When You Are Old**" is written to a woman the speaker loved. He tells her that of all the men who loved her, only he loved her for her soul. In "**The Lake Isle of Innisfree**," a poet in the city wishes for the simple country life. In "**The Wild Swans at Coole**," the speaker thinks about his past and compares himself to the swans. Swans do not change, but he has had to make many changes in his life. In "**The Second Coming**," Yeats gives his view of history. In "**Sailing to Byzantium**," Yeats says that though humans will die, art lives on.

Note-taking Guide

Use this chart to record which of the general themes of aging, loss, and change are used in each poem. Check each box that applies. Each poem may have more than one checkmark (4).

Poem	Aging	Loss	Change
When You Are Old			
The Lake Isle of Innisfree			
The Wild Swans at Coole			
The Second Coming			
Sailing to Byzantium			

Poetry of William Butler Yeats

1. **Make a Judgment:** Do you agree that in the modern world "things fall apart," as Yeats writes in "The Second Coming"? Explain.

_____

_____

2. **Literary Analysis:** A **symbol** is an image, character, object, or action that stands for something else. Find two examples in "Sailing to Byzantium" in which Yeats uses Byzantine art as a symbol of perfection.

_____

_____

3. **Literary Analysis:** Use this chart to compare the effect and meaning of the swans in "The Wild Swans at Coole" with those of the Sphinx in "The Second Coming."

Symbol	Personal / Traditional	Vivid/Flat in Effect	Rich/Poor in Associations	Easy/Hard to Interpret
swans				
Sphinx				

4. **Reading Strategy: Apply literary background** when considering the meaning of "The Second Coming." How does knowing the historical time in which Yeats wrote help you to interpret the first stanza?

_____

_____

_____

Preludes • Journey of the Magi • The Hollow Men

LITERARY ANALYSIS

Modernism was a trend in the arts that took place in the early twentieth century. A Modernist work has the following features:

- It emphasizes **images**, or words and phrases that appeal to one or more of the five senses.
- It relies on the use of the **symbol**—an image, character, object, or action that stands for something beyond itself.
- It contains **allusions**, or indirect references to people, places, events, or works of literature.
- It focuses on the spiritual troubles of modern life.

READING STRATEGY

A Modernist work of literature may suggest a theme, or a central message about people or life, without stating it directly. Follow these steps to help you **interpret** theme's in poetry.

1. Look carefully at important passages.
2. Identify key images that appear more than once.
3. Think about the ideas that these patterns of images suggest.
4. Draw a conclusion about what these patterns reveal about the meaning of the work.

Image sore-footed camels	**Image** dirty villages

Patterns discomfort, dirtiness

Conclusion the journey is difficult and unpleasant

Preludes

T.S. Eliot

Summary This poem presents a bleak vision of a world in which suffering, grime, and dreariness are the main features. Eliot may not just have been reveling in despair, however, he may have seen it as a necessary "prelude" to spiritual awakening. Each segment, or prelude, describes a different depressing urban scene. In Prelude IV, however, a new note is sounded—that of something "infinitely gentle / Infinitely suffering."

Note-taking Guide

Use this chart to record a description of each scene. Then, put a checkmark (4) in either the "despair" column or the "hopefulness" column.

Segments	Description of Scene	Hopefulness	Despair
I			
II			
III			
IV			

Journey of the Magi

T. S. Eliot

Summary In this poem, the speaker is one of the three Magi (MAY jy), or wise men, who traveled to Bethlehem to honor the baby Jesus. Now he is an old man, and he reflects on the meaning of the journey he made many years ago. He tells about the various difficulties that he and his companions encountered. Finally, he confesses that the birth he witnessed was like a death, because it was "Hard and bitter" for him and his companions. Having seen the baby Jesus, they returned to their own kingdoms. However, they no longer felt at ease among people who worshiped many gods rather than one.

Note-taking Guide

Use the following chart to record information from the poem.

Character _____

Goal _____

↓ **Difficulties encountered:**

_____

_____

_____

Result _____

Resolution ⟶ Years Later, Continuing Problems:
Or Lack of
Resolution
_____

_____

Journey of the Magi
T.S. Eliot

"A cold coming we[1] had of it,
Just the worst time of the year
For a journey, and such a long journey:
The ways deep and the weather sharp,
The very dead of winter."[2]

◆ ◆ ◆

The travelers have difficulty with the camels. The animals are stubborn and sore and don't want to move.

The speaker says the travelers miss the warm weather and the serving girls at home. Instead they meet cursing camel drivers, have trouble finding shelter, and visit unfriendly and expensive towns.

The travelers finally decide to travel at night. They have little sleep and begin to wonder if their journey is wise.

◆ ◆ ◆

---

1. The speaker is one of the three wise men, or magi, who traveled to Bethlehem to visit the baby Jesus. In this poem, the speaker reflects upon the meaning of the journey.
2. "A . . . winter": Adapted from a part of a sermon delivered by 17th-century Bishop Lancelot Andrews: "A cold coming they had of it at this time of year, just the worst time of the year to take a journey, and specially a long journey in. The ways deep, the weather sharp, the days short, the sun farthest off . . . the very dead of winter."

TAKE NOTES

Reading Check

Read the bracketed part of the poem. Circle two difficulties the wise men encountered on their journey.

Vocabulary and Pronunciation

In English, the word *dead* has several different meanings. For example, it can mean "no longer living," "very tired," "no longer in use," "the time of greatest intensity," or "dull." Which meaning of *dead* does Eliot use in the poem?

_____

English Language Development

In English, most adjectives come before the nouns they describe. For example, the adjective *long* comes before the noun *journey* in this line from the poem:

". . . and such a long journey."

In this poem, Eliot often reverses the usual placement of adjectives. List two examples from the poem in which Eliot places the adjective after the noun it describes.

1. _____

2. _____

Reading Strategy

Circle two images in the bracketed passage that might help you **interpret the theme** of hope and new life.

Literary Analysis

Which characteristic of **Modernist** poetry does Eliot use in this poem? Circle the letter of the correct answer.

(a) symbol   (b) image

(c) allusion   (d) all of these

Stop to Reflect

Is the speaker's journey positive or negative? Why do you think so?

_____

_____

_____

Then at dawn we came down to a <u>temperate</u> valley,
Wet, below the snow line,[3] smelling of <u>vegetation</u>;
With a running stream and a water-mill beating the darkness,
And three trees[4] on the low sky,

◆   ◆   ◆

The travelers arrive at a tavern but can get no information. They continue and find the place they are looking for that evening.

The speaker says that this journey took place a long time ago. He's not sure whether he witnessed a birth or a death. The miraculous birth of Jesus caused the death of his old world, his old life, and his old beliefs.

Vocabulary Development

temperate (TEM per it) *adj.* neither hot nor cold
vegetation (vej i TAY shun) *n.* the plants of an area or region

---

3. **snow line** the boundary where a snow-covered area begins.
4. **three trees** a Biblical allusion to the three crosses of Calvary, the hill outside ancient Jerusalem where Jesus and two other men were crucified.

The Hollow Men

T.S. Eliot

Summary "The Hollow Men" describes a world in which people have no faith, no courage, no spirit, and no awareness. Spoken by the hollow men themselves, the poem is a self-portrait of the typical modern person.

Note-Taking Guide

Use this cluster diagram to identify and record the images in the five parts of "The Hollow Men."

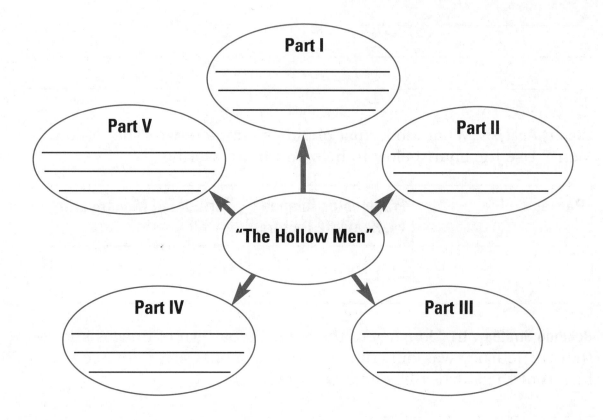

Preludes • Journey of the Magi • The Hollow Men

1. **Intrpret:** It is winter at 6:00 p.m. at the beginning of Prelude I. What cycle of time takes place from Prelude I to Prelude IV?

   _____

2. **Compare and Contrast:** The speaker in "Journey of the Magi" has gone on a journey to witness a birth. How do the descriptions of the journey compare to the descriptions of the event?

   _____

   _____

3. **Literary Analysis: Modernism** often emphasizes a concern with the spiritual ills of modern life. Identify three images in the "Preludes" that suggest the Modernist view that modern life is empty. Explain.

   _____

   _____

   _____

4. **Literary Analysis:** What Modernist qualities characterize "The Hollow Men"? Use the chart below to help you in answering.

Passage	Fragmented Images vs. Realistic Pictures	Critical of Modern Life

5. **Reading Strategy:** In "Journey of the Magi," a pattern of images shows that the journey was difficult. How does this pattern reinforce the idea that the journey has changed the Magi?

   _____

   _____

In Memory of W. B. Yeats
• Musée des Beaux Arts • Carrick Revisited •
Not Palaces

LITERARY ANALYSIS

The **theme** of a literary work is its central concern or purpose. It is the central question the poem raises. A poet may express the theme in these ways:

- Making direct statements
- Through word choice and imagery

In the poem, "In Memory of W. B. Yeats," for example, Auden looks at the link between poetry and life. Statements like "poetry makes nothing happen" speak directly to this theme.

A central theme in poetry is poetry itself. Modern poets offer many ideas on poetry.

- In "In Memory of W. B. Yeats," Auden says that poetry cannot change what is real. However, by "singing" our human weaknesses, poetry says that life is joyful.
- "Not Palaces" suggests that poems can change what is real by making social change happen.

READING STRATEGY

To understand poetry, it is often helpful to **paraphrase** difficult lines by putting the writer's words in your own words. This chart shows how you might paraphrase two lines from "In Memory of W. B. Yeats." Use the chart shown to paraphrase passages as you read.

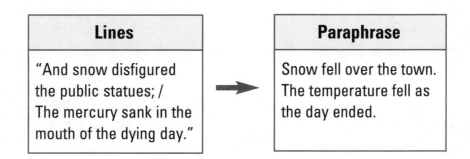

Lines		Paraphrase
"And snow disfigured the public statues; / The mercury sank in the mouth of the dying day."	→	Snow fell over the town. The temperature fell as the day ended.

In Memory of W. B. Yeats
• Musée des Beaux Arts
W. H. Auden

Carrick Revisited
Louis MacNeice

Not Palaces
Stephen Spender

Summary These poems are about looking—looking back, looking away, and looking ahead. "**In Memory of W. B. Yeats**" memorializes Yeats's death and explores the nature of poetry. "**Musée des Beaux Arts**" describes scenes from paintings showing tragic events, such as the fall to death of Icarus, that happen while people go about their daily lives. "**Carrick Revisited**" explores how the poet feels about his childhood home. "**Not Palaces**" urges readers to leave behind the palaces of the past and take in the energy of social change in the present.

Note-taking Guide

Record the topic of or inspiration for each poem in column 2. Write the theme of the poem in column 3. This will help you understand how these poems are alike and how they differ.

Poem	Topic/Inspiration	Theme
In Memory of W. B. Yeats		
Musée des Beaux Arts		
Carrick Revisited		
Not Palaces		

In Memory of W. B. Yeats • Musée des Beaux Arts • Carrick Revisited • Not Palaces

1. **Summarize:** Summarize what the poem "In Memory of W. B. Yeats" says about poetry.

   _____

   _____

2. **Compare and Contrast:** In "Musée des Beaux Arts," the ploughman and the ship probably see Icarus falling from the sky. How do their responses contrast with the seriousness of the event?

   _____

   _____

3. **Literary Analysis:** Use the chart below to compare the **themes in** two of the poems poems about the nature of art. The first one has been started for you. Choose a second poem to compare.

Poem	Central Issues	Supporting Passages	Interpretation
"In Memory of W. B. Yeats"	What difference does art make?	"Teach the free man how to praise."	

4. **Reading Strategy: Paraphrase** lines 32–41 of "In Memory of W. B. Yeats."

   _____

   _____

MISSION STATEMENTS

About Mission Statements

A mission statement is a document provided by a specific group. It identifies and describes the group's objectives and daily activities. A mission statement helps introduce the group or organization to the general public.

Reading Strategy

The organization of a mission statement is important to its success. The statement must make basic information easy to find. It should also contain enough facts to satisfy those who desire specific information. The following organizational strategies are commonly used in mission statements:

- Short boldface subheads to help readers find main points
- Groups of bulleted items to help readers follow ideas easily
- Points arranged in order of importance
- Details arranged in chronological order to allow readers to see what steps are taken to accomplish objectives

The National Gallery in London, was established in 1824 when Parliament bought a private collection of art. Its mission statement appears on the following pages. Use the chart to help you **interpret the organization** of the mission statement and to decide if it uses organizational strategies successfully.

Organizational Strategy	Purpose	Effectiveness

BUILD UNDERSTANDING

Knowing these terms will help you read this mission statement.

United Kingdom a region made up of Great Britain (England, Wales, and Scotland) and Northern Ireland

disseminate (di SEM i nayt) *v.* to scatter or spread far and wide

The National Gallery
Role and Objectives

Role

The National Gallery houses the national Collection of Western European paintings from around 1250 to 1900.

The Gallery's aim is to care for, enhance and study its Collection, so as to offer the fullest access to the pictures for the education and enjoyment of the widest possible public now and in the future. It aims for the highest international standards in all its activities.

The Collection belongs to the people of the United Kingdom. It is open, free of charge, to all.

The Gallery serves a very wide and diverse public, which includes:

- those who visit the Gallery of London—both those who visit frequently and those who visit only occasionally;
- those who see its pictures while they are on loan elsewhere, both inside and outside the UK, and those who know the Collection through publications, multimedia and TV;
- those who live nearby as well as those who live further away in the United Kingdom and overseas;

- every age group—from children to pensioners;
- the socially excluded and the privileged; the uninformed and the specialist; and those with special needs;
- the worldwide community of museums and galleries;
- and, most importantly, future generations.

Objectives

The Gallery aims to:

Care for the Collection

- keep the pictures in the nation's Collection safe for future generations by maintaining a secure and appropriate environment for them, monitoring their condition regularly, and undertaking suitable restoration or conservation;
- do everything possible to secure the pictures from fire, theft and other hazards;
- do everything possible to ensure that pictures loaned out are in sound enough condition to travel safely.

Enhance the Collection

- acquire great pictures across the whole range of European painting to enhance the Collection now and for future generations.

Study the Collection

- encourage all aspects of scholarship on the Collection, researching and documenting the pictures to the highest international standards, and ensuring that this work is disseminated.

Provide Access to the Collection for the Education and Enjoyment of the Widest Possible Public

- encourage the public to use the Collection as their own by maintaining free admission, during the most convenient possible hours, to as much as possible of the permanent Collection;

- display the pictures well;
- promote knowledge of the Collection and encourage the public to visit it;
- help the widest possible public both in the Gallery and beyond to understand and enjoy the paintings, taking advantage of the opportunities created by modern technology;
- offer the highest possible standards in services for our visitors.

Stand as a National and International Leader in All Its Activities
- work with other regional museums and galleries in the United Kingdom;
- enhance the national and international standing of the Gallery.

Reading Informational Materials

The bulleted list on page 276 describes strategies for organizing **mission statements**. Does the National Gallery use these strategies effectively in its mission statement?

_____

Explain.

_____

_____

_____

Thinking About the Mission Statement

1. What is the National Gallery's general purpose?"

_____

_____

2. The National Gallery Collection belongs to the people of the United Kingdom. In what way is this ownership important to the Gallery's mission?

_____

READING STRATEGY

3. 1n a mission statement, details about the same topic are often grouped together. How does grouping thses details help readers?

_____

4. How do bulleted lists help organize the mission statement for readers?

_____

_____

TIMED WRITING: DESCRIPTION (30 MINUTES)

Write a **mission statement** for a group or organization that you know well, you may wish to choose a school club or team.

- Write the name of the group or club you choose.

_____

- List two of the group's main activities.

_____

_____

- List ways that these activities help the club and its community.

_____

Use these notes to write your mission statement.

Shooting an Elephant

LITERARY ANALYSIS

Irony shows the difference between what is real and what seems to be real. It can take a few forms, including the following:

- **Verbal irony** is the difference between what you say and what you mean.

- **Irony of situation** is the difference between what you think will happen and what does happen.

Tone shows how a writer feels about the reader and the subject. Tone is put across in the words used, how the sentences are written, and other ways. Orwell's direct, simple sentences make it seem like someone is talking. He also uses tone to seem separated from his subject. As you read, notice how Orwell uses irony and tone.

READING STRATEGY

When reading, it helps to **recognize the writer's attitudes** toward the subject. Attitudes are the writer's feelings about the topic. They come through in the author's word choice, tone, and choice of details. Fill in the chart below to explain Orwell's attitudes.

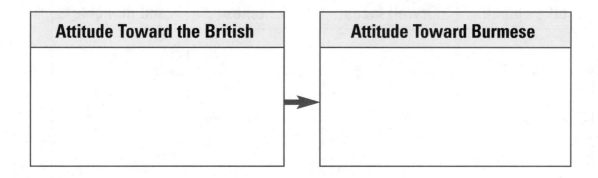

Attitude Toward the British	Attitude Toward Burmese

Shooting an Elephant

George Orwell

Summary Orwell describes his experience as a British police officer in Burma. Burma was then a British colony. Orwell secretly feels that the British should leave Burma. He is also angry with the Burmese people who insult him every day. One day, he hears that an elephant has gone wild. Orwell sends for a gun and goes looking for the beast. A large crowd follows him. The elephant has damaged property and killed a man. The animal is now peaceful. Orwell decides that he must kill it so that he does not look foolish in front of the Burmese.

Note-taking Guide Use this chart to record important details from the essay.

Details about...			
Where it takes place	**The problems Orwell faces**	**The actions he takes**	**His feelings and thoughts**

Shooting an Elephant
George Orwell

The author, George Orwell, is a police officer in Burma. He is hated in this anti-European area. The feelings of the Burmese aren't strong enough for crowds to cause a riot, but he is an individual target.

◆　◆　◆

When a <u>nimble</u> Burman tripped me up on the football field and the referee (another Burman) looked the other way, the crowd yelled with hideous laughter. This happened more than once. In the end the sneering yellow faces of young men that met me everywhere, the insults hooted after me when I was at a safe distance, got badly on my nerves. The young Buddhist priests were the worst of all. There were several thousands of them in the town and none of them seemed to have anything to do except stand on street corners and jeer at Europeans.

◆　◆　◆

Orwell is confused and upset by the behavior of the Burmese. He decides that the reason for the problem is imperialism, or the fact that Burma is a colony of Great Britain. Orwell confesses that he sides with the Burmese and opposes British rule. He hates

Vocabulary Development

nimble (NIM buhl) *adj.* quick or light in movement

TAKE NOTES

Background

In this essay, Orwell writes of the days of English rule in Burma. Burma is a country located in southeast Asia on the Bay of Bengal. Great Britain fought several wars against Burma during the 1800s. The British hoped to gain a better trade route with China. In 1885, Britain finally conquered Burma. Although the British failed to achieve the desired "golden path" to China, Burma provided Britain with other economic opportunities. For example, the British sold Burmese rice to other countries. Many Burmese, however, were unwilling to accept British rule. Opponents of the British formed the People's Volunteer Association, led by Aung San (owng sahn). This group helped win Burma's independence from Britain in 1948.

Reading Strategy

Underline two words or phrases that help you recognize **the writer's attitudes** toward the Burmese.

Reading Check

How do the Burmese view the English? Give examples to support your answer.

_____

_____

_____

In English, many words beginning with *sub* mean *lower than* something. For example, the word *subdivisional* at the beginning of this essay refers to a unit of government that is *lower than* a division. What does the word *subinspector,* underlined in blue, mean?

_____

_____

_____

Reading Check

What problem does the subinspector call Orwell about?

_____

_____

_____

_____

his job because he feels guilty about how poorly Burmese prisoners are treated by the British and because he dislikes how the Burmese treat him.

◆　◆　◆

One day something happened which in a roundabout way was <u>enlightening</u>. It was a tiny incident in itself, but it gave me a better glimpse than I had had before of the real nature of <u>imperialism</u>—the real motives for which <u>despotic</u> governments act.

◆　◆　◆

One morning a subinspector calls Orwell. An escaped elephant is destroying the market. The <u>subinspector</u> asks Orwell to do something about the problem.

◆　◆　◆

I did not know what I could do, but I wanted to see what was happening and I got onto a pony and started out. I took my rifle, an old .44 Winchester and much too small to kill an elephant, but I thought the noise might be useful. . . .

◆　◆　◆

Orwell learns that the elephant is tame. But the elephant is in a temporary, dangerous state of frenzy known as "must." The elephant had escaped from its chains, destroyed a bamboo hut, killed a cow, ate fruit at some fruit stands, and knocked over a garbage truck. Orwell joins Burmese and

---

Vocabulary Development

enlightening (en LIYT en ing) *adj.* giving insight or understanding to

imperialism (im PEE ree uh lizm) *n.* policy of forming an empire and securing economic power by conquest and colonization

despotic (de SPOT ik) *adj.* harsh, cruel, unjust

Indian police officers who question residents of a poor neighborhood to find out where the elephant has gone. The men hear a woman yelling at a group of children. Orwell investigates and finds the body of a dead Indian laborer lying in the mud. The man had been killed by the elephant. After finding the man's body, Orwell sends for his elephant rifle. Some Burmese tell Orwell that the elephant is in nearby rice fields. They are excited by the idea that he is going to shoot the elephant. A crowd gathers and follows him. Orwell spots the elephant eating grass by the side of the road.

◆　◆　◆

I had halted on the road. As soon as I saw the elephant I knew with perfect certainty that I ought not to shoot him. It is a serious matter to shoot a working elephant–it is comparable to destroying a huge and costly piece of machinery–and obviously one ought not to do it if it can possibly be avoided.

◆　◆　◆

At that moment, the elephant seems harmless. Orwell feels that the elephant's frenzy is over, and he won't be dangerous. Orwell really doesn't want to shoot him. He decides to watch the elephant for a while before going home.

◆　◆　◆

But at that moment I glanced round at the crowd that had followed me. It was an immense crowd, two thousand at the least and growing every minute. It blocked the road for a long distance on either side. I looked at the sea

Literary Analysis

Which type of **irony** does Orwell use in the sentence underlined in blue? Circle the letter of the correct answer.

(a) situational (b) verbal

Reading Check

Does Orwell think the elephant is dangerous? Why or why not?

_____

_____

_____

_____

Read the bracketed section aloud. What makes Orwell know that he will have to shoot the elephant?

_____

_____

_____

What type of **irony**—verbal or situational—lies in Orwell's comments underlined in blue?

_____

_____

_____

of yellow faces above the garish clothes—faces all happy and excited over this bit of fun, all certain that the elephant was going to be shot. They were watching me as they would watch a conjurer[1] about to perform a trick. They did not like me, but with the magical rifle in my hands I was momentarily worth watching. And suddenly I realized that I should have to shoot the elephant after all. The people expected it of me and I had got to do it; I could feel their two thousand wills pressing me forward, irresistibly . . . .

◆ ◆ ◆

Despite his position of authority, Orwell senses that he must do what the people expect him to do. He does not wish to harm the elephant, especially because the creature is worth more alive. However, he feels he has no choice. He thinks about what might happen if something goes wrong. He believes that the crowd would run him down and trample him to death if he fails to kill the animal. Orwell prepares to shoot the elephant.

◆ ◆ ◆

The crowd grew very still, and deep, low, happy sigh, as of people who see the theater curtain go at last, breathed fom innumerable throats. They were going to have their bit of fun, after all.

◆ ◆ ◆

Orwell really doesn't know how to shoot an elephant. He should aim at the ear hole.

Vocabulary Development

garish (GAR ish) *adj.*   loud and flashy
innumerable (i NYOO muhr uh bul) *adj.*   too many to be counted

1. **conjurer** (KAHN juhr uhr) *n.* a magician.

Instead, he aims in front of the ear hole, because he thinks that is where the brain is.

♦   ♦   ♦

When I pulled the trigger I did not hear the bang or feel the kick—one never does when a shot goes home—but I heard the devilish roar of glee that went up from the crowd.

♦   ♦   ♦

The elephant changes immediately. He doesn't fall, but finally he slobbers and falls on his knees. He seems to deteriorate.

♦   ♦   ♦

One could have imagined him thousands of years old. I fired again into the same spot. At the second shot he did not collapse but climbed with desperate slowness to his feet and stood weakly upright, with legs sagging and head drooping. I fired a third time. That was the shot that did for him. You could see the agony of it jolt his whole body and knock the last <u>remnant</u> of strength from his legs.

♦   ♦   ♦

The elephant appears to rise. His trunk reaches skyward as he trumpets, but his hind legs collapse.

♦   ♦   ♦

And then down he came, his belly toward me,

Vocabulary Development

remnant (REM nuhnt) *n.* what is left over

with a crash that seemed to shake the ground even where I lay.

♦   ♦   ♦

The elephant is clearly dying, but he is not yet dead. Orwell fires more shots, but the elephant still breathes.

♦   ♦   ♦

In the end I could not stand it any longer and went away. I heard later that it took him half an hour to die. Burmans were bringing dahs[2] and baskets even before I left, and I was told they had stripped his body almost to the bones by the afternoon.

Afterward, of course, there were endless discussions about the shooting of the elephant. The owner was furious, but he was only an Indian and could do nothing.

♦   ♦   ♦

In Burma, the law states that a mad elephant must be killed. Orwell feels he did the right thing. The Europeans do not agree.

♦   ♦   ♦

And afterward I was very glad that the coolie had been killed; it put me legally in the right and it gave me a sufficient <u>pretext</u> for shooting the elephant. I often wondered whether any of the others grasped that I had done it solely to avoid looking a fool.

Reading Check

(1) Why does Orwell go away?

_____

_____

_____

(2) How long does it take the elephant to die?

_____

_____

Stop to Reflect

What is Orwell's real reason for shooting the elephant?

_____

_____

_____

Vocabulary Development

pretext (PREE tekst) *n.* excuse

---

2. **dahs** (daz) *n.* knives.

Shooting an Elephant

1. **Analyze:** The Burmese hate Orwell because he is European. They also hate him because he stands for the British control of India. Why is he conflicted about this hatred?

_____

_____

2. **Interpret:** Orwell shoots the elephant to avoid looking silly. However, he is honest about why he does it. What does this show about the kind of person he is?

_____

_____

3. **Literary Analysis:** Use the chart below to understand the contrast between the words and the reality.

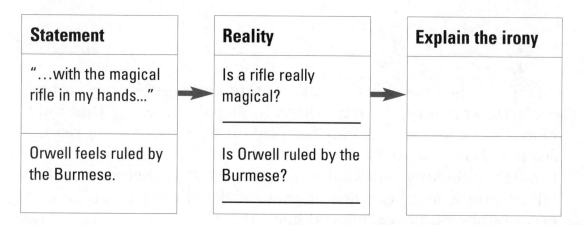

Statement	Reality	Explain the irony
"…with the magical rifle in my hands…"	Is a rifle really magical? _____	
Orwell feels ruled by the Burmese.	Is Orwell ruled by the Burmese? _____	

4. **Reading Strategy: Recognize the writer's attitudes** in this essay. Reread the paragraph beginning "It was perfectly clear to me what I ought to do." Write down details that show his thoughts and feelings.

_____

_____

_____

The Demon Lover

LITERARY ANALYSIS

A **ghost story** is a tale in which part of the past, usually a dead person, appears in the present. Many good ghost stories have these things:

- A strange or mysterious setting
- The suggestion that something unexplained is at work
- A chance that the events can be explained

As you read "The Demon Lover," study these elements of a ghost story, using a chart like the one shown.

Past ➡	Familiar ➡	Natural ➡
Present	**Unfamilar**	**Supernatural**

Some of the best ghost stories contain **ambiguity**—they can be understood in more than one way. In literature, words that have more than one meaning may be used on purpose. As you read, see how Bowen adds to the mysterious quality of her tale through ambiguity. She makes readers wonder whether the "ghost" in the story is a dead man or a vision the woman had because she never really faced her past.

READING STRATEGY

Respond to the story as you read, whether with puzzlement or fear. Note your reactions and look for what the writer has done to make you have them.

The Demon Lover

Elizabeth Bowen

Summary During World War II, Mrs. Drover returns to her shut-up London house to pick up some items. A mysterious unstamped letter has appeared on her table, but there is no clue as to how it arrived. Mrs. Drover is horrified at the realization that it appears to be from her ex-fiancé, whom she believes to have died in World War I. Referring to a vow that the engaged couple had made to each other, he now promises to return, most likely on that day, at the "hour arranged." A haunted Mrs. Drover seeks a place of safety and escapes into a taxi, only to discover that its driver is her ex-fiancé.

Note-taking Guide

Use this chart to describe the events in "The Demon Lover."

Characters:	
Setting:	
Problem:	
Event 1:	
Event 2:	
Event 3:	
Event 4:	
Event 5:	
Event 6:	
Conclusion:	

The Demon Lover

1. **Infer:** The appearance of the letter in Mrs. Drover's house is unexpected because the Post Office has been delivering the mail to their country house. Why is she so upset by this letter?

_____

2. **Literary Analysis:** Find examples in the tale of the following characteristics of a **ghost story**: *intrusion of the past* and *the suggestion of supernatural explanations for events.*

_____

_____

3. **Reading Strategy:** What was your **response** to the atmosphere at the beginning of the story? Explain.

_____

_____

4. **Reading Strategy:** Use the chart below to analyze your responses to an event in the story and the devices Bowen uses to elicit them. An example has been provided.

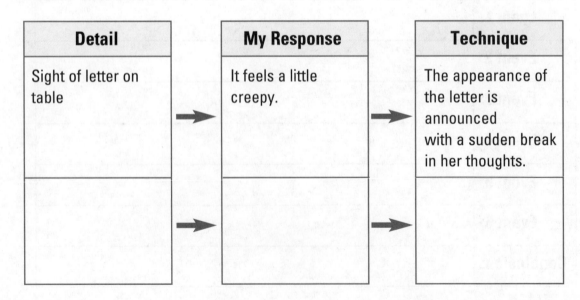

Detail	My Response	Technique
Sight of letter on table	It feels a little creepy.	The appearance of the letter is announced with a sudden break in her thoughts.

The Soldier • Wirers • Anthem for Doomed Youth • Birds on the Western Front

LITERARY ANALYSIS

The **tone** of a literary work is the writer's attitude toward the readers and toward the subject. The words and details the writer uses set the tone of a work. For example, in these lines from Rupert Brooke's "The Soldier," the underlined words set a tone of happy memories and loyalty toward England.

> Her sights and sounds; <u>dreams happy as her day</u>:
>   And <u>laughter</u>, learnt of <u>friends</u>; and <u>gentleness</u>,
>   In <u>hearts at peace</u>, under an <u>English heaven</u>.

Think about how phrases and details in these poems set different tones.

READING STRATEGY

Making Inferences

Writers often suggest, rather than state, elements like tone, theme, and speaker. Therefore, readers must **make inferences**, or educated guesses, about these elements based on clues in the text. Use the chart shown to make inferences about tone and other elements in these works.

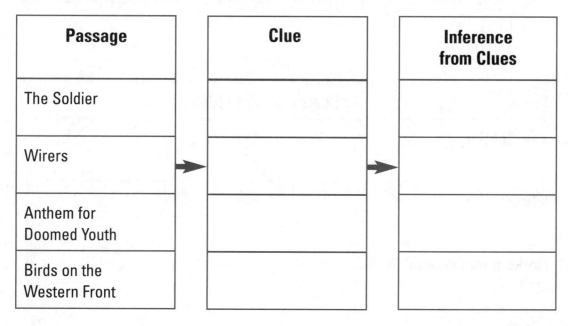

Passage	Clue	Inference from Clues
The Soldier		
Wirers		
Anthem for Doomed Youth		
Birds on the Western Front		

The Soldier

Rupert Brooke

Wirers

Siegfried Sassoon

Anthem for Doomed Youth

Wilfred Owen

'If ye break faith — we shall not sleep'

BUY VICTORY BONDS

Summaries These poems arose from the battlefields of World War I. The patriotic speaker in **"The Soldier"** imagines that his grave will be a patch of rich English dust in foreign soil. There, his soul will reflect the gentleness of England. **"Wirers"** describes a night among soldiers who repair the barbed wire around the trenches. **"Anthem for Doomed Youth"** describes the shows of emotion that must take the place of funeral rites in times of war.

Note-taking Guide

Each of these poems offers a different point of view on the topic of war. Use this chart to record the central image or idea of each poem.

Poem	Central Image / Idea
The Soldier	
Wirers	
Anthem for Doomed Youth	

Birds on the Western Front

Saki (H. H. Munro)

Summary "Birds on the Western Front" describes the behavior of different birds during the war. The narrator tells how battle has or has not affected birds in the areas of combat. He describes the ways that barn owls cope with the war's impact. He observes that noise and destruction of war do not seem to affect the rooks and other birds. He is surprised at the commitment the birds have to their surroundings. In this selection the birds' behavior stands for the behavior of humans.

Note-taking Guide

Use this chart to record the birds' reactions to war in the selection.

Birds	Reaction
Owls	
Crows and ravens	
Chaffinches	
Rook	
Lark	
Buzzards	

The Soldier • Wirers • Anthem for Doomed Youth • Birds on the Western Front

1. **Evaluate:** Which of the two poems, "Wirers" or "Anthem for a Doomed Youth," does a better job of showing the horrors of war? Explain.

   _____

   _____

2. **Literary Analysis:** Use the chart to briefly describe the **tone** in a key passage from one of these works.

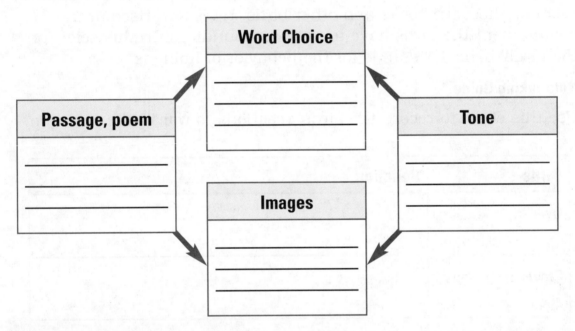

3. **Literary Analysis:** Which of these selections has the most surprising tone or mixture of tones? Explain.

   _____

   _____

4. **Reading Strategy: Make inferences** about the poet's reason for changing funeral rituals in lines 9-14 of "Anthem for Doomed Youth." Explain.

   _____

   _____

Wartime Speech
• Defending Nonviolent Resistance

LITERARY ANALYSIS

A **speech** is a talk on an important subject. The purpose of a speech is the reason it is given. The occasion is what prompts it. The audience is the people who hear it at the time or who hear or read it later.

Both Churchill and Gandhi use **rhetorical devices**, or special patterns of language. These devices make ideas dramatic and stir up feelings. Rhetorical devices include:

• **Repetition**, the repeating of key words and ideas

• **Parallelism**, like ideas expressed in like forms

• **Allusions**, references to well-known people, places, and events

• **Dramatic alternatives**, statements made one after another that differ sharply

Churchill and Gandhi do not use these devices in the same ways. As you read, compare these speakers' use of devices.

READING STRATEGY

The **main points** in a speech are the key ideas that the speaker wishes to get across. The **support** consists of the facts, examples, or reasons that explain these ideas. Use this chart to show main points and support as you read these speeches.

Speech	Main Point	Support
Wartime Speech		**Facts:**
		Examples:
		Reasons:
Defending Nonviolent Resistance		**Facts:**
		Examples:
		Reasons:

Wartime Speech

Winston Churchill

Summary In "Wartime Speech," made during World War II, Churchill describes the German invasion of France. He assures the British people that England and France will work together to defend France. He also calls upon them to make sacrifices to combat the Germans in the greatest struggle of all time.

Note-taking Guide

Use the chart below to record the phrases that Churchill uses to describe England, the Allies, and the enemy.

Phrases describing specific moment in England's history:	
Phrases describing the Allies (British and French troops):	
Phrases describing the enemy (Germany):	

Defending Nonviolent Resistance

Mohandas K. Gandhi

Summary In "Defending Nonviolent Resistance," Gandhi explains his journey from British supporter and public servant to a motivator of Indian protest against the British colonial presence. He talks about his experiences in South Africa, where he was categorized as socially inferior for his Indian race. He also discusses the massacre that happened in Jallianwala Bagh. Gandhi is proud to seek independence for his people, despite the need to break laws he had previously upheld. In this way, Gandhi is able to show his deep love for his country.

Note-taking Guide

Use the chart below to record details from Gandhi's speech.

What does Gandhi ask the judge to do?	
Why is Gandhi against violence?	
What examples of unfair British rule does Gandhi cite?	

Wartime Speech • Defending Nonviolent Resistance

1. **Draw Conclusions:** Think about the tone of Churchill's speech. It sounds urgent and dramatic. Do you think he is confident that the public will support him? Explain.

_____

_____

2. **Draw Conclusions:** Gandhi gives the following reasons for his "disaffection" with British rule: 1. British support for South African racial policies; 2. British action against Indian civilians at Punjab; and 3. British exploitation of Indian workers and resources. Why does Gandhi say it is a privilege to be charged with "promoting disaffection"?

_____

_____

3. **Literary Analysis:** A **speech** is an oral presentation in which a speaker addresses an important issue. Use the chart below to identify the following elements in either Churchill's or Gandhi's speech.

Speaker	Purpose	Audience	Occasion

4. **Reading Strategy:** To identify **main points and support**, find the most important ideas in a work and the examples that strengthen them. Identify two main points in Churchill's speech. List several details he uses to support each point.

_____

_____

Follower • Two Lorries • Outside History

LITERARY ANALYSIS

A writer must make choices about diction and other elements of style:

- **Diction** refers to the words the writer uses. The words may be formal or informal, down to earth or scholarly.
- **Style** takes in the whole of how a writer expresses him or herself. Style includes word choice, use of forms and rhythms, and themes and imagery.

A poem is a work in words. The message of the poem is important. However, the style and diction used by the poet are just as important to what a poem is and how it affects you. As you read, look for the styles that the writers use.

READING STRATEGY

Summarizing a poem means rewriting its key points using fewer words. This can help you think about the poem's central images and ideas. You might summarize a whole poem or just one stanza. Use a chart like the one shown to summarize the poems or stanzas in them.

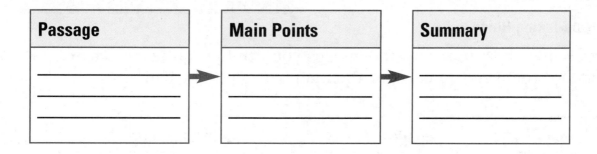

Passage		Main Points		Summary
_____	→	_____	→	_____
_____		_____		_____
_____		_____		_____

Follower • Two Lorries
Seamus Heaney

Outside History
Eavan Boland

Summaries In "**Follower**," the speaker recalls stumbling and tripping behind his father as he plowed the fields. Now, he says, his father stumbles behind him. In "**Two Lorries**," the speaker remembers two trucks. One truck was driven by a coal man who flirted with his mother. The other truck carried explosive that blew up the bus station. In "**Outside History**," the speaker says she will not be like the stars which are outside history. She will be a part of her country's own history, even though she is too late to help those who have already died.

Note-taking Guide

Use this chart to record the images you see in each poem. Then, record the central image, or the main concept, of each.

Poem	Images	Central Image
Follower		
Two Lorries		
Outside History		

Follower • Two Lorries • Outside History

1. **Interpret:** In "Follower," why does the boy want "To close one eye" and "stiffen my arm"?

   _____

   _____

2. **Recall:** What two incidents are described in "Two Lorries"?

   _____

   _____

3. **Literary Analysis:** Which words in "Follower" support the idea that Heaney's **diction** is homespun, or simple and ordinary?

   _____

4. **Literary Analysis:** Complete this chart to analyze Boland's **style** in "Outside History." Then, summarize the distinctive elements of her style.

	Diction	Imagery	Rhythm/ Rhyme	Form
Examples				
Conclusion				

5. **Reading Strategy:** Write a **summary** of "Two Lorries," including a comparison of the two incidents the poet recalls.

   _____

   _____

No Witchcraft for Sale

LITERARY ANALYSIS

British colonialism was the rule of other countries, called colonies, by Britain. Many stories of the mid-twentieth century show the disagreements between the native people and the British. These types of disagreements are called **cultural conflicts**.

Every conflict has at least two sides, so the **point of view** from which a struggle is reported is important.

- **First person point of view:** The narrator is a character in the story. The narrator refers to himself or herself as "I."

- **Limited third-person point of view:** The narrator is not part of the story but tells how things are experienced by one character.

- **Omniscient third-person point of view:** The narrator is not part of the story and tells the reader more information than any one character could know.

READING STRATEGY

To understand a story that has cultural conflicts, **analyze cultural differences**. That is, study the differences in beliefs and values that cause the problems in a story. Use this diagram to analyze cultural conflicts in the story, As you read, write the qualities, beliefs, and values that go with the Farquars in the left column and with Gideon in the right column. Write any qualities, beliefs, and values that they share in the center space.

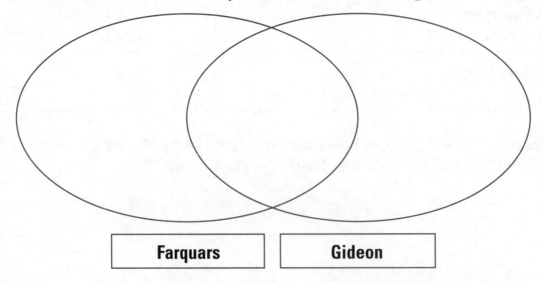

| Farquars | Gideon |

No Witchcraft for Sale

Doris Lessing

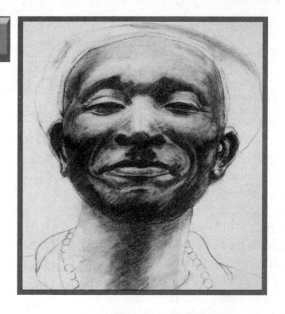

Summary The Farquars are a white couple who own a farm in southern Africa. They have a young son named Teddy. An African man named Gideon works for the family as a cook. Gideon is very fond of Teddy. One day, a snake spits poison into Teddy's eyes. Gideon saves Teddy's sight with medicine from the root of a plant. The Farquars are grateful to Gideon and reward him with gifts and a raise in pay. A scientist calls on the Farquars to find out what plant Gideon used in his cure. The Farquars never expect that Gideon will refuse to share this information.

Note-taking Guide

Use this chart to record key events from the story. Write at least one detail about each event.

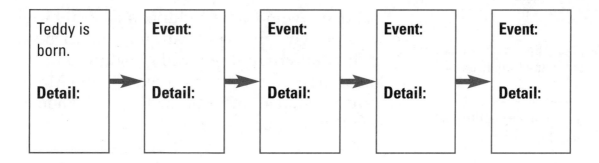

| Teddy is born. Detail: | → | Event: Detail: | → | Event: Detail: | → | Event: Detail: | → | Event: Detail: |

No Witchcraft for Sale
Doris Lessing

The Farquars, a white couple in southern Africa, who had been childless for years, finally have their first child. Their servants bring gifts, and they love the baby's blonde hair and blue eyes.

♦ ♦ ♦

They congratulated Mrs. Farquar as if she had achieved a very great thing, and she felt that she had—her smile for the lingering, admiring natives was warm and grateful.

♦ ♦ ♦

Gideon, the Farquars' cook, affectionately nicknames Teddy "Little Yellow Head." Gideon plays with the little boy and helps him learn how to walk. Mrs. Farquar recognizes Gideon's love for her son and rewards him with a raise in pay. Gideon and Mrs. Farquar notice what happens when a native child and Teddy meet. The children curiously stare at one another's skin, eye, and hair color.

♦ ♦ ♦

Gideon, who was watching, shook his head wonderingly, and said: "Ah, missus, these are both children, and one will grow up to be a baas,[1] and one will be a servant"; and Mrs. Farquar smiled and said sadly, "Yes, Gideon, I was thinking the same."

♦ ♦ ♦

Gideon knows that this is God's will. Gideon and the Farquars share the common bond of being very religious.

♦ ♦ ♦

---

1. **baas** (BAHS) *n.* boss.

Teddy was about six years old when he was given a scooter, and discovered the <u>intoxications</u> of speed.

◆　◆　◆

Teddy races around the farm and into the kitchen. He scares the farm animals and family pets. Gideon laughs as he watches this activity.

◆　◆　◆

Gideon's youngest son, who was now a herdsboy, came especially up from the compound to see the scooter. He was afraid to come near it, but Teddy showed off in front of him. "Piccanin,"[2] shouted Teddy, "get out of my way!" And he raced in circles around the black child until he was frightened, and fled back to the bush.

◆　◆　◆

Gideon blames Teddy for frightening his son. Teddy rudely replies that Gideon's son is only a black boy.

Gideon's feelings toward Teddy change. He realizes that Teddy will soon grow up and go away to school. Gideon treats Teddy kindly but acts much less friendly. Teddy, in turn, begins to treat Gideon more like a servant.

◆　◆　◆

But on the day that Teddy came staggering into the kitchen with his fists to his eyes, shrieking with pain, Gideon dropped the pot full of hot soup that he was holding, rushed to

TAKE NOTES

Stop to Reflect

Teddy and Gideon's son are the same age. But their futures will be very different. What is the difference?

_____

_____

_____

Reading Check

How does Teddy get hurt?

_____

_____

_____

Vocabulary Development

intoxications (in TAHKS i KAY shunz) *n.* great excitement

---

2. **piccanin** (PIK uh nin) *n.* an offensive term for a native child.

the child, and forced aside his fingers. "A snake!" he exclaimed.

◆ ◆ ◆

As Teddy rested on his scooter, a tree-snake spat right into his eyes. Mrs. Farquar sees that Teddy's eyes are already swollen. She is terrified that Teddy will go blind.

◆ ◆ ◆

Mrs. Farquar and Gideon react differently to Teddy's injury. Underline two words, phrases, or sentences in the bracketed passages that reveal their **cultural differences**.

Gideon said: "Wait a minute, missus, I'll get some medicine." He ran off into the bush.

Mrs. Farquar lifted the child into the house and bathed his eyes with permanganate.[3] She had scarcely heard Gideon's words; but when she saw that her <u>remedies</u> had no effect at all, and remembered how she had seen natives with no sight in their eyes, because of the spitting of a snake, she began to look for the return of her cook, remembering what she heard of the <u>efficacy</u> of native herbs.

◆ ◆ ◆

What does Mrs. Farquar remember about natives she's seen that really frightens her?

_____

_____

_____

Terrified, she holds her son and waits for Gideon to return. He soon appears with a plant. He shows her the root and assures her that it will provide a cure for Teddy's eyes.

◆ ◆ ◆

Without even washing it, he put the root in his mouth, chewed it <u>vigorously</u>, and then held the spittle there while he took the child forcibly

---

Vocabulary Development

remedies (REM i deez) *n.* medicines or therapies that take away pain or cure diseases

efficacy (EF i kuh see) *n.* power to produce intended effects

vigorously (VIG uhr uhs lee) *adv.* forcefully; energetically

---

3. **permanganate** (per MANG guh nayt) *n.* salt of permanganic acid used as a remedy for snake poison.

from Mrs. Farquar. He gripped Teddy down between his knees, and pressed the balls of his thumbs into the swollen eyes, so that the child screamed and Mrs. Farquar cried out in protest: "Gideon, Gideon!"

♦   ♦   ♦

Gideon ignores her and opens Teddy's eyes to spit into them. When Gideon is finished, he promises Mrs. Farquar that Teddy will be fine. But she finds this hard to believe.

♦   ♦   ♦

In a couple of hours the swellings were gone: the eyes were <u>inflamed</u> and tender but Teddy could see. Mr. and Mrs. Farquar went to Gideon in the kitchen and thanked him over and over again.

♦   ♦   ♦

They do not know how to express their gratitude. They give Gideon gifts and a raise, but nothing can really pay for Teddy's cured eyes.

♦   ♦   ♦

Mrs. Farquar said: "Gideon, God chose you as an instrument for His goodness," and Gideon said: "Yes, missus, God is very good."

♦   ♦   ♦

The story of how Gideon saved Teddy's eyesight spreads throughout the area. The whites are frustrated because they do not know what plant Gideon used. The natives will not tell them. A doctor in town hears the story but does not really believe it.

One day, a scientist from the nearby laboratory arrives. He brings a lot of equipment.

♦   ♦   ♦

Vocabulary Development

inflamed (in FLAYMD) *adj.* reddened

TAKE NOTES

Literary Analysis

What is the cause of the **cultural conflict** in this passage? Circle the letter of the correct answer.

(a) Teddy's feelings of superiority

(b) Gideon's knowledge of native medicine

(c) Mrs. Farquar's religious beliefs

Reading Check

(1) What is the result of Gideon's medicine?

_____

_____

(2) What do the Farquars do to reward Gideon?

_____

_____

_____

_____

Read Fluently

Read the bracketed paragraphs aloud. What three words or phrases suggest the Farquars' mixed feelings about the scientist's visit?

1. _____
2. _____
3. _____

Vocabulary and Pronunciation

In English, most words beginning with *dis* mean *not* something. For example, the word *discomfort* in this paragraph means *lack of comfort*. What does the word *distasteful* mean?

_____
_____
_____

Reading Check

How does Gideon respond when he hears the reason for the scientist's visit?

_____
_____
_____
_____

Mr. and Mrs. Farquar were flustered and pleased and flattered. They asked the scientist to lunch, and they told the story all over again, for the hundredth time. Little Teddy was there too, his blue eyes sparkling with health, to prove the truth of it.

◆ ◆ ◆

The scientist explains that people everywhere would benefit if the drug that helped Teddy could be available to them. The Farquars are pleased at the idea of being able to help.

◆ ◆ ◆

But when the scientist began talking of the money that might result, their manner showed discomfort.

◆ ◆ ◆

They do not want to think of money in connection with the miracle that has happened. The scientist realizes how they feel and reminds them that they can help others.

After eating their meal, the Farquars tell Gideon why the scientist came to visit. Gideon seems surprised and angry. Mr. Farquar tells Gideon that thousands of people could be cured by the medicine he used to save Teddy. Gideon listens but stubbornly refuses to reveal what root he used. The Farquars realize Gideon will not tell them what they want to know. To Gideon, the Africans' traditional knowledge of plant medicine, which is passed on from generation to generation, represents power and wisdom. Suddenly, however, Gideon agrees to show the root to the Farquars and the scientist. On an extremely hot afternoon, the group silently walks for two hours. Gideon appears to search for the root.

◆ ◆ ◆

At last, six miles from the house, Gideon suddenly decided they had had enough; or perhaps his anger <u>evaporated</u> at that moment.

♦ ♦ ♦

Gideon finally picks up flowers just like the ones they have seen all along their journey. He hands them to the scientist and leaves the group to go home.

When the scientist stops in the kitchen to thank Gideon, he is gone. He's back to prepare dinner, but it is days before he and the Farquars are friends again.

♦ ♦ ♦

The Farquars made inquiries about the root from their laborers. Sometimes they were answered with distrustful stares. Sometimes the natives said: "We do not know. We have never heard of the root."

♦ ♦ ♦

A cattle boy who has worked for the family for a long time tells them to ask Gideon. He says that Gideon is the son of a famous medicine man and can cure anything, although he is not as good as a white doctor.

♦ ♦ ♦

After some time, when the soreness had gone from between the Farquars and Gideon, they began to joke: "When are you going to show us the snake-root, Gideon?" And he would laugh

---

Vocabulary Development

evaporated (ee VAP uh ray tid) *v.* disappeared

TAKE NOTES

Literary Analysis

Is the **cultural conflict** resolved? Why or why not?

_____

_____

_____

English Language Development

You have probably used the words *double* and *up* separately many times. When the two words are used together, however, they form a single verb that has a special meaning. The verb *double up* means "to bend suddenly, as in pain or laughter." Write a sentence about Teddy in which you use the verb *double up*.

_____

_____

_____

Stop to Reflect

What do you think Gideon's last words to Teddy mean?

_____

_____

_____

and shake his head, saying, a little uncomfortably: "But I did show you, missus, have you forgotten?"

◆   ◆   ◆

Later, Teddy even teases Gideon about tricking everyone about the cure for the snake bite.

◆   ◆   ◆

And Gideon would <u>double</u> up with polite laughter. After much laughing, he would suddenly straighten himself up, wipe his old eyes, and look sadly at Teddy, who was grinning <u>mischievously</u> at him across the kitchen: "Ah, Little Yellow Head, how you have grown! Soon you will be grown up with a farm of your own. . . ."

Vocabulary Development

mischievously (MIS chuh vuhs lee) *adv.* playfully

No Witchcraft for Sale

1. **Infer:** Gideon saves Teddy's sight with a special plant. What does this event show about Gideon?

_____

_____

2. **Literary Analysis:** Use the chart below to examine how three events in the story show a **cultural conflict**. Write down the event in the middle column. Write down how the Farquars and Gideon feel about the event in the other columns.

Statement	Question
Man will never conquer space.	*Never* is a strong word. Is this statement well supported?

3. **Literary Analysis:** This story is told from the limited third person **point of view**. This means that the narrator tells the thoughts and feelings of only one character. What kinds of things might you learn if Gideon were the narrator instead?

_____

_____

4. **Reading Strategy:** This story is full of **cultural differences** between characters. Find two events that show Teddy feels more important than the black Africans on the farm. Explain your choices.

_____

_____

The Lagoon • Araby

LITERARY ANALYSIS

A **plot device** is a particular technique used to build a story. Writers often use plot devices to achieve a special effect. One kind of plot device developed by James Joyce is an epiphany.

- An **epiphany** is a character's sudden insight.
- It reveals an important truth.
- It occurs during an ordinary event or situation.
- It forms the climax, or high point of interest, of the story.

READING STRATEGY

When you read a story, use your imagination to help you picture the action and situation. This strategy may help you understand the characters, the setting, or the events in a story.

1. Briefly stop when you come to a difficult passage.
2. Try to picture the scene in your mind.
   - What is happening? Where is it happening?
   - How do the characters react to these events?
3. Use the chart to put what you "see" into words.

Story	Passage	Action and Situation	Character's Inner Responses
The Lagoon	A breath of warm air touched the two men's faces and passed on with a mournful sound	Arsat pauses in his story. In the silence, a wind passes	Both characters may be uneasy—Arsat because of his memories and the narrator because of Arsat's distress.
Araby			

The Lagoon

Joseph Conrad

Summary In this story, a white man visits Arsat, a Malay who lives by a jungle lagoon. Arsat's wife is dying, and the visitor learns her history. She and Arsat had run away from a Malaysian ruler with the help of Arsat's brother. They were pursued, and Arsat abandoned his bother to save the woman. While Arsat tells the story, his wife dies, and Arsat decides to return to face his former pursuers.

Note-taking Guide

Use this chart to record the action of the story Arsat tells his friend.

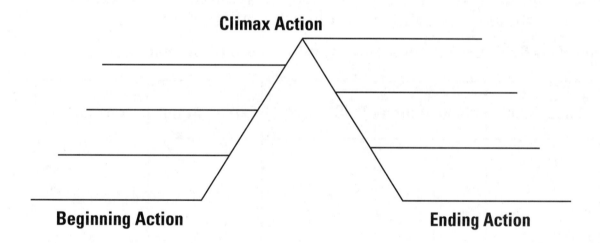

Climax Action

Beginning Action

Ending Action

Araby

James Joyce

Summary The narrator tells about an experience he had as a boy growing up in Dublin, Ireland, in the late nineteenth century. He had a crush on another boy's sister. The first time she spoke to him, she asked whether he was going to a fair called Araby. She herself could not go. However, he offered to bring her something from Araby. He asked his uncle—he lived with his uncle and aunt—for the money to go to the fair. The night of the fair, his uncle came home late, and it was after nine when he gave the narrator the money. By the time the narrator arrived at the fair, it was nearly over. The big hall in which the fair was being held was already dark. At one stall, a young woman with an English accent was talking and laughing with two young men. The narrator refused her offer to serve him. He suddenly realized that he had been foolish about everything, and he felt both grief and anger.

Note-taking Guide Use the chart to examine the plot of Araby.

Exposition	Rising Action	Climax	Falling Action	Resolution

Araby
James Joyce

The narrator, or storyteller, lives on a quiet, dead-end street. He enjoys playing on the street with his friends. They explore the dark alleys, gardens, and stables behind the houses. In the winter, the boys stay out until dark. From the shadows they watch the narrator's uncle come home. They also watch the sister of a boy whose last name is Mangan. The narrator has a serious crush on Mangan's sister. Every morning he watches her door until she comes out. Then he follows her when she goes to school. He even thinks about her when he helps his aunt with her shopping in the busy, dirty markets in Dublin. Although the narrator has strong feelings for Mangan's sister, he has never said a single word to her.

◆　◆　◆

At last she spoke to me. When she <u>addressed</u> the first words to me I was so confused that I did not know what to answer. She asked me was I going to *Araby*. I forget whether I answered yes or no. It would be a splendid bazaar,[1] she said; she would love to go.

"And why can't you?" I asked.

While she spoke she turned a silver bracelet round and round her wrist. She could not go, she said, because there would be a retreat[2]

Vocabulary Development

addressed (uh DREST) *v.* directed to

---

1. **bazaar** (buh ZAHR) *n.* a market or fair where various goods are sold in stalls.
2. **retreat** (ri TREET) *n.* period of retirement or seclusion for prayer, religious study, and meditation.

Background

This story takes place in Dublin, Ireland, in the early 1900s. The main character is a boy who lives on North Richmond Street and goes to a bazaar. Like the narrator in "Araby," James Joyce, the story's author, once lived with his family on North Richmond Street. When Joyce was twelve years old, he went to the Araby bazaar held in Dublin in May 1894. Look at a library book, a social studies textbook, or the Internet to find a map of Dublin. Use the map to answer the following questions:

• What river flows through the city?

_____

• What is the name of one park in Dublin?

_____

• In what part of Dublin does the narrator live with his aunt and uncle?

_____

Reading Strategy

Circle words and phrases in the bracketed paragraph here and on page 177 that help you form a mental **picture** of the scene.

Read Fluently

Read the first bracketed paragraph out loud. Before you read, skim through the paragraph to look for words you do not know. Make sure you know what they mean and how to pronounce them, so that you can read smoothly.

Reading Check

Why does the narrator have to wait to go to the bazaar?

_____

_____

_____

Reading Strategy

In this paragraph, the narrator hears his uncle coming in. Circle the details that tell him what his uncle is doing.

that week in her convent.[3] Her brother and two other boys were fighting for their caps and I was alone at the railings. She held one of the spikes, bowing her head towards me. The light from the lamp opposite our door caught the white curve of her neck, lit up her hair that rested there and, falling, lit up the hand upon the railing. It fell over one side of her dress and caught the white border of a petticoat,[4] just visible as she stood at ease.

◆　◆　◆

Mangan's sister is happy for the narrator. He promises to bring her something from the bazaar.

The narrator cannot stop thinking about Mangan's sister. He is excited about going to the bazaar. He has trouble doing his schoolwork, and he daydreams in class. On Saturday morning the narrator reminds his uncle that he wants to go to the bazaar that night. His uncle leaves for the day. While the narrator eagerly waits for his uncle to return and give him money, he stares at the clock. He stands at the window for an hour and watches his friends play outside. He pictures Mangan's sister in his mind.

◆　◆　◆

At nine o'clock I heard my uncle's latchkey in the hall door. I heard him talking to himself and heard the hallstand rocking when it had received the weight of his overcoat. I could interpret these signs. When he was midway through his dinner I asked him to give me the money to go to the bazaar. He had forgotten.

"The people are in bed and after their first sleep now," he said.

---

3. **convent** (KAHN vent) *n.* school run by an order of nuns.
4. **petticoat** (PET ee koht) *n.* a woman's slip that is sometimes full and trimmed with lace or ruffles.

I did not smile. My aunt said to him energetically:

"Can't you give him the money and let him go? You've kept him late enough as it is."

My uncle said he was very sorry he had forgotten. He said he believed in the old saying: *All work and no play makes Jack a dull boy.* He asked me where I was going and, when I had told him a second time he asked me did I know *The Arab's Farewell to His Steed.*[5] When I left the kitchen he was about to recite the opening lines of the piece to my aunt.

◆　◆　◆

The narrator leaves the house with money his uncle gives him. He rides an empty train to the bazaar. The train arrives just before ten o'clock. The narrator pays the fee and enters a large, dark hall. Because it is late, most of the stalls are closed. The bazaar is as quiet as a church.

◆　◆　◆

Remembering with difficulty why I had come I went over to one of the stalls and examined porcelain[6] vases and flowered tea sets. At the door of the stall a young lady was talking and laughing with two young gentlemen. I remarked their English accents and listened vaguely to their conversation.

"O, I never said such a thing!"

"O, but you did!"

"O, but I didn't!"

"Didn't she say that?"

"Yes. I heard her."

"O, there's a . . . fib!"

Vocabulary Development

remarked (ri MARKT) *v.* noticed

---

5. **The Arab's . . . His Steed** *n.* popular nineteenth-century poem.
6. **porcelain** (POR suh lin) *n.* a hard, white type of clay pottery also known as china.

TAKE NOTES

Read Fluently

Read the bracketed paragraph aloud. Write three words you would use to describe the narrator's uncle.

1. _____

2. _____

3. _____

Vocabulary and Pronunciation

The word *stall* has several different meanings. For example, it can mean "a sudden loss of power in an engine," "a booth at a market," or "a action for an animal in a barn." Which meaning of *stall* does Joyce use here?

_____

_____

Why doesn't the young lady spend more time helping the narrator at her stall?

Is the narrator's trip to Araby a success? Why or why not?

_____

_____

_____

The bracketed passage is the narrator's **epiphany**. Tell in your own words what the narrator realizes about himself in the **epiphany**.

_____

_____

_____

In English, many adverbs are formed by adding -*ly* to an adjective. For example, the word *slowly* is an adverb. It is formed by adding -*ly* to the adjective *slow*. What is another adverb that appears in the bracketed paragraph?

◆ ◆ ◆

The young lady offers to help the narrator. He answers that he doesn't need help, and she doesn't encourage him. She watches him as she returns to the conversation with the two young gentlemen.

The narrator lingers and pretends to be interested in the items in the stall. Then, he leaves, jingling the coins in his pocket.

◆ ◆ ◆

I heard a voice call from one end of the gallery that the light was out. The upper part of the hall was now completely dark.

Gazing up into the darkness I saw myself as a creature driven and <u>derided</u> by <u>vanity</u>; and my eyes burned with anguish and anger.

Vocabulary Development

derided (dee RYD id) *v.* made fun of

vanity (VAN uh tee) *n.* excessive pride

The Lagoon • Araby

1. **Interpret:** Following Diamelen's death in "The Lagoon," Arsat says, "I can see nothing," and the white man replies, "There is nothing." What does each statement mean?

_____

_____

2. **Literary Analysis:** In "The Lagoon," Conrad uses the **plot device** of a **story within a story.** What information would you lack if all of "The Lagoon" had been narrated in the first person by Arsat?

_____

_____

3. **Literary Analysis:** Write a paragraph describing the narrator's feelings when he experiences his epiphany in "Araby."

_____

_____

_____

4. **Reading Strategy:** Write a paragraph describing a scene in "The Lagoon." Use the following chart to help you.

Exposition	Rising Action	Climax	Falling Action	Resolution

The Lady in the Looking Glass: A Reflection • The First Year of My Life

LITERARY ANALYSIS

Writers often experiment with **point of view**, the perspective from which a story is told. These experiments help them to capture the pace of modern life.

- **Stream-of-consciousness** narration follows the flowing, branching thoughts inside a character's mind.
- An **omniscient** narrator has more information than any single character could have.

Woolf uses the stream-of-consciousness technique in "The Lady in the Looking Glass." Spark's omniscient narrator in "My First Year" is herself—as a baby who knows "everything." As you read, think about how these experiments affect the way you see events in the stories.

READING STRATEGY

Experimental works offer great rewards but also place great demands on readers. Find your way in the story by continually **asking questions** as you read. Use the chart below to help you.

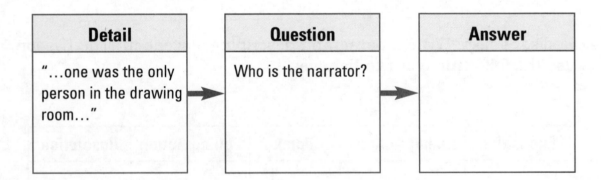

Detail	Question	Answer
"...one was the only person in the drawing room..."	Who is the narrator?	

The Lady in the Looking Glass: A Reflection

Virginia Woolf

Summary Isabella Tyson is a wealthy woman who lives alone. The narrator looks at the objects in Isabella's home and at Isabella's reflection in a mirror. The descriptions of her home and of her reflection show that she is happy and successful. While she picks flowers from her garden, a mailman delivers letters. Isabella returns from the garden and looks at herself in the mirror. At that moment, we see Isabella's true nature.

Note-taking Guide

Use this chart to record information from the story about how the narrator describes Isabella.

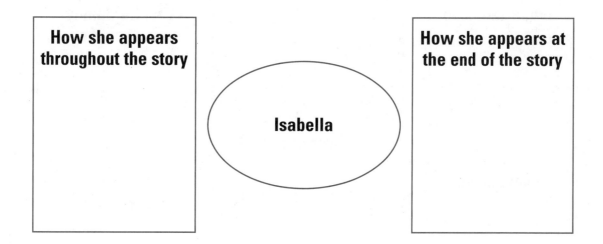

How she appears throughout the story

Isabella

How she appears at the end of the story

The First Year of My Life

Muriel Spark

Summary The narrator of "The First Year of My Life" is a child. She narrates the events that took place in 1918, the year she was born. The world is involved in World War I. As a baby, she has the power to hear and see things that are going on around the world. All the while, her family notices that she does not smile. On her first birthday, she finally hears something that makes her smile.

Note-taking Guide

Use this chart to list information about the narrator in the story.

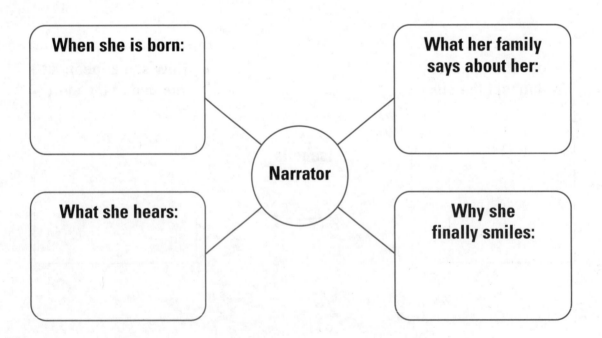

The Lady in the Looking Glass: A Reflection
• The First Year of My Life

1. **Interpret:** In "The Lady in the Looking Glass: A Reflection," Isabella is seen through a looking glass, or mirror. How does the looking glass "guide" the narrator to an understanding of Isabella?

_____

_____

_____

2. **Literary Analysis:** **Stream-of-consciousness** narration presents the flow of thoughts in a character's mind. Give three examples of the use of **stream-of-consciousness** in Woolf's story.

_____

_____

_____

3. **Literary Analysis:** Use the chart below to compare Spark's narrative techniques to Woolf's.

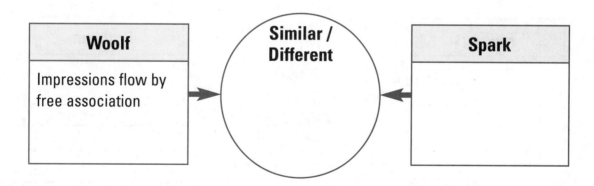

4. **Reading Strategy:** In Woolf's story, what **questions** did you ask about the narrator while reading?

_____

_____

The Rocking-Horse Winner
• A Shocking Accident

LITERARY ANALYSIS

Most short stories have a **theme**. A theme is a central idea or question that the writer explores. Writers often show the theme through a **symbol**. This is a person, thing, or action that brings to mind a deeper meaning. Look for symbols as you read.

Each of these stories is told from a **third-person point of view**. This means that the narrator does not take part in the action. As you read, compare the ways in which both authors use this point of view to show their themes. Note that each author tells what the characters are thinking and uses symbols to suggest meanings. Ask yourself how the third-person point of view is different in each story.

READING STRATEGY

Identifying with a character means putting yourself in a character's place. This helps you understand the character's feelings, needs, problems, and goals. It can also help you understand the theme of a work. Choose one of the main characters from the stories, and complete this chart to help you identify with that character.

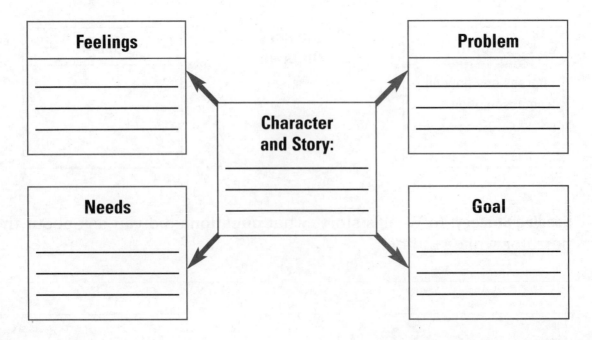

Feelings

Problem

Character and Story:

Needs

Goal

The Rocking-Horse Winner

D. H. Lawrence

Summary: This story explores the cost of greed. An unhappy, greedy woman feels little for her children and complains about a lack of money. She tells her son, Paul, that luck is the only thing that brings money. Paul wants to make his mother happy, so he tries to become lucky. He discovers that when he sits on his rocking horse, he suddenly knows which horses will win at the races. He wins a small fortune by betting. He secretly gives money to his mother, but she is not satisfied. Paul drives himself nearly crazy trying to please her.

Note-taking Guide

Use this chart to record the main events in the story.

The mother wants more money.	She tells Paul that luck brings money.	

A Shocking Accident

Graham Greene

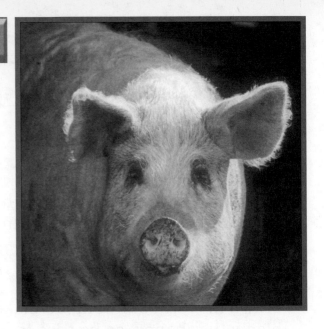

Summary: In this story, Jerome learns that his beloved father has been killed in a freak accident. A pig fell on him from a balcony as the man walked down the street. It is difficult for Jerome to share this story because he hates to see people try not to laugh. He worries about telling his fiancée the story. He fears that if he sees her trying not to laugh, he will not be able to marry her.

Note-taking Guide

Fill in the chart to help you better understand Jerome's Character.

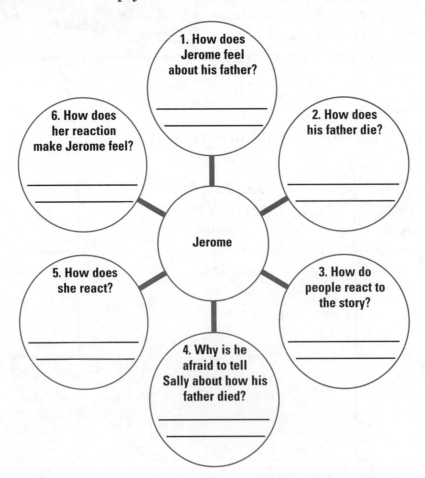

1. How does Jerome feel about his father?

2. How does his father die?

6. How does her reaction make Jerome feel?

Jerome

3. How do people react to the story?

5. How does she react?

4. Why is he afraid to tell Sally about how his father died?

The Rocking-Horse Winner
• A Shocking Accident

1. **Draw Conclusions:** Do Jerome's uncomfortable feelings about his father's death go away at the end of "A Shocking Accident"? Why or why not?

_____

_____

2. **Literary Analysis:** Complete the chart below by noting passages that show the **symbolic** meanings of the rocking horse. Explain how these meanings connect to the overall **theme** of the story.

Symbolic Meanings	Passages That Illustrate	Links to Overall Theme
Effort to satisfy a need that cannot be satisfied Frightening power of desire and wishes		

3. **Literary Analysis:** How is the use of the **third-person point of view** similar in both "The Rocking-Horse Winner" and "A Shocking Accident"?

_____

_____

4. **Reading Strategy: Identify with the character** Paul in "A Rocking-Horse Winner." What is his most important goal?

_____

_____

_____

Do Not Go Gentle into That Good Night • Fern Hill • The Horses • The Rain Horse

LITERARY ANALYSIS

The **voice** of a poet is his or her "sound" on the page. A poet's voice is based on word choice, sound devices, pacing, attitude, and even patterns within words. Dylan Thomas and Ted Hughes have different voices. Thomas's words tumble out in a rush and Hughes "speaks" in little blips of images:

- *Thomas*, in "Fern Hill": "All the sun long it was running, it was lovely . . ."
- *Hughes, in "The Horse"*: "Not a leaf, not a bird."

Listen for the different voices of these poets as you read their poems.

Because they have different "voices," these two poets use different poetic forms and rhythms. To go along with his tight, closed way of speaking, Hughes uses loose, non-rhyming lines and free verse. In contrast, Thomas uses regular poetic forms like the **villanelle**—a nineteen-line poem in which lines 1 and 3 of the first stanza appear regularly throughout and the rhyme scheme is *aba aba aba aba aba abaa*. In reading these poets, consider how their voices match the forms and rhythms they use.

READING STRATEGY

When **judging a writer's message**, test what a writer says against your own experience and past reading. Choose one of the poems. In the chart below, write what you think the poet's message is, what your past experience has shown, and your own evaluation of the poet's message.

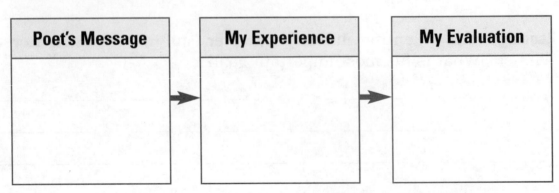

Poet's Message	My Experience	My Evaluation

Do Not Go Gentle into That Good Night • Fern Hill

Dylan Thomas

The Horses • The Rain Horse

Ted Hughes

Summaries These three poems and a story provide different views of nature. In "**Do Not Go Gentle into That Good Night**," the speaker advises readers to resist death with all of their strength, not to yield quietly to it. In "**Fern Hill**," the speaker recalls his childhood on a farm, when he was innocent of the knowledge that he was growing older. "**The Horses**" describes an early morning encounter with a herd of wild horses. "**The Rain Horse**" tells the story of a young man who is revisiting a childhood place when he seems to be attacked by a wild horse in the rain.

Note-taking Guide

Use this chart to record the writer's message in each work.

Poem	Main Idea / Writer's Message
"Do Not Go Gentle"	
"Fern Hill"	
"The Horses"	
"The Rain Horse"	

Do Not Go Gentle into That Good Night • Fern Hill • The Horses • The Rain Horse

1. **Literary Analysis:** A writer's **voice** is his or her "sound" on the page. It includes word choice, sound devices, phrasing, pace, and attitude. Fill in this chart to look at aspects of Thomas's **voice**.

Quality	Examples
Words tumble out in a rush	
Shows an attitude of wonder about life	
Uses complex poetic forms	

2. **Literary Analysis:** Explain how "Do Not Go Gentle into That Good Night" is a **villanelle**. What is the effect of repeated lines in this poem?

_____

_____

3. **Reading Strategy:** To **judge a writer's message**, decide whether what a writer says matches your own ideas and experiences. In "Fern Hill," Thomas suggests that children do not have worries or an awareness of death. Do you think this is true? Explain.

_____

_____

4. **Reading Strategy:** In "The Horses" and " The Rain Horse," Hughes seems to be saying that people who live in cities are cut off from nature. Do you think this is true? Explain.

_____

_____

An Arundel Tomb • The Explosion
• On the Patio • Not Waving but Drowning

LITERARY ANALYSIS

Free verse is poetry without regular end rhymes and regular rhythm, or **meter**. The rhythm of a free verse poem suits the poem's meaning. Redgrove's poem "On the Patio" is an example.

In contrast, Larkin uses regular meters. These meters are named for the stresses in each group of syllables, or foot, and for the number of feet per line. An **iamb** is a foot made up of one unstressed and one stressed syllable (˘´). A **trochee** is a foot with a stressed and an unstressed syllable (´˘). The word **tetrameter** describes a verse with four feet per line.

"An Arundel Tomb" is written mostly in **iambic tetrameter**. "The Explosion" uses **trochaic tetrameter**, with some lines of iambic tetrameter.

READING STRATEGY

To understand the meaning of a poem, **read in sentences.** Do not automatically stop at the ends of lines. Although poems are written in sentences, each sentenc˘e does not always coincide with the end of a poetic line. To read in sentences, notice the punctuation. Do not pause or make a full stop at the end of a line unless there is a period, comma, colon, semicolon, or dash. Use the following chart to record sentences from the poems.

Poem	Sentence	Meaning

An Arundel Tomb
• The Explosion
Philip Larkin

On the Patio
Peter Redgrove

Not Waving but Drowning
Stevie Smith

Summaries: The two poems by Philip Larkin describe the effects of death on those who are still living. **"An Arundel Tomb"** describes the statues of an earl and a countess on their ancient tomb. **"The Explosion"** recounts the events on the day of an explosion in a coal mine. **"On the Patio"** uses the image of the poet draining a glass and allowing the thunderstorm to refill it as a symbol of a person willing to be open to nature. **"Not Waving but Drowning"** uses the water that drowned a man as a symbol of the coldness and isolation that he felt his whole life and finally led to his death.

Note-Taking Guide Use this chart to compare and contrast the poems.

Poem	Important Symbols and Their Meanings	Theme
"An Arundel Tomb"		
"The Explosion"		
"On the Patio"		
"Not Waving but Drowning"		

An Arundel Tomb • The Explosion • On the Patio • Not Waving but Drowning

1. **Iterpret:** In the final image of "The Explosion," one of the dead miners shows the unbroken eggs to his wife. What does this image mean?

   _____

   _____

2. **Connect:** How do the images in "On the Patio" link what occurs in the sky with what occurs below the earth?

   _____

   _____

3. **Draw Conclusions:** In the poem "Not Waving but Drowning," what might the "dead man" mean when he moans, "I was much too far out all my life"?

   _____

4. **Literary Analysis:** Use this chart to analyze Larkin's use of **iambic** and **trochaic tetrameter** in his two poems. Note the pattern of stresses in each line, using (´) to indicate stressed syllables and (˘) to indicate unstressed ones.

"An Arundel Tomb"	"The Explosion"
Their proper habits vaguely shown	It was said, and for a second
As jointed armor, stiffened pleat . . .	Wives saw men of the explosion . . .

5. **Reading Strategy:** When you **read in sentences**, where do you pause at the end of the lines in "The Explosion" and where do you stop?

   _____

   _____

B. Wordsworth

LITERARY ANALYSIS

The point of view of a story affects how you see and understand the events.

- A **first-person narrator** takes part in the events of the story. This narrator calls himself or herself "I." This type of narrator shares his or her own thoughts and feelings.

- A **third-person narrator** is outside the action. This kind of narrator calls the characters "he" or "she" and shows the thoughts and feelings of many characters.

In "B. Wordsworth," Naipaul uses a first-person narrator. You learn about the narrator through what he says, does, and thinks. You see B. Wordsworth though the narrator's eyes, so you can only guess what he thinks. As you read, remember that the narrator is not the same person as the author. Ask yourself how the narrator's point of view affects the story.

READING STRATEGY

You will become more involved in a story by **responding to characters**. Note how you feel when you read their words, actions, and thoughts. Use this chart to record your responses as you read.

Character's Words, Deeds, or Thoughts	Your Response

B. Wordsworth

V. S. Naipaul

Summary This story is told by a young boy who lives in Trinidad. One day, a poet comes to the boy's house. He asks to watch the bees. The poet calls himself B. Wordsworth. The man talks strangely. When he leaves, the boy wants to see him again. The two become friends. B. Wordsworth teaches the boy to appreciate beauty. He helps the boy escape the pain in his life. One day, the boy visits the poet and thinks that he looks old and weak. B. Wordsworth reveals something that makes the boy question everything he knows.

Note-taking Guide

Use the chart below to record what you learn about B. Wordsworth.

B. Wordsworth

1. **Draw Conclusions:** What experience does the boy gain from knowing B. Wordsworth?

   _____

   _____

2. **Literary Analysis:** The boy is the **first-person** narrator in this story. We see events through his eyes. Fill in the chart to show how the story might change if B. Wordsworth were the first-person narrator.

Narrator	Characters' First Meeting	Knowledge of B. Wordsworth's Past	Mystery About B. Wordsworth
Boy			
B. Wordsworth			

3. **Reading Strategy:** To which of the main characters do you **respond** more strongly? Explain.

   _____

   _____

   _____

4. **Reading Strategy:** B. Wordsworth believes that it is possible and desirable to "cry for everything." Explain what you think he means. Then, say whether or not you agree.

   _____

   _____

   _____

   _____

The Train from Rhodesia

LITERARY ANALYSIS

A **theme** is the main idea, or message, of a story. Writers often show themes by showing characters in **conflict**. Conflict is an inner or outer struggle. The conflict between a good character and a bad one is a simple theme: Good will triumph over evil. Conflicts are not always this simple, however. As you read, think about the questions or problems the characters face in "The Train from Rhodesia."

Sometimes a writer does state a theme directly. A writer may show a theme through conflicts, images, symbols, and other ways. That is called an **implied theme**. The theme in "The Train from Rhodesia" is implied. Think about why the writer chose to show the theme indirectly instead of stating it directly.

READING STRATEGY

Writers do not always give away every detail about a situation in a story. You can often **read between the lines** to learn what the writer means. Reading between the lines means thinking about details or connections that the writer suggests, but does not state. Use the chart below to help you read between the lines of this story.

Passage	What Is Missing	What Is Implied

The Train from Rhodesia

Nadine Gordimer

Summary In this story, a train from Rhodesia pulls into a station in a poor section of South Africa. Native people try to sell wooden carvings to the passengers. A newly married young woman wants to buy a carved lion. She decides it is too expensive. Later, her husband convinces an old man to sell the lion for very little money. When the husband gives his wife the lion, she does not accept it the way he thought she would.

Note-Taking Guide

Use the chart below to write down details about this story.

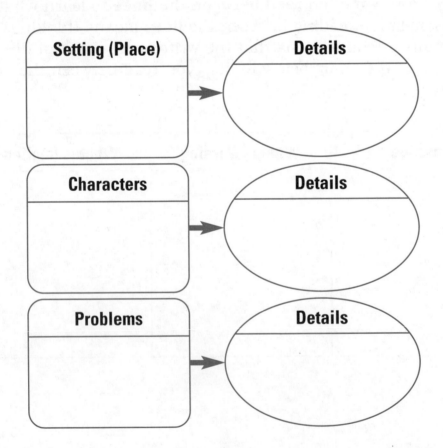

Setting (Place) → Details

Characters → Details

Problems → Details

The Train from Rhodesia

1. **Draw Conclusions:** The woman learns that her husband has qualities she does not like. What do you think will happen in their marriage?

   _____

   _____

2. **Literary Analysis:** A **conflict** is a struggle. The woman has a conflict with her husband. Tell one conflict she has with herself.

   _____

   _____

3. **Literary Analysis:** Writers may use conflicts, images, or symbols to set up an **implied theme**. When the train arrives at the beginning of this story, many details set up a theme. Fill in the chart below to explain how three details from the description of the train's arrival set an implied theme. One has been done for you.

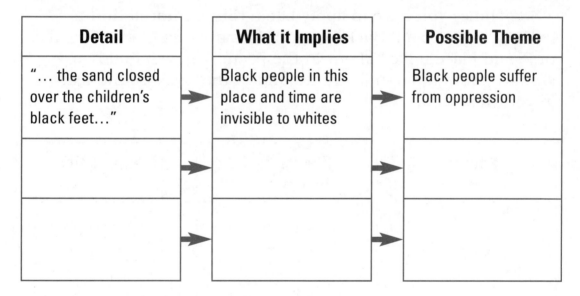

Detail		What it Implies		Possible Theme
"… the sand closed over the children's black feet…"	→	Black people in this place and time are invisible to whites	→	Black people suffer from oppression
	→		→	
	→		→	

4. **Reading Strategy: Read between the lines** to understand ideas that a writer does not state directly. Explain how these lines tell you that the young woman thinks beauty is something of great value: "One-and-six. One-and-six for the wood and the carving and the sinews…"

   _____

   _____

from Midsummer XXIII • from Omeros from Chapter XXVIII

LITERARY ANALYSIS

The **context** of a poem is the time and place in which the action of the poem takes place. The **theme** is the main message of the poem. You can better understand the theme of a poem by understanding its context. The theme of these poems is about the responsibilities of the artist and the problems of society. The context is about the differences between the British and Caribbean peoples.

The poet uses allusions to show the reader the theme and context of his poems. **Allusions** are short comments about literary works, people, or events. An allusion suggests that the writer and the reader share a common culture.

READING STRATEGY

Sometimes you have to **apply background information** to understand a poem. Background information is the historical time and place talked about in the poem. You will find background information in footnotes and in the Background feature in your textbook.

Passage	Background Information	Interpretation

from Midsummer XXIII

Derek Walcott

Summary This poem reflects the author's West Indian background and experience. The poem shows the speaker's responses to the Brixton riots. It tells his mixed feelings about British culture and power. The speaker also talks about his own racial background. He considers his position as a black Caribbean poet in white British society.

Note-taking Guide

Use this chart to list context details from the poem that directly relate to the conflict in the poet's mind.

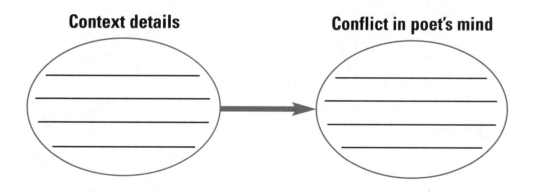

Context details

Conflict in poet's mind

from Omeros from Chapter XXVIII

Derek Walcott

Summary This part of the poem looks at the painful past of how Africans were brought to America and the Caribbean and forced to work as slaves. An African storyteller, called a griot, tells the story in song. The story he tells is about the horrible experiences on the slave ships. Another speaker talks about how slavery still affects the people today.

Note-taking Guide In the chart, list details that support the theme.

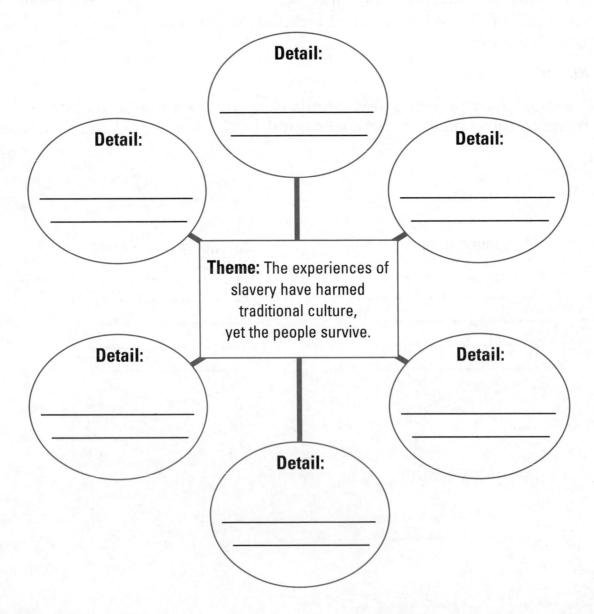

Detail: _____

Detail: _____

Detail: _____

Theme: The experiences of slavery have harmed traditional culture, yet the people survive.

Detail: _____

Detail: _____

Detail: _____

from Midsummer XXIII
• from Omeros from Chapter XXVIII

1. **Interpret:** Reread lines 31–33 in "Omeros." What does Walcott mean when he says, "Now each man was a nation / in himself"?

_____

_____

_____

2. **Literary Analysis:** What is the general **theme** in *Midsummer*?

_____

_____

3. **Literary Analysis:** Use this chart to identify Walcott's use of **allusion** in *Midsummer* or in *Omeros*.

Allusion	Literary/ Scholarly	News/Popular Trends	Historical
"our skulls on the scorching decks"			inhuman treatment on slave ships

4. **Reading Strategy:** Walcott talks about a griot in Omeros. What **background knowledge** helps you find out what a griot is?

_____

_____

A Devoted Son

LITERARY ANALYSIS

Characters in stories often change as the story moves along. Some characters remain the same.

- **Static characters** do not change. They may represent a social role or an attitude.
- **Dynamic characters** have a major change. The change may be one they have chosen or one that happens to them. Writers use such characters to develop truths about life.

In "A Devoted Son," there is only one character who is dynamic. Think about whether this character likes change, or whether this character is forced by events to change.

Writers sometimes use static characters as symbols to stand for ideas or general thoughts. When you read a story with many static characters, think about how the writer is using these characters as symbols to stand for beliefs, roles, or social trends.

READING STRATEGY

Characters make choices just like people in real life. You can **evaluate a character's decisions** just as you would your own. To evaluate means to look at and judge the character's choices. Ask questions about how the character's choices change his or her life. Use the organizer below to evaluate Rakesh's decision to become a doctor.

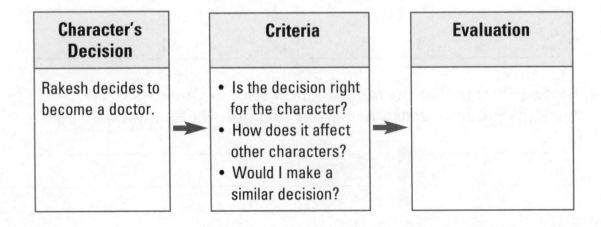

Character's Decision	Criteria	Evaluation
Rakesh decides to become a doctor.	• Is the decision right for the character? • How does it affect other characters? • Would I make a similar decision?	

A Devoted Son

Anita Desai

Summary This story takes place in a suburb in India. A vegetable seller and his family sacrifice to send their son, Rakesh, to medical school. Rakesh is very successful, but he dutifully returns home to his family after graduating. A devoted son, Rakesh fulfills the traditional expectations of his family. Rakesh's father is proud of his son, but as the father grows old and ill and Rakesh assumes more authority, the two come into conflict. The father comes to resent Rakesh's control of his diet and health matters and wishes to die in peace.

Note-taking Guide

Use the chart below to note whether Rakesh and Varma are static or dynamic characters. Then record details that support your choice.

Character	Details	Dynamic	Details
Rakesh			_____ _____ _____ _____ _____
Varma			_____ _____ _____ _____ _____

A Devoted Son

1. **Interpret:** How do the disagreements between Rakesh and Varma reflect the central conflict of the story?

_____

_____

2. **Literary Analysis:** Are Rakesh's mother and wife static or dynamic characters? Explain your classifications.

_____

_____

3. **Literary Analysis:** Use the chart below to interpret Rakesh's actions. List three of Rakesh's decisions or actions, and note whether they fit traditional or modern ideals.

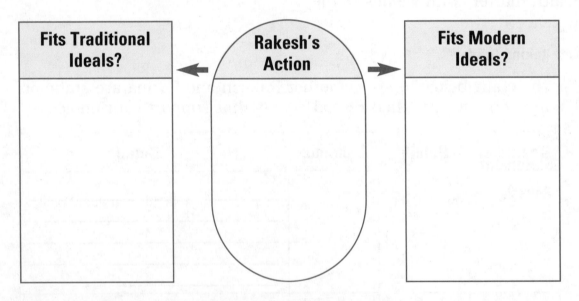

Fits Traditional Ideals?	**Rakesh's Action**	**Fits Modern Ideals?**

4. **Reading Strategy:** Do you think it was a wise decision for the family to make sacrifices for Rakesh's education? Explain.

_____

_____

We'll Never Conquer Space

LITERARY ANALYSIS

We all make guesses, or predictions, about the future. In a **prophetic essay,** a writer makes bold predictions and supports them with evidence. A prophetic essay has these qualities:

- It is a short work of nonfiction.
- It makes predictions about the future of a large group, such as a nation, people, or planet.
- It may give warnings.
- It uses words and phrases readers will remember.

An **analogy** helps readers understand an idea by showing how it is like another idea we already know. Clarke uses many analogies to explain unfamiliar things. As you read, notice how his analogies help you understand hard-to-picture ideas.

READING STRATEGY

When you **challenge a text**, you question what it says. You treat it like a friend you can argue with rather than like someone whose words you must accept. When you read something that you are not sure about in this essay, ask yourself a question about it. Use the chart below to keep track of your questions. One question has been included for you.

Statement	Question
Man will never conquer space.	*Never* is a strong word. Is this statement well supported?

We'll Never Conquer Space

Arthur C. Clarke

Summary This essay begins with the statement "Man will never conquer space." The author claims that space is too large for humanity to conquer. The speed of light limits how quickly people can communicate with one another. People living in different galaxies will be unable to have conversations. They will only be able to hear about events years later. Those who colonize space will lose their ties with Earth.

Note-Taking Guide

There are three subheadings in Clarke's essay. Use this chart to record the most important thought in each subheading.

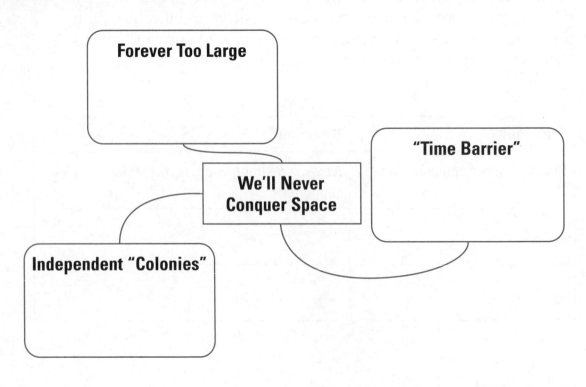

We'll Never Conquer Space

1. **Classify:** Clark says people will be able to send messages to people on other planets. They will not be able to have a real conversation. What is the difference between sending a message and having a conversation?

   _____

   _____

2. **Literary Analysis:** A **prophetic essay** makes predictions about the future. Clarke predicts that people will not be able to conquer space. Write two ideas he uses to support his prediction.

   _____

   _____

3. **Literary Analysis:** Clarke makes the **analogy** that people in space will be like "ants crawling on the face of the earth." Use the chart below to interpret this analogy. In the left column, write the two things the analogy compares. In the middle column, write how the two things are the same. In the third column, write the idea this analogy helps makes clear.

Things Compared	Similarities	What is Explained

4. **Reading Strategy: Challenge a text** by asking questions about it. Clarke writes, "Man has always accepted whatever price was necessary for his explorations . . .." Write one question that challenges this statement.

   _____

   _____

PART 2: TURBO VOCABULARY

The exercises and tools presented here are designed to help you increase your vocabulary. Review the instruction and complete the exercises to build your vocabulary knowledge. Throughout the year, you can apply these skills and strategies to improve your reading, writing, speaking, and listening vocabulary.

PREFIXES

The following list contains common prefixes with meanings and examples. On the blank lines, write other words you know that begin with the same prefixes. Write the meanings of the new words.

Root	Meaning	Example and Meaning	Your Words	Meanings
Anglo-Saxon fore-	before	*foreword:* a short piece of writing that comes before the main part of the book		
Greek a-	without; not	*amoral:* without moral standards		
Greek apo-	away; separate	*apothecary:* drug-gist; one who puts away prescriptions		
Greek auto-	self	*automatic:* done without thought; involuntary		
Greek mono-	single; alone	*monorail:* a railway with a single track		
Latin circum-	around	*circumscribed:* limit-ed; having a boundary around		
Latin con-	with; together	*concoct:* to make by combining		
Latin dis-	apart; not	*dissatisfied:* not satisfied		

Root	Meaning	Example and Meaning	Your Words	Meanings
Latin ex-	out	*expect:* to look out for		
Latin inter-	between; among	*international:* between or among nations		
Latin mal-	bad	*malformed:* abnormally or badly formed		
Latin multi-	many; much	*multicultural:* having to do with many cultures		
Latin ob-	against; opposed to	*object:* to complain or protest against		
Latin omni-	all; every	*omnivorous:* eating all types of food		
Latin sub-	under; lower	*substandard:* lower than what is acceptable		
Latin trans-	across; through	*transplant:* to remove from one place and settle in another		

WORD ROOTS

The following list contains common word roots with meanings and examples. On the blank lines, write other words you know that have the same roots. Write the meanings of the new words.

Root	Meaning	Example and Meaning	Your Words	Meanings
Greek -chron-	time	*chronology:* arranged in order of occurrence		
Greek -top-	place; surface	*topographical:* relating to a map of the surface of a place		
Latin -cert-	sure	*certify:* to make sure		
Latin -cred-	belief	*credible:* believable		
Latin -dict-	the idea of something said	*diction:* choice of words		
Latin -duc-	to lead	*inducted:* led into a group		
Latin -fid-	faith	*fidelity:* faithfulness		
Latin -fort-	strength	*fortitude:* strength to endure pain		

Root	Meaning	Example and Meaning	Your Words	Meanings
Latin -loc-	place	*dislocation:* being out of place		
Latin -mort-	death	*immortal:* living forever; not ever dying		
Latin -puls-	push; drive	*impulse:* driving forward with sudden force		
Latin -sol-	to comfort	*solace:* an easing of grief; comfort		
Latin -spec-	to look; see	*inspector:* one who looks carefully		
Latin -spir-	breath; life	*aspire:* to yearn or seek after		
Latin -turb-	to disturb	*turbulence:* commotion or disorder		
Latin -voc-	voice	*vocalist:* one who sings		

SUFFIXES

The following list contains common suffixes with meanings and examples. On the blank lines, write other words you know that have the same suffixes. Write the meanings of the new words.

Suffix	Meaning	Example and Meaning	Your Words	Meanings
Anglo-Saxon -fold	a specific number of times or ways	*manifold:* many times		
Anglo-Saxon -ful	full of	*forgetful:* apt to forget		
Anglo-Saxon -hood	state or quality of	*childhood:* the state of being a child		
Anglo-Saxon -less	without	*penniless:* without a penny; very poor		
Anglo-Saxon -ness	the state of being	*randomness:* the state of lacking purpose		
Anglo-Saxon -some	tending toward being	*worrisome:* having the tendency to worry		
Greek -ate	forms verbs	*orchestrate:* to coordinate		
Greek -itis	disease; inflammation	*appendicitis:* inflammation of the appendix		

Suffix	Meaning	Example and Meaning	Your Words	Meanings
Greek -logy	the science of study of	*sociology:* the study of human society and social relations		
Latin -able/-ible	able to	*incredible:* not able to be believed		
Latin -ade	the act of; the result of	*barricade:* the result of barring the way		
Latin -age	condition or result of	*vintage:* the wine produced in a particular place and time		
Latin -ance/-ence	quality of; state of being	*dependence:* state of being dependent or needing someone or something		
Latin -ness	the state of being	*happiness:* the state of being happy		
Latin -ous	full of	*glorious:* full of glory		
Latin -tion	the act or process of	*participation:* the process of taking part or participating		

Etymology is the history of a word. It shows where the word came from, or its origin. It also shows how it got its present meaning and spelling. Understanding word origins, or etymology, can help you understand and remember the meanings of words you add to your vocabulary.

A good dictionary will tell you the etymology of a word. The word's etymology usually appears in brackets, parentheses, or slashes near the beginning or the end of the dictionary entry. Part of the etymology is the language from which the word comes.

Abbreviations for Languages	
Abbreviation	**Language**
OE	Old English
ME	Middle English
F	French
Gr	Greek
L	Latin

You can find these abbreviations and more in a dictionary's key to abbreviations.

Words from other languages

The English that you speak today began in about the year 500. Tribes from Europe settled in Britain. These tribes, called the Angles, the Saxons, and the Jutes, spoke a Germanic language. Later, when the Vikings attacked Britain, their language added words from Danish and Norse. Then, when Christian missionaries came to Britain, they added words from Latin. The resulting language is called Old English, and it looks very different from modern English.

For example, to say "Listen!" in Old English, you would have said "Hwaet!"

The Normans conquered Britain in 1066. They spoke Old French, and the addition of this language changed Old English dramatically. The resulting language, called Middle English, looks much more like modern English, but the spellings of words are very different.

For example, the word *knight* in Middle English was spelled *knyght*, and the word *time* was spelled *tyme*.

During the Renaissance, interest in classical cultures added Greek and Latin words to English. At this time, English started to look more like the English you know. This language, called Modern English, is the language we still speak.

Modern English continues to add words from other languages. As immigrants have moved to the United States, they have added new words to the language.

For example, the word *boycott* comes from Ireland and the word *burrito* comes from Mexico.

Note-taking Using a dictionary, identify the language from which each of the following words came into English. Also identify the word's original and current meaning.

Word	Original language	Original meaning	Current meaning
comb			
costume			
guess			
mile			
panther			

Words that change meaning over time

English is a living language. It grows by giving new meanings to existing words and by incorporating words that have changed their meaning over time and through usage.

For example, the word *dear* used to mean "expensive."

Note-taking Using a dictionary, identify the original meaning and the current meaning of each of the following words.

	original meaning	current meaning
1. havoc	_____	_____
2. magazine	_____	_____

Words that have been invented, or *coined*, to serve new purposes.

New products or discoveries need new words.

For example, the words *paperback* and *quiz* are coined words.

Note-taking Identify one word that has been coined in each of the following categories.

Category	Coined word
sports	
technology	
transportation	
space travel	
medicine	

Words that are combinations of words or shortened versions of longer words

New words can be added to the language by combining words or by shortening words.

For example, the word *greenback* is a combination of the words *green* and *back*, and the word *flu* is a shortened version of the word *influenza*.

Note-taking Generate a word to fill in the blanks in each of the following sentences correctly. Your word should be a combination of two words or a shortened version of a longer word.

Jerome served one of our favorite dinners, spaghetti and _____.

Many years ago, people might take an omnibus to work, but today they would call that vehicle a _____.

We took the most direct route to Aunt Anna's house, which meant driving forty miles on the _____.

We thought we could get to shelter before the storm started, but we did not quite make it. A few _____ dampened our jackets.

A dictionary lists words in alphabetical order. Look at this sample dictionary entry. Notice the types of information about a word it gives.

Example of a Dictionary Entry

dictionary (dik′ shə ner′ ē) n., pl. –aries
[ML *dictionarium* < LL *dictio*) 1 a book of
alphabetically listed words in a language,
with definitions, etymologies, pronunciations,
and other information 2 a book of alphabetically
listed words in a language with their equivalents
in another language [a Spanish-English
dictionary]

Answer the questions based on the dictionary entry.

1. What is the correct spelling?_____

2. How do you form the plural? _____

3. What language does the word come from? _____

4. How many definitions are there? _____

5. What example is given? _____

Here are some abbreviations you will find in dictionary entries.

Pronunciation Symbols	Parts of Speech	Origins of Words
′ means emphasize this syllable as you say the word	adj. = adjective	Fr = French
‾ means pronounce vowel with a long sound, such as -*ay*- for a and -*ee*- for e	adv. = adverb	Ger = German
ə means a sound like -*uh*-	n. = noun	L = classical Latin
o͞o means the sound of *u* in *cute*	v. = verb	ME = Middle English OE = Old English

As you read, look up new words in a dictionary. Enter information about the words on this chart.

My Words

New Word	Pronunciation	Part of Speech	Origin	Meanings and Sample Sentence

ACADEMIC WORDS

Academic (A kuh DEM ik) words are words you use often in your schoolwork. Knowing what these words mean will help you think and write better.

On the next two pages, you will find a list of these words. You will also see how to pronounce each word and what it means. On the lines below each word, write sentences from your reading in which the word appears. Then, using your own words, explain what the sentence means.

apply (uh PLY) tell how you use information in a specific situation

_____

_____

_____

_____

clarify (KLA ri FY) make something more understandable

_____

_____

_____

_____

conclude (KUHN klood) use reasoning to reach a decision or opinion

_____

_____

_____

_____

define (dee FYN) tell the qualities that make something what it is

_____

_____

_____

_____

demonstrate (DEM uhn STRAYT) use examples to prove a point

_____

_____

_____

evaluate (ee VAL yoo AYT) determine the value or importance of something

_____

_____

_____

identify (y DEN ti FY) name or show you recognize something

_____

_____

_____

label (LAY bel) attach the correct name to something

_____

_____

_____

predict (pree DIKT) tell what will happen based on details you know

_____

_____

_____

recall (ri KAWL) tell details that you remember

_____

_____

_____

When you are reading, you will find many unfamiliar words. Here are some tools that you can use to help you read unfamiliar words.

PHONICS

Phonics is the science or study of sound. When you learn to read, you learn to associate certain sounds with certain letters or letter combinations. You know most of the sounds that letters can represent in English. When letters are combined, however, it is not always so easy to know what sound is represented. In English, there are some rules and patterns that will help you determine how to pronounce a word. This chart shows you some of the common **vowel digraphs**, which are combinations like *ea* and *oa*. Two vowels together are called vowel digraphs. Usually, vowel digraphs represent the long sound of the first vowel.

Vowel Digraphs	Examples of Usual Sounds	Exceptions
ee and *ea*	steep, each, treat, sea	head, sweat, dread
ai and *ay*	plain, paid, may, betray	
oa, ow, and *oe*	soak, slow, doe	rot, box
ie, igh, and *y*	lie, night, my, delight	with, lit, myth

As you read, sometimes the only way to know how to pronounce a word with an *ea* spelling is to see if the word makes sense in the sentence. Look at this example:

The water pipes were made of *lead*.

First, try out the long sound "ee." Ask yourself if it sounds right. It does not. Then try the short sound "e." You will find that the short sound is correct in that sentence.

Now try this example.

Where you *lead*, I will follow.

WORD PATTERNS

Recognizing different vowel-consonant patterns will help you read longer words. In the following section, the **V** stands for "vowel" and the **C** stands for "consonant."

Single-syllable Words

CV–go: In two letter words with a consonant followed by a vowel, the vowel is usually long. For example, the word *go* is pronounced wiht a long o sound.

In a single syllable word, a vowel followed only by a single consonant is usually short.

CVC-got: If you add a consonant to the word *go*, such as the *t* in *got*, the vowel sound is a short *o*. Say the words *go* and *got* aloud and notice the difference in pronunciation.

Multi-syllable Words

In words of more than one syllable, notice the letters that follow a vowel.

VCCV–robber: A single vowel followed by two consonants is usually short.

VCV–begin: A single vowel followed by a single consonant is usually long.

VCe–beside: An extension of the VCV pattern is vowel-consonant-silent *e*. In these words, the vowel is long and the *e* is not pronounced.

When you see a word with the VCV pattern, try the long vowel sound first. If the word does not make sense, try the short sound. Pronounce the words *model, camel,* and *closet*. First, try the long vowel sound. That does not sound correct, so try the short vowel sound. The short vowel sound is correct in those words.

Remember that patterns help you get started on figuring out a word. You will sometimes need to try a different sound or find the word in a dictionary.

As you read and find unfamiliar words, look the pronunciations up in a dictionary. Write the words in this chart in the correct column, to help you notice patterns and remember pronunciations.

Syllables	Example	New Words	Vowel Sound
CV	go		long
CVC	got		short
VCC	robber		short
V • CV	begin open		long long
VC • V	closet		short

FAQS ABOUT THE SAT®

What is the SAT®?

- The SAT® is a national test intended to predict how well you will do with college-level material.

What does the SAT® test?

- The SAT® tests vocabulary, math, and reasoning skills in three sections:
  - Critical Reading: two 25-minute sections and one 20-minute section
  - Math: two 25-minute sections and one 20-minute section
  - Writing: one 35-minute multiple-choice section and one 25-minute essay

Why should you take the SAT®?

- Many colleges and universities require you to submit your SAT® scores when you apply. They use your scores, along with other information about your ability and your achievements, to evaluate you for admission.

How can studying vocabulary help improve your SAT® scores?

- The Critical Reading section of the SAT® asks two types of questions that evaluate your vocabulary.
  - Sentence Completions ask you to fill in one or more blanks in a sentence with the correct word or words. To fill in the blanks correctly, you need to know the meaning of the words offered as answers.
  - Vocabulary in Context questions in Passage-based Reading ask you to determine what a word means based on its context in a reading passage.
- With a strong vocabulary and good strategies for using context clues, you will improve the likelihood that you will score well on the SAT®.

Using Context Clues on the SAT®

When you do not know the meaning of a word, nearby words or phrases can help you. These words or phrases are called *context clues*.

Guidelines for Using Context Clues

1. Read the sentence or paragraph, concentrating on the unfamiliar word.

2. Look for clues in the surrounding words.

3. Guess the possible meaning of the unfamiliar word.

4. Substitute your guess for the word.

5. When you are reviewing for a test, you can check the word's meaning in a dictionary.

Types of Context Clues

Here are the most common types of context clues:

- formal definitions that give the meaning of the unfamiliar word

- familiar words that you may know that give hints to the unfamiliar word's meaning

- comparisons or contrasts that present ideas or concepts either clearly similar or clearly opposite to the unfamiliar word

- synonyms, or words with the same meaning as the unfamiliar word

- antonyms, or words with a meaning opposite to that of the unfamiliar word

- key words used to clarify a word's meaning

Note-taking List several new words that you have learned recently by figuring out their meanings in context. Then, explain how you used context to decide what the word meant.

New Word	How You Used Context to Understand the Word

Sample SAT® Questions

Here are examples of the kinds of questions you will find on the SAT®. Read the samples carefully. Then, do the Practice exercises that follow.

Sample Sentence Completion Question:

Directions: The sentence that follows has one blank indicating that something has been omitted. Beneath the sentence are five words or sets of words labeled A through E. Choose the word or set of words that, when inserted in the sentence, best fits the meaning of the sentence as a whole.

1. Though he is _____, his nephew still invites him to Thanksgiving dinner every year.

A cheerful

B entertaining

C misanthropic

D agile

E healthy

The correct answer is *C*. The uncle is *misanthropic*. You can use the context clues "though" and "invites him" to infer that the uncle has some negative quality. Next, you can apply your knowledge of the prefix *mis-* to determine that *misanthropic*, like *mistake* and *misfortune*, is a word indicating something negative. Eliminate the other answer choices, which indicate positive or neutral qualities in this context.

Sample Vocabulary in Context Question:

Directions: Read the following sentence. Then, read the question that follows it. Decide which is the best answer to the question.

Martin Luther King, Jr., whose methods motivated many to demand equal rights in a peaceful manner, was an <u>inspiration</u> to all.

1. In this sentence, the word *inspiration* means—

   A politician

   B motivation to a high level of activity

   C the process of inhaling

   D figurehead

The correct answer is *B*. Both *B* and *C* are correct definitions of the word *inspiration*, but the only meaning that applies in the context of the sentence is "motivation to a high level of activity."

Practice for SAT® Questions

Practice Read the following passage. Then, read each question that follows the passage. Decide which is the best answer to each question.

Many people are becoming Internet <u>savvy</u>, exhibiting their skills at mastering the Web. The Internet is also becoming a more <u>reliable</u> source of factual information. A <u>Web-surfer</u> can find information provided by <u>reputable</u> sources, such as government organizations and universities.

1. In this passage, the word *savvy* means—

   A incompetent

   B competent

   C users

   D nonusers

2. The word *reliable* in this passage means—

   A existing

   B available

   C dependable

   D relevant

3. In this passage, the term *Web-surfer* means—

A someone who uses the Internet

B a person who uses a surfboard

C a person who know a great deal about technology

D a student

4. The word *reputable* in this passage means—

A an approved Internet provider

B well-known and of good reputation

C purely academic

D costly

Practice Each sentence that follows has one or two blanks indicating that something has been omitted. Beneath the sentence are five words or sets of words labeled A through E. Choose the word or set of words that, when inserted in the sentence, best fits the meaning of the sentence as a whole.

1. "I wish I had a longer _____ between performances," complained the pianist. "My fingers need a rest."

A post-mortem   C prelude   E solo

B circumlocution   D interval

2. Instead of revolving around the sun in a circle, this asteroid has a(n) _____ orbit.

A rapid   C interplanetary   E regular

B eccentric   D circular

3. He was the first historian to translate the _____ on the stone.

A impulsion   C excavation   E inscription

B aversion   D circumspection

4. To correct your spelling error, simply _____ the i and the e.

A translate   C transcent   E integrate

B transpose   D interpolate

5. Spilling soda all over myself just when the movie got to the good part was a(n) _____ event.

A fortunate   C tenacious   E constructive

B premature   D infelicitous

Diction

Diction is a writer's or a speaker's word choice. The vocabulary, the vividness of the language, and the appropriateness of the words all contribute to diction, which is part of a writing or speaking style.

- Hey, buddy! What's up?
- Hi, how're you doing?
- Hello, how are you?
- Good morning. How are you?

These four phrases all function as greetings. You would use each one, however, in very different situations. This word choice is called *diction*, and for different situations, you use different *levels of diction*.

Note-taking Here are some examples of levels of diction. Fill in the blanks with the opposite level of diction.

Level of Diction	Formal	Informal
Example	Good afternoon. Welcome to the meeting.	
Level of Diction	Ornate	Plain
Example		I need more coffee.
Level of Diction	Abstract	Concrete
Example		The mayor has asked for volunteers to pick up litter along the river next Saturday.
Level of Diction	Technical	Ordinary
Example	My brother is employed as a computer system design manager.	
Level of Diction	Sophisticated	Down-to-Earth
Example	Thank you very much. I appreciate your help.	
Level of Diction	Old-fashioned	Modern/Slangy
Example	Yes, it is I. Shall we sample the bill of fare?	

With close friends and family, most of your conversations will probably be informal, down-to-earth, even slangy. In school or in elegant surroundings, or among people you do not know well or people who are much older than you, you will probably choose language that is more formal. Sometimes the distinctions can be subtle, so try to take your cues from others and adjust your diction accordingly.

Note-taking Complete the following activities.

1. Make a list of words and phrases that would be appropriate for you to use as you escort a visiting school board member on a tour of your school.

_____

_____

_____

_____

2. Make a second list of words and phrases that you might use as you escort your teenage cousin on a tour of your school.

_____

_____

_____

_____

3. Study the following pairs of phrases. Then, identify one phrase in each pair as formal and the other as informal.

	Phrase	Formal / Informal	Phrase	Formal / Informal
1.	Hello, it's nice to meet you		How do you do?	
2.	What is your opinion, Professor Hughes?		What do you think, Pat?	
3.	Please accept my deepest sympathy.		That's too bad.	
4.	Sorry. I didn't hear you.		I beg your pardon. Please repeat the question	
5.	I don't get it.		I do not quite understand.	

4. List several common phrases. Then, identify whether each phrase is formal or informal, and give its formal or informal opposite.

	Phrase	Formal / Informal	Phrase	Formal / Informal
1.				
2.				
3.				
4.				
5.				

Etiquette: Using the Vocabulary of Politeness

No matter how many words you know, the way you use those words will impact how your friends, your family, your teachers, and all the people in your life react to you. For almost every interaction you have, choosing a vocabulary of politeness will help you avoid conflicts and communicate your ideas, thoughts, and feelings effectively to others.

When in doubt, always choose the polite word or phrase.

Formal or Informal?

Polite vocabulary does not have to be formal. In fact, the definition of the word *polite* is "behaving or speaking in a way that is correct for the social situation." People often think that *etiquette*, which consists of rules for polite behavior, applies only in formal situations. All interactions with other people, though, should follow the etiquette that is appropriate for the situation.

Etiquette for Classroom Discussions

Use the following sentences starters to help you express yourself clearly and politely in classroom discussions.

To Express an Opinion

• I think that _____.
• I believe that _____.
• It seems to me that _____.
• In my opinion, _____.

To Agree

• I agree with _____ that _____.
• I see what you mean.
• That's an interesting idea.
• My idea is similar to _____'s idea.
• I hadn't thought of that.

To Disagree

- I don't completely agree with _____ because _____.
- My opinion is different from yours.
- My idea is slightly different from yours.
- I see it a different way.

To Report the Ideas of a Group

- We agreed that _____.
- We concluded that _____.
- We had a similar idea.
- We had a different approach.

To Predict or Infer

- I predict that _____.
- Based on _____, I infer that _____.
- I hypothesize that _____.

To Paraphrase

- So you are saying that _____.
- In other words, you think _____.
- What I hear you saying is _____.

To Offer a Suggestion

- Maybe we could _____.
- What if we _____.
- Here's something we might try.

To Ask for Clarification

- Could you explain that another way?
- I have a question about that.
- Can you give me another example of that?

To Ask for a Response

- What do you think?
- Do you agree?
- What answer did you get?

Practice With a partner, discuss an issue about which you disagree. At the end of five minutes, list five or more polite words or phrases that you used to communicate your conflicting opinions.

_____

_____

Use this page to write down academic words you come across in other subjects, such as social studies or science. When you are reading your textbooks, you may find words that you need to learn. Following the example, write down the word, the part of speech, and an explanation of the word. You may want to write an example sentence to help you remember the word.

dissolve *verb* to make something solid become part of a liquid by putting it in a liquid and mixing it

The sugar *dissolved* in the hot tea.

_____

_____

_____

_____

_____

_____

_____

_____

_____

_____

_____

_____

_____

_____

_____

_____

_____

_____

VOCABULARY FLASH CARDS

Use these flash cards to study words you want to remember. The words on this page come from Unit 1. Cut along the dotted lines on pages V29 through V32 to create your own flash cards or use index cards. Write the word on the front of the card. On the back, write the word's part of speech and definition. Then, write a sentence that shows the meaning of the word.

fervent	grievous	redress
sentinel	compassionate	rapture
admonish	rancor	winsomeness

adjective
having or showing great warmth of feeling

There were *fervent* arguments both for and against school uniforms.

---

adjective
causing sorrow; hard to bear

The earthquake was a *grievous* disaster.

---

noun
compensation, as for a wrong

The courts provide the means of *redress* for victims of crime.

---

noun
person or animal that guards

The German shepherd sat by the door like a *sentinel*.

---

adjective
sympathizing; pitying

The *compassionate* man adopted the kitten that had been abandoned.

---

noun
joy; great pleasure

He stared in *rapture* at his baby son.

---

verb
advise; caution

The lifeguard *admonished* Hal never to swim alone.

---

noun
ill will

Jim and Carla ended their relationship with no *rancor*.

---

noun
charm; delightfulness

The young girl's smile was an example of *winsomeness*.

VOCABULARY FLASH CARDS

Use these flash cards to study words you want to remember. Cut along the dotted lines on pages V29 through V32 to create your own flash cards or use index cards. Write the word on the front of the card. On the back, write the word's part of speech and definition. Then, write a sentence that shows the meaning of the word.

Use these flash cards to study words you want to remember. Cut along the dotted lines on pages V29 through V32 to create your own flash cards or use index cards. Write the word on the front of the card. On the back, write the word's part of speech and definition. Then, write a sentence that shows the meaning of the word.

VOCABULARY FOLD-A-LIST

Use a fold-a-list to study the definitions of words. The words on this page come from Unit 1. Write the definition for each word on the lines. Fold the paper along the dotted line to check your definition. Create your own fold-a-lists on pages V35 through V38.

reparation _____

_____

solace _____

_____

purge _____

_____

writhing _____

_____

massive _____

_____

loathsome _____

_____

innumerable _____

_____

stranded _____

_____

solicitous _____

_____

garnished _____

_____

Fold

VOCABULARY FOLD-A-LIST

Write the word that matches the definition on each line.
Fold the paper along the dotted line to check your work.

something making up for
a wrong or an injury   _____

comfort; relief   _____

purify; cleanse   _____

making twisting or
turning motions   _____

big and solid; bulky   _____

disgusting   _____

too many to count   _____

forced into shallow
water or onto a beach;
left helpless   _____

showing care or concern   _____

decorated; trimmed   _____

Fold

VOCABULARY FOLD-A-LIST

Write the words you want to study on this side of the page. Write the definitions on the back. Then, test yourself. Fold the paper along the dotted line to check your answers.

Word: _____

_____

Word: _____

_____

Word: _____

_____

Word: _____

_____

Word: _____

_____

Word: _____

_____

Word: _____

_____

Word: _____

_____

Word: _____

_____

Word: _____

_____

Fold

VOCABULARY FOLD-A-LIST

Write the word that matches the definition on each line.
Fold the paper along the dotted line to check your work.

Definition: _____

_____

Definition: _____

_____

Definition: _____

_____

Definition: _____

_____

Definition: _____

_____

Definition: _____

_____

Definition: _____

_____

Definition: _____

_____

Definition: _____

_____

Definition: _____

Fold

Write the words you want to study on this side of the page. Write the definitions on the back. Then, test yourself. Fold the paper along the dotted line to check your answers.

Word: _____

_____

Word: _____

_____

Word: _____

_____

Word: _____

_____

Word: _____

_____

Word: _____

_____

Word: _____

_____

Word: _____

_____

Word: _____

_____

Word: _____

_____

Fold ▸

VOCABULARY FOLD-A-LIST

Write the word that matches the definition on each line.
Fold the paper along the dotted line to check your work.

Definition: ______________________________

____

Definition: ______________________________

____

Definition: ______________________________

____

Definition: ______________________________

____

Definition: ______________________________

____

Definition: ______________________________

____

Definition: ______________________________

____

Definition: ______________________________

____

Definition: ______________________________

____

Definition: ______________________________

Fold

COMMONLY MISSPELLED WORDS

The list on these pages presents words that cause problems for many people. Some of these words are spelled according to set rules, but others follow no specific rules. As you review this list, check to see how many of the words give you trouble in your own writing. Then, add your own commonly misspelled words on the lines that follow.

abbreviate	auxiliary	census	deficient
absence	awkward	certain	definitely
absolutely	bandage	changeable	delinquent
abundance	banquet	characteristic	dependent
accelerate	bargain	chauffeur	descendant
accidentally	barrel	chief	description
accumulate	battery	clothes	desert
accurate	beautiful	coincidence	desirable
ache	beggar	colonel	dessert
achievement	beginning	column	deteriorate
acquaintance	behavior	commercial	dining
adequate	believe	commission	disappointed
admittance	benefit	commitment	disastrous
advertisement	bicycle	committee	discipline
aerial	biscuit	competitor	dissatisfied
affect	bookkeeper	concede	distinguish
aggravate	bought	condemn	effect
aggressive	boulevard	congratulate	eighth
agreeable	brief	connoisseur	eligible
aisle	brilliant	conscience	embarrass
all right	bruise	conscientious	enthusiastic
allowance	bulletin	conscious	entrepreneur
aluminum	buoyant	contemporary	envelope
amateur	bureau	continuous	environment
analysis	bury	controversy	equipped
analyze	buses	convenience	equivalent
ancient	business	coolly	especially
anecdote	cafeteria	cooperate	exaggerate
anniversary	calendar	cordially	exceed
anonymous	campaign	correspondence	excellent
answer	canceled	counterfeit	exercise
anticipate	candidate	courageous	exhibition
anxiety	capacity	courteous	existence
apologize	capital	courtesy	experience
appall	capitol	criticism	explanation
appearance	captain	criticize	extension
appreciate	career	curiosity	extraordinary
appropriate	carriage	curious	familiar
architecture	cashier	cylinder	fascinating
argument	catastrophe	deceive	February
associate	category	decision	fiery
athletic	ceiling	deductible	financial
attendance	cemetery	defendant	fluorescent

foreign
fourth
fragile
gauge
generally
genius
genuine
government
grammar
grievance
guarantee
guard
guidance
handkerchief
harass
height
humorous
hygiene
ignorant
immediately
immigrant
independence
independent
indispensable
individual
inflammable
intelligence
interfere
irrelevant
irritable
jewelry
judgment
knowledge
lawyer
legible
legislature
leisure
liable
library
license
lieutenant
lightning
likable
liquefy
literature
loneliness
magnificent
maintenance
marriage
mathematics
maximum
meanness
mediocre
mileage
millionaire
minimum

minuscule
miscellaneous
mischievous
misspell
mortgage
naturally
necessary
neighbor
neutral
nickel
niece
ninety
noticeable
nuisance
obstacle
occasion
occasionally
occur
occurred
occurrence
omitted
opinion
opportunity
optimistic
outrageous
pamphlet
parallel
paralyze
parentheses
particularly
patience
permanent
permissible
perseverance
persistent
personally
perspiration
persuade
phenomenal
phenomenon
physician
pleasant
pneumonia
possess
possession
possibility
prairie
precede
preferable
prejudice
preparation
previous
primitive
privilege
probably
procedure

proceed
prominent
pronunciation
psychology
publicly
pursue
questionnaire
realize
really
recede
receipt
receive
recognize
recommend
reference
referred
rehearse
relevant
reminiscence
renowned
repetition
restaurant
rhythm
ridiculous
sandwich
satellite
schedule
scissors
secretary
siege
solely
sponsor
subtle
subtlety
superintendent
supersede
surveillance
susceptible
tariff
temperamental
theater
threshold
truly
unmanageable
unwieldy
usage
usually
valuable
various
vegetable
voluntary
weight
weird
whale
wield
yield

PHOTO AND ART CREDITS

Cover: *Big Ben*, Andre Derain, ©2005 Artists Rights Society (ARS), New York/ADAGP, Paris, Giraudon/Art Resource, NY; **3:** *Ships with Three Men, Fish*, The Bodleian Library, University of Oxford; **4:** *Susanna in Bath* (detail), Albrecht Altdorfer, Wasserholendes Madchen, Munchen, Alte Pinakothek, Munich. Photo: Blauel/Artothek; **7:** ©Karen Loccisano; **17:** Snark/Art Resource, NY; **26:** *The Monk*, Arthur Szyk for The CANTERBURY TALES, Reproduced with permission of Alexadra Szyk Bracie and Irvin Ungar; **36:** *The Pardoner*, Arthur Szyk for The Canterbury Tales, Reproduced with permission of Alexadra Szyk Bracie and Irvin Ungar; **39:** *The Wife of Bath*, Arthur Szyk for The CANTERBURY TALES, Reproduced with permission of Alexadra Szyk Bracie and Irvin Ungar; **42:** Three Knights Returning from a Tournament. French miniature from "Recueil de Traites de Devotion." Ms. 137/1687, fol. 144 r.c.1371-78, Giraudon/Art Resource, NY; **43:** Department of Printing and Graphic Arts, The Houghton Library, Harvard College Library; **52:** The Granger Collection, New York; **53:** ©Michael Giannechini/Photo Researchers, Inc.; **56:** Corel Professional Photos CD-ROM™; **59:** Getty Images; **62:** Courtesy of the Library of Congress; **65:** Corel Professional Photos CD-ROM™; **67:** Portrait of Queen Elizabeth I, Donne Bryant/Art Resource, NY; **71:** *Il Buon Pastore* (The Good Shepherd), Early Christian, 4th century, Vatican Museum, Scala/Art Resource, New York; **72:** Corel Professional Photos CD-ROM™; **73:** *The Return of the Prodigal Son*, Lionello Spada/Erich Lessing/Art Resource, NY; **76:** Pearson Education/PH School Division; **79:** Pearson Education/PH School Division; **82:** Pearson Education/PH School Division; **85:** Pearson Education/PH School Division; **88:** Pearson Education/PH School Division; **102:** Corel Professional Photos CD-ROM™; **103:** Romilly Lockyer/Getty Images; **108:** Corel Professional Photos CD-ROM™; **111:** *Young Man Writing*, Joos van Craesbeeck (follower of), Musee des Beaux-Arts, Nantes, France, Giraudon/The Bridgeman Art Library, London/New York; **114:** istockphoto.com; **115:** © Chris Hellier/CORBIS; **123:** Bildarchiv Preussischer Kulturbesitz; **126:** The Granger Collection, New York; **132:** The Granger Collection, New York; **135:** The Granger Collection, New York; **139:** The Granger Collection, New York; **142:** *The Barge*, 1895-1896, (detail), Aubrey Beardsley from "The Rape of the Lock," Smithers, 1896 from The Best of Beardsley, Collected and edited by R.A. Walker, ©1948 by The Bodley Head, Published in the U.S. A. by Excalibur Books, plate 63; **145:** The Granger Collection, New York; **146:** ©British Museum; **149:** Lenore Weber/Omni-Photo Communications, Inc.; **152:** Corel Professional Photos CD-ROM™; **151:** © National Portrait Gallery, London; **151:** The Granger Collection, New York; **153:** The Granger Collection, New York; **156:** The Granger Collection, New York; **164:** ©R.J. Erwin/Photo Researchers, Inc.; **167:** ©Archive Photos; **170:** ©Barson Collection/Archive Photos; **173:** The Granger Collection, New York; **178:** *Storming of the Bastille, 14 July 1789*, Anonymous, Chateau, Versailles, France, Giraudon/Art Resource, NY; **181:** Michael Jenner/Robert Harding World Imagery; **185:** The Granger Collection, New York; **193:** Lord Byron, shaking the dust of England from his shoes, from The Poet's Corner pub. by William Heinemann, 1904 (engraving) by Max Beerbohm (1872-1956), Central Saint Martins College of Art and Design/Bridgeman Art Library, London/New York; **196:** Corel Professional Photos CD-ROM™; **199:** John Keats, 1821, Joseph Severn, by courtesy of the National Portrait Gallery, London; **200:** GREEK VASE, TERRACOTTA c. 460 B.C., Attributed to the Orchard Painter, Column Krater (called the "Orchard Vase"), Side A:Women Gathering Apples, The Metropolitan Museum of Art, Rogers Fund, 1907, (07.286.74) Photograph © 1984 The Metropolitan Museum of Art; **205:** Power loom weaving, 1834 (engraving) by Thomas Allom (1804-72) (after), Private Collection/Bridgeman Art Library, London/New York; **206:** Brown Brothers; **210:** istockphoto.com; **211:** Corel Professional Photos CD-ROM™; **216:** *The Stages of Life*, c.1835 (oil on canvas) by Caspar-David Friedrich (1774-1840), Museum der Bildenden

Kunste, Leipzig/Bridgeman Art Library, London/New York; **217:** Superstock; **224:** *Antea, (Portrait of a Lady),* Parmigianino, Museo Nazionale di Capodimonte, Naples/ Scala/Art Resource, NY; **227:** Culver Pictures, Inc.; **230:** The Granger Collection, New York; **235:** Springer/CORBIS-Bettmann; **243:** Culver Pictures, Inc.; **244:** The Granger Collection, New York; **321:** ©Kim Sayer/ CORBIS; **247:** *Woman Begging at Clonakilty,* James Mahony, The Illustrated London News, 1847. Photo by Grace Davies/Omni-Photo Communications, Inc.; **248:** Culver Pictures, Inc.; **256:** ©Gregory K. Scott/Photo Researchers, Inc.; **259:** Corel Professional Photos CD-ROM™; **260:** CORBIS-Bettmann; **264:** Corel Professional Photos CD-ROM™; **267:** Courtesy of the Library of Congress; **268:** Eric Meola/Getty Images; **271:** Chuck Carlton/Index Stock Photography, Inc.; **274:** istockphoto.com; **283:** Jeremy Homer/ CORBIS; **282:** ©Orwell Archive; **291:** *Ox House, Shaftesbury,* 1932, John R. Biggs, Wood Engraving; **294:** Photri; **295:** CORBIS-Bettmann; **298:** Snark/Art Resource, NY; **299:** Culver Pictures, Inc.; **302:** ©D'Lynn Waldron; **305:** Pearson Education; **315:** Emma Lee/Getty Images; **316:** *St. Patrick's Close,* Walter Osborne, National Gallery of Ireland; **323:** Corel Professional Photos CD-ROM™; **324:** Getty Images; **327:** Culver Pictures, Inc.; **328:** Corel Professional Photos CD-ROM™; **331:** Corel Professional Photos CD-ROM™; **331:** © Jim Ballard/Stone; **334:** *Tombstones of Tiberius Julius Rufus and his son,* Petronius Rufus and their wives, Erich Lessing/Art Resource, NY; **337:** *The Red House,* Carlton Murrell, Courtesy of the artist; **340:** © Richard A Cooke III/Stone; **343:** ©Bettmann/CORBIS; **344:** istockphoto.com; **347:** Dinodia/Omni-Photo Communications, Inc.; **350:** NASA;